Rule-Following Skepticism in Contemporary Epistemology

About the Author

Gopal Sahu, a Ph.D. in Philosophy from Indian Institute of Technology (IIT), Bombay, is presently teaching in the Department of Philosophy, University of Allahabad, Allahabad. To his credit, Dr. Sahu has several publications in the area of naturalized epistemology, skepticism, philosophy of science, consciousness and applied ethics. Dr. Sahu is a recipient of the prestigious Jawaharlal Nehru Doctoral Scholarship for History and Philosophy of Science. He was the managing editor of the esteemed philosophy journal, *The Philosophical Quarterly*, published from Pratap Center of Philosophy, Amalner from 1997 to 2002.

Rule-Following Skepticism in Contemporary Epistemology

Gopal Sahu

CONCEPT PUBLISHING COMPANY PVT. LTD.
NEW DELHI-110059

ISBN-13: 978-93-5125-243-6

First Published 2017

Published and Printed by

Concept Since 1974

Concept Publishing Company Pvt. Ltd.
Regd. Office:
A/15-16, Commercial Block, Mohan Garden,
New Delhi-110059 (INDIA)
Phones : 25351460, 25351794, *Fax* : 091-11-25357109
E-mail : publishing@conceptpub.com
Website: www.conceptpub.com

Editorial Office: H-13, Bali Nagar, New Delhi-110 015, India.

Cataloging in Publication Data—DK Courtesy: D.K. Agencies (P) Ltd. <docinfo@dkagencies.com>

Sahu, Gopal, author.
Rule-following skepticism in contemporary epistemology / Gopal Sahu.
pages cm
Includes bibliographical references and index.
ISBN 9789351252436

1. Skepticism. 2. Knowledge, Theory of. I. Title.

201.S24 2017 DDC 149.73 23

Dedicated to
My Parents

Dr. Ganesh Prasad Das
Formerly, Professor of Philosophy,
Utkal University & Formerly
Sr. Research Fellow,
Indian Council of Philosophical Research
'RUTAYANI', 396, Paika Nagar,
Bhubaneswar-751003, Odisha

Tel: 0-674-2560000
Cell: 0-9437195757
Email: gpdas45@gmail.com

Foreword

The conception of philosophy, which has emerged consequent upon the work of Ludwig Wittgenstein and his followers, is that philosophy is a conceptual and logical study and that meaning of sentences and discourse constitutes its field. Sharply distinguished from sciences that directly deal with facts, philosophy remains as a critique of other modes of thinking, or, what is the same, thinking about thinking. As an activity of clarification and elucidation, it banishes metaphysics as being devoid of sense, christens epistemology as philosophy of psychology and revamps ethics as logic of moral discourse or metaethics. It was not comfortable for philosophers to break with the past and soon brought in old things in the new garb: traditional metaphysics as "Descriptive Metaphysics", traditional epistemology as "Naturalised Epistemology" and traditional ethics as "Applied Ethics".

Skepticism is an old philosophical problem, which has its origin in Greek philosophy with Cratylus (mid-late fifth century BCE) and Pyrrho (360-270 BCE) as its champions. The most complete surviving account of skepticism is given by the Roman skeptic Sextus Empiricus (160-210 CE). According to him, there are three types of investigators: (i) those, who claim finality of discovery of truth—they have discovered the truth, or they have not discovered the truth; (ii) those, who proclaim that truth cannot be apprehended; and (iii) those, who avow their investigation is still going on. The first group is dogmatists, the second one academics and the third one skeptics. The quintessence of skepticism is the claim that to every account, there is an equal and opposite account. They are, more often than not, misunderstood to have created hindrance to the practical and natural activity of men. But what they ask is whether the existing things are such as they appear to be. What they investigate is not what is apparent, but what is said about what is apparent.

In the mid-twentieth century, A.J. Ayer brought out a book *The Problem of Knowledge*, in which he took skepticism as the problem of knowledge. Skepticism, as he understood it, does not claim that, "every theory, or hypothesis, will eventually break down, but that the accumulation of favourable instances, however long continued, affords us no good reason for believing it." The actual course of our experience neither justifies, nor rejects the validity of the skeptic's contention.

During the same period of time, Wittgenstein's *Philosophical Investigations* was published giving a fillip to the new trend of philosophical thinking. Skeptical doubts were brought to bear upon not knowledge of truths, but upon understanding of meaning of words and sentences of language. His objective was to show that logic does not lean on philosophy in its area of operation, but rather the reverse is the case. In particular, he wanted to show that understanding is not a mental state or process that happens in private space of the person when he comes to understand something that he previously did not. It is all about human activity in the public space. Wittgenstein raised doubts and he himself resolved some of them and kept other open for debate, but he was sanguine that doubting has an end with due deference to Descartes.

Saul Kripke does not allow doubts to wither away. Wittgenstein got the principle settled that language is a rule-governed activity as games are. Kripke holds that doubts could always be raised about rule-following, thus giving a jolt to the very foundation of the institution of language that acts like a bridge between human being in a society. His skeptic leads us towards the conclusion that no language, no knowledge and no values are possible.

This has roused Gopal Sahu, the author of the present title *Rule-Following Skepticism in Contemporary Epistemology* to meet the skeptic in a head-on challenge by trying to prove that the skeptic's contention is not logically tenable. The attempt is a valiant one, but it is difficult to say how far it is successful. Ayer was of the view that philosophy is an exercise in rhetoric and he found that the skeptic emerges victorious, but his victory is a bloodless one.

The author ropes in philosophers other than Kripke like Nelson Goodman with his new riddle of induction and W.V.O. Quine with his indeterminacies trio for treatment at par with Kripke's skepticism. Wherever there is rule-following, be it in the use of language or logic, or description and prediction in the sciences, the same hiatus between the "rule followed so far" and "rule to be followed in the case next" yawns and the skeptic can always stand by his claim that there is no viaduct to ensure continuity. The conceptual and the factual domains suffer from the same fate. The two are not categorically distinct fields of human investigation. The conceptual is an extension of the factual and both are empirical as well as normative.

It is a commendable piece of research work by Gopal Sahu on contemporary logico-linguistic philosophy. I hope that it would be widely and profitably used by students, teachers and researchers, who have involvement in the philosophic quest from age to age.

Bhubaneswar
April 30, 2016

(Ganesh P. Das)

Preface

Epistemology, the philosophical theorization on knowledge, has been the core area of philosophy. Traditionally epistemology is concerned with the definition, nature, scope, justification and kinds of knowledge. Since these methodological, conceptual and logical issues cut across many subjects, both in empirical and social sciences, epistemology has gone beyond philosophy. As a result, the scope and application of the contemporary epistemology are vast, varied, complex and trans-disciplinary. However, the entire contemporary epistemological issues such as defining important epistemological concepts (truth, belief, rationality etc.), analysis of knowledge (Gettier's problem, fallibilism etc.) and structure of knowledge (foundationalism, coherentism etc.) centre around the problem of skepticism—whether and how knowledge is possible? No wonder, epistemology has its origin in skepticism as an attempt to justify the claim that knowledge is possible. If epistemology is the core of philosophy, skepticism is the core of epistemology. Skepticism comes in many forms depending on the nature and degree of doubt. Traditionally, skepticism has played bigger roles in connection with doubting our knowledge claims about perception, memory, self and induction. However, skepticism has evolved into even more complex and multi-dimensional in the contemporary time. The latest and the more comprehensive form of the skepticism have come in the form of rule-following skepticism in the contemporary epistemology. The book explains the much talked about rule-following skepticism and its attempted solutions in the contemporary epistemology. The most innovative way of posing the rule-following skeptical issue can be found in the works of Saul A. Kripke.

Kripke poses a radical and all pervasive skeptical problem in the context of rules and their following by hypothesizing another rule just like our arithmetical rule of addition with one important difference. The other rule which he calls *quus function* is different from the plus function in some unobserved cases, while it is identical to the *plus function* on all observed cases. Kripke demonstrates that any rule governed behaviour of an individual in the act of adding numbers is equally a rule-governed behaviour of using *quus function*. By generalizing from this, Kripke is in a position to claim that any rule governed behaviour of a person can be interpreted in more than one way since the behaviour fits many competing rules. There are no facts physical or mental which can lend us help in identifying the rule that is being followed. Moreover, even the person who follows the rule cannot be sure of which rule he had followed in the past since even he cannot have access to his own past intentions.

Rule-following skepticism is a very powerful form of skepticism for it strikes the very vital cord of knowledge, i.e., it makes language impossible. It denies ascription of meaning to any symbol and makes understanding, thought, and communication impossible. Thus, it enters every segment of human life leaving no room for rule-governed activity.

Kripke's skeptic is demanding that, first, we should be in a position to identify the rule that we follow now is the same as the one which we have used up till now. Second, we should have some mechanism to determine the infinite future applications of rules which are yet to take place independent of the actual applications we have made thus far. In other words, skeptic is demanding a *normative guideline* to determine infinite applications of rules in the future.

Kripke concedes the argument of his skeptic and argues that skeptic cannot be answered on his own conditions. However, he provides a *skeptical-solution* to the skeptical problem by compromising with the skeptic on the ground that life should go on and for that man should be granted the status of human by adopting the right attitude towards him. Kripke is of the opinion that we cannot provide always truth-conditions, i.e., necessary and sufficient conditions for certain sentences. He claims that truth-conditions have to be replaced by assertive conditions, i.e., whether the situation is linguistically fertile to assert certain statements irrespective of whether we are able to discover whether the statement is true or false. This requires change in attitude, immediately after observing the pain behaviour. Instead of asking whether someone is really in pain, we do ask now: what can we do to help the individual? On the skeptical-solution, we have the ways of ascribing concepts to others and claim whether the rules followed are the same with reference to present and past behaviours of an agent. However, this cannot silence Kripke's skeptic, since the assertive condition of a rule provides only the history of the use of the rule, but does not have any guiding force for future applications. Thus, Kripke's assertive condition is nothing more than a descriptive answer to a normative question.

Since, this form of skepticism operates at the level of language, it has far reaching consequences on other issues, namely, hypothesizing, induction, generalization, projection, prediction, scientific theory, etc. In nutshell, on every walk of rational activity rules and rule-following are inevitable. On this background, the thesis makes an attempt to interpret and evaluate Nelson Goodman's *New Riddle of Induction* as a rule-following skepticism in the context of induction, hypothesis and projection, Quine's *three indeterminacies* are interpreted as problems of rule-following arising in the issue of knowledge, theory and translation and L. Wittgenstein's use theory of meaning in the case of meaning and use of words.

Making use of linguistic liberty, Goodman defines the term *grue* in such a way that each and every observation of emerald after specific time support two incompatible hypotheses equally, namely, "all emeralds are green" and "all emeralds are grue", similar to the problem of multiplicity of rules. From this Goodman argues that there is no syntactic and semantic criterion to differentiate lawlike statements from contingent generalizations.

Goodman's theory of projection adopts a descriptive attitude to the problem of skepticism, as it is based on the history of the projection or entrenchment of a term in the given society. He would base his projection on the strength of entrenchment and the purpose served by the use of words in the society. Goodman's theory of projection as a solution to skepticism would remain inconclusive as it offers a descriptive answer to the skeptic.

W.V.O. Quine entertains three main skeptical issues. First, the indeterminacy of reference which shows that ontology cannot be fixed since it is relative to the perspective. This leads to the problem of deciding as to what we mean by a sentence if its scope is different when perspectives change. Second, the indeterminacy of translation shows that the notion of proposition as sentence meaning is untenable, since translation depends on the manual of translation. And third, what the empirical under-determination of theory shows is that there are various defensible ways of conceiving the world.

All the three skeptical issues share the same feelings of Kripke's skeptic: given the behaviour or data which rule or theory do we fit to the context? In the context of indeterminacy of reference, the issue is: how do we interpret the quantified sentence if the predicate term refers to different ontologies or different perspectives? In the context of translation, the issue is that of finding the exact translation from one language to another given the verbal behaviour in addition to the individual's sense perception. Furthermore, if a theory is never deduced from the available data and if the theory is transcending the observations made, and if two theories are empirically equivalent, the underdetermination of theory may be put as: how do we choose one theory against another?

Quine attempts to answer skeptic by establishing objectivity on the basis of unification of science through theoretical kinds and naturalization of epistemology. He hopes to achieve unification on the ground that natural kinds can eventually evolve into theoretical kinds, and predicate logic would take over natural language. Though, Quine speaks of normative element in his naturalized epistemology, because of the problem in theoretical kinds and his immanent theory of truth, his goal of the unification of science remains ideal.

The Wittgensteinian formulation of the paradox of rule is this: how can we say that we have grasped the meaning of a word when meaning lies in use and use is spread over time? We argue that Wittgenstein presents the skeptical problem to reject it as part of his method of *reductio-ad-absurdum* argument. Though, Wittgenstein's *philosophical grammar* and *form of life* can very much accommodate the normative aspect of rules, he considers the said grammar and the task of philosopher to be descriptive and fails to meet the requirement of Kripke's skeptic.

In fact, the skeptic doubts the possibility of objective and necessary knowledge. If we can establish the objectivity of knowledge, and make it the foundation of science, then this would be an adequate answer to all forms of skepticism, i.e., the riddle of induction, indeterminacies etc. Objectivity of knowledge can be the foundation of our value system as well. It can be the basis of communication, induction, prediction, explanation, translation etc. And it would, in fact, touch all the aspects of engineering and sciences on the one hand, culture and value on the other.

We have tried to achieve the normativity, thus the necessity and objectivity in rule by inducting universal character and commitment into linguistic rules. It should be noted that we have accepted the Wittgensteinian framework of philosophical grammar to establish the objectivity and normativity of knowledge with only one minor modification. As is known, grammar is a set of free-floating conventional linguistic rules which are descriptive. As it stands, the arbitrary set of rules cannot provide the basis of the objectivity and necessity. But once, we infuse our commitment and universalize its use, a rule acquires normativity. For example, the simple rule of addition becomes normative rule when we universalize it by adding 'so on *ad infinitum*' to the explanatory examples.

But the question is how can we utilize the linguistic rule to explain the world? In other words, if rules of grammar are merely conventional set of guidelines, how it can be used to explain the laws of nature, which are supposed to be independent of our thought and language? To say that a sentence is true by virtue of linguistic rule need not make us think that they are not true synthetically because language does not contradict reality. Since, language and reality are in harmony, since, they belong to different realms, there is no reason to believe that an analytic statement which is true by virtue of language cannot be true in any other sense. If we accept the regularity in nature conventionally as a rule, there is no reason to believe that the necessity achieved would be of a lesser kind. For instance, this simple property of fire that it burns can be conventionally accepted as a rule for the use of the term "fire". Having accepted it conventionally as a rule, it is true by definition that "fire burns". If it is true by definition, even a skeptic cannot doubt it. If a skeptic doubts a truth by definition, then he is refusing to use a language which has sense and if a skeptic uses the language which lacks sense, nothing needs to be proved to him. If there can be analytic sentences in ordinary language, there could as well be analytic sentences in the language of science. A good example would be "Water is H_2O" or "Heat is molecular agitation".

We may be permitted to say that the words that constitute natural laws are also governed by linguistic rules, yet linguistic rules themselves do not yield natural laws. Philosophers, for having failed to notice the fact that language is also playing crucial rule in generalizing the natural laws, conclude that there are conjectures and refutations of various kind. Goodman, Quine and Karl Popper all seem to believe that hypotheses are somehow formed having no logic. We think that there is logic to hypothesis formation; the logic is comparable to the rule formation in language. Having observed some cases of a certain type, we may propose a hypothesis on the analogy of our proposing the rule of addition after doing some additions. If we have formulated our rules on the basis of our observation in the regularity in nature, what happens is that the rules that are formulated provide us the linguistic necessity. In case we discover the regularity in nature in a way that two rules we formulate in language are related necessarily, certain analytic statements would be applicable to the world exactly the way that natural laws are applicable to the world. There is nothing that stops a natural scientist accepting the natural laws to be linguistic laws. All that he requires to do is to align himself to the laws of nature while formulating linguistic rules to govern natural laws.

Since, language is in perfect harmony with reality, natural laws have been part of our culture and that the skeptic cannot contradict himself, there are at least some cases wherein rule-following is certain, I cannot be saying that a cup of tea is hot and mean that it is cold. For instance, if I have dropped an object and the object fell down, this cannot be doubted by a skeptic. Even if the skeptic is not very happy about the example, one can construct several examples carefully choosing the cases where natural laws have been adapted culturally by invoking certain conventions to prove the point.

To conclude, the strongest sense of necessity that one could have is the sentence which is found to be true on three counts: linguistic, empirical and metaphysical. Are there such sentences? We tend to say, 'yes'. As we have mentioned above, 'fire burns', 'water boils', 'birds fly', 'individuals have parents' are all the examples of statements which are true on the said counts. Linguistically if you call someone a human being, you need to presuppose that he is born to his parents, this is found to be empirically true and scientifically justified. Moreover, any possible perspective or world we imagine where we speak of the individual in question, we need to grant that he has parents and hence is true even in the metaphysical sense. Thus, one could conclude that there are many examples of this kind and the notion of necessity involved is the strongest possible one.

Writing this book has its root in my Ph.D. Thesis completed under the supervision of Prof. P.R. Bhat and submitted to Indian Institute of Technology (IIT), Bombay. Taking this opportunity I place on record my deepest gratitude and obligation to Prof. P.R. Bhat for his personal and keen involvement in all stages of the writing of this book. I am thankful to Prof. Ganesh P. Das, my teacher from Utkal University, Bhubaneswar, who has been a constant guide for me and to have written the "Foreword" for the book. Over the years, teaching and lectures at various institutes and forums have significantly sharpened the central ideas and argumentation of the book. From the conceptualization through the writing and editing of the book, I have been helped by many people, particularly by Prof. Debashis Guha, my senior colleague from the Department of Philosophy, University of Allahabad.

It is too formal on my part to thank my parents, brothers and sisters, but I must acknowledge their help and support, particularly my wife Hrudeswari and two sons Swapnil and Sahil in whatever ways they could provide in writing this book.

Allahabad **Gopal Sahu**
April 30, 2016

Contents

1
Introduction

The Skeptical Problem

Skepticism as a philosophical approach doubts the certainty and the possibility of knowledge by questioning the source, nature and the reliability of knowledge-claims made by anyone. One could speak of skeptics of different degrees: the one who believes knowing anything for certain is impossible. There are skeptics of a moderate kind who believe that you know your own mental states but not anything external to you. There are skeptics more liberal in their approach. They believe that they know their mental states for sure, they also know the external physical world, they are also reasonably sure of the observable behaviour of others, but not what other's think, feel and value. The skeptic questions our ontological assumptions, epistemic foundations, linguistic competence and basis of our values. For instance, we know many objects around us that stimulate our senses. We normally trust our senses unless there are good grounds to doubt them. If the medium and the stimulus are very weak, the doubt about the certainty of knowledge derived from senses might naturally arise. The skeptic will not grant certainty to any knowledge derived from the senses, not because there are natural doubts, but because they *can be* doubted. The skeptical argument is simple and straightforward. There are instances where senses mislead, such as, optical illusions. There is no mechanism inbuilt in the senses that they can distinguish right perceptions from the wrong ones. The senses cannot ensure that there are no distortions and aberrations in perceptions. Since, one is not sure which perception is defective, and how to distinguish defective one from the non-defective one, all that is sensual is rejected as not trustworthy. Moreover, even the mind cannot ensure what is derived from the senses are legitimate and not distorted, for it has not independent method of knowing what there is apart from what has been given as input only through the senses. One cannot ensure what is reported in a news paper is authentic by referring to another copy of the same newspaper. Unless the conditions have changed, even the sensual verification of what is claimed does not add any value. The optical illusion is a case in point. If our perception of ourselves in the mirror is distorted, it is of no value in verifying our own image repeatedly. Mirror image gives us a sense that when I raise my left hand, it appears that I raise my right hand. This cannot be corrected by repeated observation. The conclusion the skeptic would draw from this is: since, there is no single way of segregating defective perception from the non-defective ones, all sense perceptions have to be rejected as not worthy of trust.

An extension of the above argument would be handy for the skeptic to deny the knowledge of the existence of external objects. It takes the following line of argument. Since, sense perceptions cannot be trusted, the contents of the sense perceptions also cannot be trusted. The existence of an object cannot be asserted simply because our sense perception has given us a sense that the object exists. There are, as a matter of fact, experiences which give us certain sensations, but they are necessarily unreliable. For instance, the illusion that we get that two railway lines meet one another far away from here. One can also produce a hologram which gives us the false perception of a three dimensional object. One cannot, thus, jump to the conclusion that the object exists because we perceive it. There is no independent way of knowing whether an object exists apart from the perceptual mode of knowing. Hence, the inevitable conclusion that one cannot claim that any object other than my own sense perception exits for sure.

Having lead us this far, a skeptic finds it very easy to persuade us to believe that there is no way of knowing the thoughts, feelings and values of others. By way of giving us the maximum concession, he would admit that we have the observational data about the behaviours of others. The skeptic objects to our trusting the data we have gathered about others. Since, we are aware of the possibility of pretensions, even if the behaviours of others are true reflections of what they think, one cannot conclude what they think from their behaviour. Thus, in one stroke the skeptic denies the authenticity of our knowledge of what others know, feel or value. The same argument is extended to cover the domain of the speech of others. Even if the other person takes an oath and claims certain things, one cannot trust such statements since, he is capable of cheating us and there is no independent mechanism to segregate authentic statements of others from that of inauthentic ones. Thus, the skeptic goes for wholesale rejection of our knowledge of other minds.

With respect to the values that we hold, a skeptic finds problems with all of them. He finds no base for supporting one set of values as opposed to another set since, values and the degree with which importance is attached to them vary from society to society and from time to time. Some values seem to spring from human nature and the need and some others seem to be consequences of certain religious beliefs. For instance, the values that we attach to food and shelter spring from human need. In contrast, the religious values such as universal brotherhood and concern for others spring from certain religious teachings. Yet, another set of values we find in the conventions and rituals of certain cultures and some are said to be aesthetic values. For instance, the design of the house the marriage rituals are based on the cultural conventions. The values attached to paintings and music have aesthetic base. Since,, there is no universal basis for values; the skeptic argues that the values are temporary and contextual.

In the hands of Kripke, the modern linguistic skeptic has a different approach to the problem of skepticism from a linguistic point of view. As is known to philosophers, language is an institution built on agreement. Language is a rule governed institution. One is able to understand the meaning of words and sentences because the rules of language are public. Furthermore, using all behavioural inputs in addition to the linguistic inputs human communication is made possible. Thus, the bridge between individuals is established through the institution of language. Kripke's rule-following skeptic destroys this very foundation of linguistic institution. This he achieves by showing how rule-following is impossible. He shows how one cannot know what rules others are following and consequently one would not be able to follow what others express in their statements. Since, one is not able to follow the rules of others, one cannot know the meaning attached to different words and sentences that are uttered by others. As if this is not enough, the skeptic shows how one cannot even be sure whether one is following the same rule which was followed in the past, thus, failing to ensure the consistency in the use of rules themselves. By destroying the concept of rule and rule-following, the skeptic shows the impossibility of the institution of language. As a consequence, anything that is achieved through language is also is suspect. Thus, the thoughts, desires, intentions, experiences, feelings expressed through language cannot be trusted. This seems to be the logical limit of the skeptical exercise. Even the solipsist known to the philosophers so far in the history of philosophy seems to be better placed. The solipsist is at least sure of the existence of himself and his thoughts. The rule-following skeptic denies even the knowledge of his own past intentions and thoughts since, he is not sure of what rules he had followed in the past. This is the case, the Kripke's skeptic argues because human memory cannot give us the guarantee as to what rules we had followed in the past, and the facts about our past are incapable of giving us the rules. The rules cannot be read off from the behaviour of a person. This is because, the skeptic argues, each behaviour is over-determined by rules. In other words, each pattern of behaviour can fit more than one formulation of rules and thus, justify multiplicity of rules. That is to say, one is lead to multiple abstractions of rules from the same set of behaviour patterns. To give an analogy, one cannot conclude from the fact that a person buys a ticket for a film does not mean that he enjoys the film. It could as well be the case that he wants to give company to someone else. Alternatively, it might be the case that he would like to hide himself from the police and going to a film theater is one best way of hiding since, lights are off in the theater when the film is being screened. One cannot, thus, read off the intention of the person from his behaviour. This analysis applies to all linguistic behaviours in all contexts. It is in the nature of a rule that it has innumerable applications and given this any set of human behaviour can fit and satisfy several possible rules. The rules that we abstract from the behaviour is after all a rule, and this rule can differ from the one which our friends abstract from the same set of behaviour and further there is no surprise if the person who is under observation followed entirely different rule. This is the reason why one cannot know the rule that is being followed by an individual from his limited behaviour. Thus, the skeptic succeeds in frustrating our last effort to save our optimism.

Having rejected the very possibility of language, Kripke's skeptic could easily show how one cannot meaningfully talk about knowledge. Simple unit of knowledge may be said to be of a substance having a property which is presented in a simple subject predicate sentence. However, if rules are not possible, even the predicate terms will not be possible. If predication is not possible, no description is possible. This analysis would apply to even subjective experiences, values and so on. Without rules it is not possible to have even predicate terms, as a consequence it is not possible to speak of values, or even comprehend values. Thus, Kripke's skeptic takes us to the logical conclusion that no language, no knowledge and no value are possible.

Traditional Responses to Skepticism

Enthusiastic and optimistic philosophers find Kripke's skeptic unbearable. They feel the urgency to answer Kripke's skeptic so that they create some breathing space for themselves. One may, of course, reject outright the claim of rule-following skeptic by calling him unreasonable. One may opine that life would go on as usual despite the challenge of rule-following skeptic. There would not have been a single rule-following skeptic who ever survived on this earth, yet the challenges he poses are like bumps on the smooth roads. The skeptic poses the intellectual challenge and philosophers are in the habits of taking up such intellectual and paradoxical challenges to comfort our rationality. The skeptics, like logical paradoxes, make us feel small and limited and shake our faith in the rational human endeavours.

Though skepticism has never been a school in the history of philosophy, it has appeared and reappeared in different forms parallel to development of thoughts. The history of skepticism dates back to pre-Socratic period. Skeptical arguments were advanced by the early Epicurians and Greek philosophers. The Pyrrohnian School, however, provides the most systematic arguments in favour of skepticism. Sextus Empiricus, the pioneer of the school argues that we should suspend our judgements about the objects, because the relativity in our sense experience, memory and other sources of knowledge give only contradictory account of the world.

The beginning of the modern period saw a great deal of discussion on skepticism. Descartes, in the process of answering the skeptic, himself provided a very novel and radical skepticism. He examined all alleged sources of knowledge and found that perception, authority etc. are vitiated in contradiction. Perception is not veridical since, it is possible to imagine the worldly experiences to be series of dreams caused by a mischievous demon. He tried to establish a set of "clear" and "distinct" criteria to answer skeptic once and for all.

Locke's representative realism and his distinction between primary and secondary qualities ultimately land him in "I-do not-know-what" view about the world. Locke is known for his empiricism. He certainly upholds the view that the properties of objects and things are perceived through sense perception. But when it is the matter of *real essence*, no sense organ could help him. The Berkelian subjective idealism proposes an extreme form of skepticism about the knowledge of the external world and other minds and treats them as our "ideas" only. His claim *esse est percipi* goes to show that he is extremely cautious about asserting anything except mental phenomena. Only by invoking a good benevolent God like Descartes, could he ensure that there are inter-subjective and objective realities and their knowledge.

Hume also held a very radical skeptical view about our conception of the world, self and other minds. He made the distinction between *matter of fact* and the *relation of ideas*. Matters of fact cannot be known in any other manners than perception. There is no way one can perceive a universal truth except through repeated observation. Thus, he held that any knowledge of cause and effect is based on association of ideas hence, causal relation is psychological in nature. Thus, Hume believed that we have no way of knowing the ontological relationship between any two events.

Though Kant criticizes Hume's skepticism sufficiently in logical terms, he was very skeptical about the possibility of knowledge of the objective world *as it is*, i.e., the knowledge of the *things-in-themselves*. He opines that the world known to us is limited by categories of judgements within the spatio-temporal world. He had to speak of *a priori* foundation of mathematics, laws of nature and metaphysics. By invoking the *a priori* source for knowledge that is certain, Kant had to accept the charge of talking about non-phenomenal certainty. The phenomenal world remained uncertain for the skeptic.

Philosophers worked hard to answer the skeptic so that they can restore confidence in their knowledge system and make advances in their theory building activity. Sometimes, skeptic is looked at with suspicion, and sometimes with great respect. Even if there is no skeptic, yet the assumed skeptic is a friend of an epistemologist. A skeptic asks critical questions and in answering the skeptic a philosopher develops a rigorous and systematic epistemology. Therefore, there is no wonder why most of the epistemologists welcome the skeptic in order to defeat him. Skepticism as a philosophical problem is familiar to all the students of philosophy since, Greek times. Philosophers have raised skeptical issues and thought they have resolved them in one way or the other; but the skeptic is born and reborn again and again in different forms to challenge the philosophers. Kripke's skeptic is the latest and the strongest incarnation of such a skeptic.

Rule-following Skepticism

Rule-Following skepticism is the most modern and innovative way of presenting skeptical problem in the history of mankind. Rule-following skepticism is the skeptical issue raised in the context of rules and their applications. Society consists of customs and conventions including its language habits. Since, language is a fully symbolic activity, it is governed by rules. We are able to distinguish rule governed behaviour of human beings from the natural behaviour of individuals. Our only medium through which we understand the rule governed behaviour of others is in terms of observation. Observation has limitations in the sense that intentions and desires are not observable. In order to understand the rule governed behaviour, we need to read the intentions of others in their behaviour. Since, man is a free agent capable of invoking his own rules and obey them, one cannot be sure of whether rule governed behaviour of the person is indicative of any rule or not. Further, it is difficult to distinguish rule governed behaviour from that of natural behaviour. It is possible to drop one's valet and check the honesty of the other person behind him. It is also possible that the valet dropped because of the gravitational law. Therefore, even if one has behaved in the past in a certain manner that may not be sufficient ground to believe that he would behave in similar manner in future. That is to say, all the facts taken together about an individual cannot give us any certainty about what he would do in the future. There does not seem to be any fact which would justify the rule that we abstract from the behaviour of a person that can ensure his future course of actions.

The skeptic who gets all the opportunity to question the rule governed behaviour asks one basic question: How do we know that a person who behaves in a particular manner has followed a particular rule? The question is important for several reasons. The question is important especially in the context where the same behaviour fits several existing rules. To give an analogy, there can be several paths to reach a destination. From the fact that one has reached the destination does not mean that he has travelled in a specific path. Concrete example could be cited from the case of a paranoid person. If the doctor is genuinely helping this person, the behaviour of the doctor is suspected by the paranoid person and interprets the behaviour of the doctor as the murder plan. The same behaviour, however, is interpreted by the normal person as helping the patient. It is possible and sometimes real that the same behaviour is given several interpretations which fit each of these interpretations. Some of the detective films are made using such tactics to retain the interest and curiosity of the audience. Using such line of argument, the skeptic questions the authenticity of our normal interpretation of human behaviour.

There is the second reason why a skeptic doubts our understanding. Human beings are autonomous and have the habit of formulating the rules and obeying them. For instance, several of us, make time-table for ourselves and follow them. Being autonomous agents, we retain the authority to modify our own rules. If the time-table is too unrealistic, one may modify the time-table. Thus, the skeptic is very right in doubting the rule governed behaviour of other agents given the fact that they are autonomous beings and hence, could change their rule governed behaviour. To put it differently, there is no way that our skeptic can ensure that the same rule is followed by the agent exactly in the same manner without introducing any modifications to the said rule.

The problem becomes acute when the subject himself has doubted his own behaviour. For instance, if the person concerned is not sure which rule one has followed in the past in similar contexts, then this can be a genuine problem. The skeptic heavily depends on the following for his argument: there is no mental or physical fact that can guide us regarding the rules that we have followed in the past. All that is available to us as resource regarding the rules of the past is first person or third person account of our behaviour recorded in the form of videos etc. or retained in our memory.

The option available to us is of looking at this data and concluding what we did perform in the past. When an individual looks at his past, he is with equal footing on others. Memory cannot give us which rule we followed, for memory can provide data only on such things which the person has experienced. Rule-following is not over and above performing certain actions. If someone remembers his rule governed behaviour in the past, he remembers his behaviour in the past and nothing more. Given this, knowing our own past rule governed behaviour is one like observing the rule governed behaviour of others. This data or memory is raw and it requires a fresh look at it by way of finding some pattern and meaning. In order to make sense of the data or memory, we need to abstract certain rules by observing the pattern of our behaviour of the past. This is the reason why the skeptic claims that physical or mental facts cannot give us rules. Even when we speak of past rules that we have followed, we need to invoke them once again in order to give interpretation to our pattern of past behaviour. Thus, there is no physical nor mental fact that gives us the rule that we have followed in the past.

If rule-following skepticism is allowed to have its sway, even the individual who framed the rule cannot be sure whether he has followed the rule or followed modified form of it or followed entirely a different rule in a different context. This is so because each time when we understand the pattern of behaviour, the understanding could be different since, several rules fit this pattern of behaviour and as we have noted earlier our memory is of no use in resolving any doubt if there is one. If this is the level of skepticism, then it is obvious that we cannot with surety speak of the rule-governed behaviour of other persons. Thus, social building of knowledge system is impossible, and not only that the day-to-day working knowledge of the language and other transactions that are made using language is impossible. The skeptical issue being what it is, every philosopher who is aware of this problem feels intensely that the problem be solved, because consequence of skepticism is unintelligible absurdity.

This problem is very powerful, not because of any other reason, but because it operates through language and hence, pervades all sectors of our philosophical activity, namely, thinking, imagining, comprehending, communication, induction, prediction, inference, building scientific theory etc., and in nutshell, every walk of rational activity where rules and rule-following is inevitable.

Kripke's Skeptic

The explicit formulation of rule-following skepticism can be found in the work of Kripke.[1] He, in fact, should be credited with popularizing the Wittgensteinian novel method of posing skeptical issues involving rule-following.

Kripke poses the problem of rule-following skepticism by hypothesizing another rule just like our arithmetical rule of addition with one important difference. The difference being that the other rule which he calls *quus function* is different from the *plus function* in some unobserved cases while it is identical to the plus function on all observed cases. Kripke demonstrates that any rule governed behaviour of an individual in the act of adding numbers is equally rule governed behaviour of the act of adding numbers using *quus function*. By generalizing from this, Kripke is in a position to claim that any rule governed behaviour of a person can be interpreted in more than one way since, the behaviour of the person in question fits many competing rules similar to *quus*.

There are critics of Kripke who hold the view that Kripke has not interpreted Wittgenstein faithfully.[2] We do not enter into this debate here. However, Kripke himself explicitly remarks that he may be charged with misinterpreting Wittgenstein, yet believed that there is something which merits philosophical consideration in the rule-following skepticism of his formulation even if it is not Wittgensteinian.[3] Without involving ourselves with this debate, we take Kripke and Wittgenstein as two independent thinkers involving themselves with the issue of skepticism and its solution.

Our understanding of what Wittgenstein does is quite different from that of Kripke. Wittgenstein seems to be using private language argument and the rule-following skepticism as a *reductio-ad-absurdum* argument to show that the skeptic is wrong. Skeptical argument constructed in this fashion is not a conclusion of Wittgenstein, rather a starting point to build epistemological foundation on a firm ground of rules of language. His notion of form of life, use theory of meaning, agreement in action etc. all refers to the community notion of language. This is quite the opposite of the notion of private language and Wittgenstein rejects the very possibility of a private language. Keeping the autonomy of language in tact, he links language with reality through a very general notion of the philosophical grammar. This philosophical grammar lays the foundation for objective knowledge.

In contrast, Kripke believes that Wittgenstein grants the skeptic his due. According to Kripke's understanding, Wittgenstein sees no possibility of answering the skeptic. Thus, Kripke feels that

Wittgenstein handles the skeptic exactly the way Hume did. Kripke invokes the notion of skeptical solution to the skeptical problem. According to Kripke, Hume gave a skeptical solution to the skeptic and Wittgenstein too used the same method. However, Kripke admits that the skeptical problem does not affect our ordinary life. He gives an account of how understanding takes place because of mutual trust among the members of the society and due to our institution of language having agreement in action, forms of life and criteria. Granting the skeptic his point and yet speaking of change in attitude towards life and its issues Kripke calls this the "skeptical-solution to the skeptical problem".[4]

One may agree or disagree with Kripke on his ascription of skeptical problem to Wittgenstein, but this formulation of skepticism perhaps is an ingenious one. We believe that the credit should go to Kripke rather than Wittgenstein for the formulation of this issue, and rightly scholars have recognized "rule-following skepticism" as Kripke's rather than Wittgenstein's. However, but for Wittgenstein, Kripke would not have thought of posing the skeptical problem in this radical fashion.[5] In this sense Wittgenstein too deserves some credit for this new formulation of skeptical problem of rule-following.

We may note that Wittgenstein recognized rule-following to be the best manner in which one can explain language and human behaviour. He described language as a *form of life*. That is to say, language cannot be understood in abstraction. It is always intimately related to action. Wittgensteinian strategy of subjecting the philosophical issues to the rule governed behaviour has mainly two advantages: (1) this approach avoids the use of mentalistic terms; and (2) it gives the dynamic account of language in action. As rightly pointed out by Kripke, Wittgenstein is able to present some of the epistemic issues in a more focused and direct way using the notion of rule and rule-following.

Goodman and the New Riddle of Induction

Nelson Goodman, another name in the contemporary philosophy long before Kripke published his work had posed a philosophical puzzle called the *New Riddle of Induction*.[6] Goodman formulates the problem of induction making use of the concept of rules and their arbitrary nature. He innovatively uses the predicates green and the predicate blue to form a new predicate '*grue*'. Both green and blue behave exactly the way they are used in our ordinary language, while his new hybrid of green and blue behaves in a peculiar manner. It behaves as if it were green for till time t, and behaves as if it were blue after time. This behaviour of grue is legitimate in the sense that rules of language are arbitrary. This predicate grue helps Goodman to formulate a paradox using the notion of induction. On a closer examination, one would be convinced that what Goodman has presented in the form of the *New Riddle of Induction* or his problem of grue is a problem of rule-following. By invoking the notion of *grue* in an arbitrary manner, Goodman builds a situation where it would be impossible to project the future instances of a certain kind on the basis of the past and present behaviour of the stipulated rules. Since, rules are conventional and arbitrary, Goodman would make use of this in building the *grue* problem. By showing that green is projectible because it is entrenched, he concludes that the reason for *grue* not being projectible lies in its being an arbitrary predicate. The simple point he emphasizes is that arbitrary rules which are not practical or applicable in our life activity cannot be used in building the knowledge system. This *New Riddle of Induction* is a problem comparable to Kripke's rule-following skepticism on one count, i.e., both of them invokes rules which are not part of practical life and exploit the arbitrary nature of rules fully in posing skeptical problem.

The solution offered by Goodman to the new riddle of induction is also comparable to Kripke's skeptical-solution in the sense that both base their solution in community living which involves agreement in action, shared values and principles and other related aspects. By using the concepts of entrenchment and projectibility, Goodman is in a comfortable position to demonstrate that those rules which are accepted and adopted by the society have the element of projectibility while any arbitrary rule may not have this property. Thus, he grounds his knowledge on the lived experience of people at large.

Unavoidable Uncertainties of Quine

Quine, a celebrated American philosopher had his own way of raising skeptical issues. He speaks of different forms of uncertainties. We see these uncertainties largely due to rule-following problem. Underdetermination of theories, inscrutability of reference and the uncertainty about translation are the three uncertainties which Quine raises are basically springing from the problem of rule-following.

The underdetermination of theories holds that logically incompatible theories may fit all possible evidences. There may be pairs of empirically equivalent theories while not contradicting each other use radically different theoretical notions. There is no easy way to choose one theory against another competing theory, thus, leading to skeptical problem. Underdetermination of the theory arises as an issue because of the lack of necessary link between theory and observation. However, the observational sentence itself may be infested with many controversies. For instance, an issue that is related to the observation sentence is the indeterminacy of reference. In other words, the ontological relativity of such observational sentences does not allow us to fix the reference. This in turn has serious implication for translation whether one considers word to word translation or sentence translation within a language or across the languages. All these aspects put together make the skeptic the winner. He has his say on all the three indeterminacies of Quine.[7]

We note that this problem of theory choice is in spirit similar to that of *quus* and *grue* problems. Theories are constituted by cluster of inter-related concepts. And the relation between theories and its application or observation is comparable to rules and their applications. Though not explicitly stated by Quine even in his later works, his three indeterminacies are essentially Kripkean problem of multiplicity of interpretations of rules. We are convinced that Kripke was not wrong in thinking that the three indeterminacies can also be viewed as rule-following skepticism.

Naturalized epistemology popularized by Quine as an attempt to overcome the two indeterminacies, at least the indeterminacy of reference and underdeterminacy of the theory, is viewed as an attempt to answer skeptic. Quine believed that since, knowledge is natural to man, there must be a scientific way of studying it and theorizing it. He advanced the view that science and philosophy should work together since, philosophy cannot provide foundation to science. He also pleaded for wiping the boundaries between philosophy and psychology on the one hand, philosophy and linguistics on the other. With the help of scientific method and making use of the backlog theory, he hoped that we can move steadily towards the unification of science having all the normative characteristics inbuilt within the epistemology which our traditional epistemology stood for. This is his programme of naturalizing epistemology.

Though Wittgenstein had everything that was required to provide an able answer to skeptic, unfortunately he does not do a systematic job for it. His own remarks seem to cut the edge of other arguments propounded by him. Not that showing by using *reductio-ad-absurdum* argument is any inferior; one would have welcomed it more had it been the straight answer to his skeptic. We find Wittgenstein's attempt to answer skeptic quite satisfying and yet not fully happy with his solution. The reason for our unhappiness lies in the manner in which he failed to answer the skeptic on normative issue. Kripke's skeptic wants the theory of meaning to have some teeth to bite, but no descriptive theory has this teeth to bite. For certain unknown factors, Wittgenstein makes his theory of meaning a descriptive one and hence, the required teeth do not grow.

The Proposed Solution

Skepticism and paradoxes are to be avoided at any cost because they are not life- conducive. This is the reason all the efforts are made to answer a skeptic. We may find several methods of answering skeptic and well known ones are: (a) do not acknowledge any skeptical question at all. Dismiss every skeptical question as uninteresting, useless, wasteful exercise; (b) answer the skeptic in a diplomatic manner, granting him his philosophical due and carrying on our daily activities without heeding much to a skeptic; and (c) face the skeptic head on and try to show that skepticism is not logically tenable philosophy. We shall adopt the last strategy to face the skeptic head on and show him that he could be answered in straight manner.

Kripke thought that the straight solution to the skeptical problem consists of providing necessary and sufficient truth conditions. We believe that there are other ways of answering the skeptic as well. One can show to the skeptic that his assumptions are wrong. For instance, the knowledge of certain mental fact is required to justify which rule one had followed in the past cannot be provided. We for instance, by showing how our past behaviour fitted a rule appropriately, argue that the identity of rule and intention get established if our present behaviour also fits the same rule. This attempt is made at the end of the second chapter. The other attempt is made in chapter 6 by giving an account of how objective knowledge is possible. The skeptic can be shown that certainty is possible. Then one could advance the other thesis as to how the scientific method could be developed in order to build a system of knowledge, how induction, prediction, expectation, verification etc. can take place in a justified manner. This method of answering the skeptic can also be considered straight solution.

Our straight solutions to the skeptical problem, one at the end chapter 2 as immediate response and the other in chapter 6, involve in what follows. We largely accept Wittgenstein's framework, but want to add a few features which not all Wittgensteinian scholar might agree to attribute them to Wittgenstein. (1) We would like to outline a normative theory of meaning. Though, 'use' can be said to be a criterion of meaning, it cannot be made into a full theory of meaning. (2) We recognize the normative element in rule, this aspect is not recognized by many, though some philosophers do recognize this feature. Rules having regularity in use acquire *normative* features in the context of human dwelling. They become *prescriptive* and *prohibitive* as they entrench themselves in the life of the individuals. (3) Our theory of meaning derives its normativity from universality of rules. That is to say, it is normative only to the extent that we are rational, use language consistently and so on. The objective knowledge and the cohesive nature of rules etc. are only applicable to a rational man. Use of language is itself a rational activity since, it works like a calculus. There is nothing that applies to a non-rational person. We assume a skeptic to be rational in this minimum sense that he would be governed by the rule of consistency for instance, he would not assert self-contradictory statements etc. adhering to which is a must for any one to have a language.

One tends to think that the community view of meaning and justification, unless qualified properly, will result in an utterly relative theory and encourage a trend of 'any thing goes'. It is true that neither description of the world nor the logical structure of mind is enough to define what is justification, but it is also true that meaning is not 'free creation'. We cannot freely create a belief system by ignoring the contribution of the external world in our belief formation and subsequently in its meaning. Our grammar, though is autonomous, is restricted by the world. This is the reason why certain combination of words does not make sense. Wittgenstein would readily agree that certain sentences, for instance, the one which Russell sites "Saturday is sleeping furiously" does not make sense because our grammar does not permit such a combination of words. Though grammar is conventional, it would have limitation; yet it cannot allow self-contradiction for instance. Given the thesis of Wittgenstein that rules determine their extension, it is possible to predict what we are going to count as an instance of the rule well in advance. If we speak of natural laws that have been adopted in our language, the instances of the laws can be equally predicted well in advance. There is no element of uncertainty in our prediction. Moreover, a skeptic cannot fail to obey the laws of nature. Given the fact that laws of nature are already embedded in our language, skeptic has no scope to disobey the rules. In addition to this, the skeptic on his own admission cannot be self-contradictory.

Since, language is in perfect harmony with reality and natural laws have been part of our culture, and that the skeptic cannot contradict himself, there are at least some cases where rule-following is certain. For instance, parallel lines never meet are an example which is true linguistically and true empirically. There is no single instance, without changing the rules for the use of the terms involved where two lines are parallel to each other and yet meet at some point is not possible in the language of Euclid. There would be no single instance where I can speak of meaningfully that someone has dropped an object and the object has not fallen down.

Having seen how at least in some cases the skeptic cannot question the rule governed behaviour, one can extend this to answer Goodman. Quite correctly, if something is a law of nature, then it is projectable if that law is also accepted by the society in the form of a linguistic rule. However, the natural law may involve many other aspects in addition to the linguistic rules governing the use of words. For instance, a complicated law of gravitation, e.g. $S = ut + 1/2\ gt^2$, where the relationship among, distance, time, and the gravitational force do involve quantitative aspects in addition to rules and their following. Therefore, it would be quite correct to say that the formulation of laws involve rule-following whereas rule-following are not adequate to form a natural law. However, this does not affect our thesis as long as we are interested in answering only the skeptic. A skeptic is answered by the laws of nature if those laws of nature also have terms which are rule governed and use those rules in such a manner that we form certain analytic sentences, one like "water is H_2O".

Similarly, one can answer Quine's skeptical issues underlying underdetermination of theory. The failure of naturalized epistemology need not result in embracing skepticism. As pointed out above, there are cases of knowledge that are definite and certain. Using this, one can achieve the goal of naturalized epistemology without having the disadvantages of the three indeterminacies. Since, the observation sentence does not have two interpretations given the necessity, we are able to avoid the uncertainties that are linked to the behavioural aspect of the rule-following. For instance, the observation sentence "This stick has two ends" is true linguistically, empirically and in all possible perspectives and hence, would not entertain the indeterminacy of reference, translation or that of underdeterminacy of the theory about the nature of the stick.

An Overview of the Essay

Inspired by Kripke's formulation of skepticism, this thesis makes an attempt to understand the skeptical issues in the writings of modern philosophers, Kripke, Goodman, Quine and Wittgenstein. Kripke himself has tried to discuss the problem of skepticism in the background of Goodman and Quine. Many thinkers may find this to be extrapolation. However, we agree with Kripke, if not in every detail that the issue of grue in the context of Goodman and the issue of the indeterminacies which Quine speaks of are closely linked to the issue of rule-following. We make a fresh and humble attempt here to interpret the works of Goodman and Quine in this light taking their major concerns into consideration and their solutions. This work is an attempt to look at the epistemic issues from this perspective of rule-following. We therefore, do not fancy surveying historically classic works on skepticism. However, we believe that the import of the traditional skeptical views is best represented in the modern form of skepticism in the form of rule-following skepticism. For instance, the skeptical argument forwarded by Cartesians may run as follows: given the same behaviour one cannot know whether one is actually seeing the behaviour of the person or one is dreaming the seeing of the behaviour. This may be considered a rule-following skepticism by interpreting the behaviour in two different perspectives.[8] Thus, rule-following skepticism is not a new skeptical problem; it is the new way of raising the old skeptical problem. Therefore, it would be a mistake to think that old skeptical problems are forgotten and we are tackling new issues. It is like pouring old wine into new bottle though an attractive one.

We find similar problems with Goodman, Quine and Wittgenstein who tried to build the system of knowledge by answering the skeptic. One may differ in one's opinion as to the last thinker, namely, Wittgenstein whether he had any plan to systematically build a knowledge base. There is no doubt that he had made such an attempt earlier in *Tractatus* and the skeptic remained his enemy even in his later phase of life to whom he was directly responding to. Thus, rule-following skepticism is not a new skepticism, but is the new way of formulating old skepticism. We are aware that Wittgenstein has shifted the focus of discussion from the philosophy of mind to philosophy of language. For instance, he preferred to speak of the role played by a philosophical term in language rather than examine its meaning and reference. He was quite aware that the questions about meaning and reference of a term like "pain" lead to unresolvable paradoxes and instead of getting tied down by our own rope, we should reformulate the question in such a way that these traps are avoided. In this process of shifting the philosophers' attention, he formulated what is now popularised by Kripke as rule-following skepticism.

In addition to the above consideration, there is also an academic criterion that was overweighting in our mind. Goodman explicitly uses the terms of rules, and we consider the new riddle is a sample case of rule-following problem. Quine of course is highly rigorous philosopher, perhaps the most systematic one of this century and yet he faces some of the basic philosophical issues which he calls three indeterminacies. Since, Quine is involved in the issue of providing a sound ground for philosophical knowledge in naturalizing epistemology, we thought that it would be a good idea to examine his answer against the skeptical argument of the Kripke's skeptic. In the process, we learnt that even Quine's model is not devoid of the problems which Kripke's skeptic face.

Skepticism in this new form is not simply an issue to be discussed in the context of Wittgenstein or what is known as the issue of private language. In fact, it has far-reaching consequences. All those who have made some attempt to give some foundation for knowledge are affected either directly or indirectly, whether they address the issue of rule-following skepticism in the latest form or not. For instance, the issues that Goodman was dealing with to a large extent can be reformulated by the skeptic of Kripke, and similarly, the issues that Quine dealt with can be looked at by the skeptic of Kripke. Why only this, in fact, the skeptic of Kripke can reformulate the skeptical issue with reference to most of the epistemologists.

We are interested, not in any details of any particular model, for once we see that the answer offered by Kripke, Goodman and Quine are not satisfactory; we turn to Wittgenstein to see why he proposed this skeptical theory at all. We felt that Kripke has missed the point of Wittgenstein marginally. Though Kripke's interpretation is quite authentic of Wittgenstein, he read perhaps more than what was there in Wittgenstein. Not that Wittgenstein does not raise the issue of skepticism in the manner in which Kripke has developed the theme in his book, but the point of raising the skeptical issue was to make the argument of the skeptic more forceful. As we see, Wittgenstein himself answers the skeptic, by providing the notion of philosophical grammar which takes care of the issues the skeptic has raised to some extent. Since, the manner in which these remarks are written, it does not become obvious what Wittgenstein intended in several of these passages. No doubt that one has to admit that it is a matter of *seeing*, and we see the works of Wittgenstein in this way. An implication that follows is that, both the views that of Kripke's and ours may be justified interpretations. That is to say, in order to assert our thesis, we need not reject the thesis of Kripke. We see the writings of Wittgenstein differently do not mean Kripke's understanding is wrong, it only means that there are other ways of looking at the works of Wittgenstein.

The concept of objectivity of knowledge is thought to be a good solution to many philosophical issues. On the one hand, the objectivity of knowledge can be the foundation of science, on the other; it can give an adequate answer to all forms of skepticism. Objectivity of knowledge can be the foundation of our value system. It can be the basis of communication, translation and it would in fact touch all the sectors of engineering and sciences on the one hand, culture and value on the other.

What one would notice is that the discussion has been centered around only the primary sources and when each one of the thinkers had many followers and critics and there is hardly any mention about those developments. The reason is simple and practical. It would have not been practical to go through the inner debates on any one of the issues further. For instance, the published works on the new riddle of induction itself runs into more than 300 articles.[9] And similarly, Quine himself has written and published vociferously. And the literature on

Wittgenstein cannot be read by one person in his life time.[10] And the writings on Kripke are not less though not comparable to these scholars. Yet, the responses to his writing are not by any standard is less. The main reason is not that we wanted to avoid going into the details of these scholars and the issues, but our purpose for which we deal with these scholars is different. We need their general stand on the issue of skepticism and we would like to show that there is a new way of looking at the old issues that are dealt with these prominent scholars. Of course, we could have dealt with may be traditional scholars, for instance, Berkeley; for many of the problems which Wittgenstein faced are faced by Berkeley. And we could also have gained by the discussion of some of the issues Goodman has raised by studying Hume and Hobbes for instance. Since, the thrust of the issue is on rule formation and rule-following, we thought that it would be quite prudent to restrict ourselves to four major thinkers of later half of this century. Though Wittgenstein can be said to belong to the first half of this century, most of his later works became known to the readers only after fifties.

A word about foundation of philosophy is necessary here. Wittgenstein, by no means, believes that philosophy can provide foundation for knowledge. Philosophy only describes and leaves everything as it is. At best it puts sign posts, so that the philosopher travels in the right direction. We may note that this very act of putting sign post is a great job in philosophy. By providing proper account of use of words, philosophy gives an account for objective knowledge. It distinguishes knowledge from nonsense on the one hand, knowledge from philosophical puzzles on the other. Wittgenstein does not believe in *a priori* foundation of knowledge; nor does he believe in first philosophy. He holds that philosophy is born along with language and language is found to exist with humans even in the ancient period. No one knows the beginning of philosophy, nor there be a day when all philosophical problems are solved.

We said that skeptic challenges the foundationist, but he also challenges the evolutionist and relativist. If one could reject Cartesian attempt on the ground that no *a priori* philosophy is possible, the skeptic would reject even the empirical basis of our philosophy. No amount of empirical experience can permit any sweeping generalization. There does not seem to be an easy solution to the skeptical problems since, neither a priori foundation can be given nor the empirical foundation can be thought of to counter a skeptic.

We need to consider this seriously and find an inter-subjective or objective ground for knowledge, belief and values. Evolution of knowledge is possible if we grant the possibility of knowledge first. Growth theory of knowledge holds that we accumulate knowledge bit by bit and eventually we have large body of scientific knowledge. This ambitious project starting with a small bit of indubitable knowledge is possible only if the scientist is allowed to make a beginning. Similarly, the relativist position on epistemology is conceivable if and only if something as knowledge is feasible in the first instance. Without admitting anything as knowledge, the talk of relative knowledge would make no sense.

The best analogy we may give to explain the dynamic nature of rule-following skepticism is from the language of computers. A virus, like any other package, is a designed programme with malicious intentions. A typical manner in which it works is that it attaches itself with other files when they are activated. By attaching itself to other files of other programmes, it propagates itself silently. Some of the variants of viruses convert some normal commands into another kind. If you issue a command to open a file, it would execute the command "delete" and thus, destroys the file itself. The presence of the virus is noticed only after it acts. Rule-following skepticism has this ability to adjust and modify itself to handle any context where other forms of skepticism arose in the past. The simple reason is that rule-following skepticism is formulated at a fundamental level of human institution. No institution can exist without rules. Any rule-governed behaviour is questioned by the rule-following skeptic. Literally all philosophical activities can be halted by an effective and intelligent rule-following skeptic.

NOTES AND REFERENCES

1. Kripke, S.A. (1982), *Wittgenstein on Rules and Private Language*, (henceforth *WRPL*), Blackwell, Oxford, 1982.
2. There are numerous philosophers who have questioned the authenticity of Kripke's interpretation of Wittgenstein. The strongest criticism, however, comes from Baker, G.P. and Hacker, P.M.S., (1984) *Skepticism, Rules and Language*, Basil Blackwell, pp. 1-50. They say, "Kripke's interpretation flew flagrantly against Wittgenstein's manifest intentions....misconstruing their meaning, misidentifying their target and misreading their thrust", p. vii. McGinn, Marie, "Kripke on Wittgenstein's skeptical Problem",

Ratio, 1984, pp. 19-32 and Malcom (Malcom, *Wittgenstein: Nothing Is Hidden*, Basil Blackwell, 1986, pp. 154-181) have also expressed their doubt in Kripke's interpretation of Wittgenstein).

3. See *WRPL*, pp. 5, 7.
4. *Ibid.*, p. 66.
5. See Preface to *WRPL*.
6. Goodman, Nelson, (1965) *Fact, Fiction and Forecast*, 2nd edition, Bobbs-Merrill Co. Inc., Indianpolis, pp. 59-122.
7. Please see, Quine, W.V., (1992) *Pursuit of Truth*, revised edition, Harvard University Press, Cambridge, p. 50. Also Quine, W.V., "Three Indeterminacies", in *Perspectives on Quine*, edited by Robert Barrett and Roger Gibson, 1990, Basil Blackwell, USA, p. 6.
8. E.S. Haldane and G.R. Ross, (1967) *Philosophical Works of Desecrates*, 2 Vols. Cambridge University Press. Vol. 1, pp. 145.
9. For example, the annotated bibliography of 316 articles on the new riddle of induction has been prepared by Stalker Dauglas (ed.), (1994) *Grue! The New Riddle of Induction*, The Open Court Publishing Co., US, pp. 281-458.
10. In a book guide, *Waterstone's Guide's to Books 1989-90*, it is mentioned that a bibliography on Wittgenstein lists nearly 6000 books and articles p. 651.

2

Kripke: Rule-Following Skepticism

Introduction

Kripke[1] has raised a skeptical problem for anyone who follows rules, for example, rules of meaning, in the ordinary sense of the term "rule". It is suggested that there are rules of meaning as a set of guidelines which we follow to ascribe meaning to words and expressions. Kripkean skepticism of rule-following is that there is nothing, mental or factual, which can help us to determine which rules is being followed for a given behaviour and action. There is nothing called meaning that we refer by any word and there is no reason to believe that a word refers to this thing and not any other things.

Kripke has attributed the rule-following skepticism to Wittgenstein and strongly argued that the latter Wittgenstein's work on rule involves the skeptical puzzle. This is a very debatable claim and many scholars of Wittgenstein argue that Kripke is not faithful in presenting Wittgenstein's view on rule. We do not want to debate on the matter.[2] In fact, majority of the critics of Kripke have concentrated on debating this issue and we feel that in the process they have missed the real issue involved in the rule-following skepticism. We believe that Kripke's problem of skepticism can be studied independently of Wittgenstein. The problem merits separate philosophical discussion without any reference to Wittgenstein. This is because, Kripke is the first philosopher to have presented the problem of rule-following skepticism in a systematic and novel manner. The problem *per se* does have serious philosophical implications to be taken independently. Moreover, Kripke seems to argue that the problem as expounded is neither "Wittgenstein's nor Kripkean, "rather Wittgensteinian argument as it is struck Kripke, as it presented a problem for him,"[3] which Wittgenstein may not himself approve. The discussion of the rule-following skepticism is centred on the assumption that Kripke has attempted to "develop the paradox in his own way".[4]

As understood by Kripke, Wittgenstein has shown much concern regarding philosophy of mind and philosophy of mathematics. He does not view these dual interests in two separate and distinct ways.[5] The basic structure of Wittgenstein's approach is said to be as follows: A certain problem of "skeptical paradox" is presented concerning the notion of rule. Following this, a skeptical solution is presented.

The Rule-Following Paradox

Kripke poses the problem of rule-following skepticism by invoking another rule just like our arithmetical rule of addition. The difference between the rule of addition and the other rule, namely, *quus rule* lies in some unobserved cases while being identical to all observed cases. Kripke demonstrates that any rule governed behaviour of an individual in the act of adding numbers using plus function is equally rule governed behaviour of using *quus* function. By generalizing from this, Kripke is in a position to claim that any rule governed behaviour of a person can be interpreted in more than one way since, the behaviour fits more than one rule.

Let us consider the rule of addition. Let us suppose that I have not computed '68 + 57' previously and obtain the answer '125'. Suppose, I meet a skeptic who questions my answer and says that it should have been 5. Despite my insisting that I am correct, the skeptic continues. He says, on what basis did I perform this function? I had previously performed only finite number of cases of addition. All we have done so far involved the numbers less than 57. Kripke invokes at this juncture the notion of *quus*. This new notion is like plus as long as we deal with the number less than 57, but once we reach this number, the behaviour of the *quus-rule* is different. Thus, the skeptic says that the sum should have been 5 instead of 125 following the *quus* function.[6]

Kripke now argues that the person cannot provide the reason to choose between *plus-rule* and *quus-rule* for the future applications of the *plus-rule* involving number beyond 57. Since, the person is used to the *plus-rule* in the past, the answer he computes for 68+57, should be 125 rather than 5. He follows the rule previously he used to follow to determine the new and unique 125. But by hypothesis, the person has never told to himself that he should say 125 for this calculation. The hypothesis is true for all cases of the rule for the infinitely large number of the cases, e.g., of horses are not in the mind. The applications so far made are always limited. Thus, Kripke argues that there is no way one can say whether plus or *quus* rule the follower is following. It is possible that by plus I always meant *quus* in the past since, all my mathematical calculations involved numbers less then 57, and I misinterpreted all my past uses of the *plus-rule*. The skeptic is asking "how do we know that 68 plus 57 as we meant "plus" in the past should denote 125 and not "5"? The skeptic argues that there are equally compelling reasons for both plus and *quus* functions having been applied in this case. Thus, Kripke poses his skepticism:

> This, then, is the skeptical paradox. When I respond in one way rather than another to such a problem as '68+57', I can have no justification for one response rather than another. Since, the skeptic who supposes that I meant *quus* cannot be answered, there is no fact about me that distinguishes between my meaning plus and my meaning *quus*.[7]

The rule-following skepticism poses the most ingenious and radical[8] form of skepticism by doubting the underlying regularities in human behaviours. As rules encompass the whole civilized aspect of human beings, and since, thought and language are rule-governed, the rule-following skepticism poses a serious problem to the extent of the impossibility of language and communication. Denying that there are such things as rules of meaning, it puts in jeopardy some of our most central notions about ourselves. It denies the concept of "meaning the same" by the same words and behaviours, the understanding of the intention of others and the process of generalisation from observed to unobserved. It puts question about language as a means of communication and undermines the objective characterisation of meaning. In Kripke's own admission it makes "all languages, all concept formulation, to be impossible, indeed unintelligence."[9]

Thus, Kripke's rule-following skepticism involves three skeptical issues: (1) How does one know that I use a word with certain meaning or with the same meaning?; (2) If multiple interpretation fit the behaviours of a person, how do we know which meaning to be attached to the given behaviour?; and (3) How does one know the intention of a person given his behaviours? i.e., the problem of other minds.[10]

The rule-following skepticism says that on the basis of the given observational behaviour of the person, we cannot make out which rule the person is following to express the particular behaviour. In other words, the same behaviour can be explained by invoking two or more than two incompatible rules. We cannot ascertain the fact just by associating some verbal and overt behaviours of the person with the following of a particular rule or we cannot know the fact just by asking the person for he may be telling lies. We do not have direct access to the mental processes of the person also and even if we had, the mental events would have been always finite, and thus, would have failed to determine the future step of the calculation according to the +2 rule. None of these would have helped us to resolve the problem of multiple interpretation of rules. As Kripke says, "indeed, there is no fact about me that distinguishes between my meaning a definite function by "plus" and my meaning nothing at all."[11]

What is important to note here is that I cannot produce any fact to justify that I followed one rule rather than another in terms of either my mental facts of physical behaviour in the past or at present. Kripke adds further saying that, "there is no such thing as meaning by any word... Each new application we make is a leap in the dark, any present intention could be interpreted so to accord with anything which we choose to do."[12] Since, there is nothing that can guide us, a skeptic is free to interpret the way he deems fit and we are free to interpret our way. If any interpretation fits the behaviour since, there is no fact which goes against any interpretation, then there is no much meaning in saying that I follow one rule instead of the other. Therefore, Kripke says, "meaning one function rather than another will not make sense."[13] The so-called rules governing the meaning ascription to words and expressions are "unjustified stab in the dark, I apply the rule blindly."[14]

The example of *plus* and *quus* is not such an unusual thing. It quite often happens that we are speaking about a person by the name XX, and after quite a long discussion about him, we realise that we are talking of two different individuals with the same name. Kripke's description of the two rules has resemblance with this. Given the arbitrary nature of rules, any convention can be part of the rule and we can have two rules in such a manner that they overlap only till the cases we have examined so far. And from the given instances, it is not possible for us to conclude which rule is being followed and moreover, it is also not possible to conclude that which rule did we follow in the past. Consider Wittgenstein's own example.[15] Let us say the skeptic writes the series, 1, 5, 11, 19, 29 and asks us to continue. We may continue using the formula $a_n = n^2 + n - 1$ and write the next number as 41. If we are asked to explain which rule did we follow, we may give the formula. But the skeptic might say that we followed the rule of the series of the difference, he finds the series 4, 6, 8, 10 and you have added the number 12 to 29 to get 41 he says. The next time, you add 14 to 41 and you would get the number 55. In fact what you followed in the past is this rule of adding this latter series to the first and obtain the next number he claims. There is no way to prove that we did not follow the rule which our skeptic followed.

Kripke limits his discussion to an example from mathematics and may give an impression that the rule-following skepticism is a problem in the case of the mathematical rule only. However, such skeptical problems can very much affect our day-to-day life and it is generalizable to other fields of study. For example take the case of a person following the usage of the word "Hello". The act of saying hello can be interpreted in more than one incompatible ways. First, it may be the case that the person simply wants to express his courtesy and wants to recognize the existence of other people by greeting them. Second, the person may intend to begin his conversation by saying hello. Thirdly, the person is very cheerful today and he wants to positively relate himself to others. And from the overt behaviour of the person saying hello, we cannot know what use of the term "hello" is being put to.

Kripke's skepticism doubts two things: First that, there is any "fact about past history – nothing that was ever in my mind, or in my external behaviour – establishes what I mean by a word."[16] Second, even if we have meaning, we are not justified in having it. There is no logical justification that a particular word would necessarily mean this and not any thing else, for, "there is no justification for one response rather than others."[17] The immediate consequence of skepticism is that the meaning is *indeterminate and unjustified*[18] implying that all our present usage would only be an "unjustified leap". A particular word may mean anything and many things, even the same word at times can mean two contradictory things. If skepticism is pressed further the notion of world as an objective and independent entity would vanish; the conception of the meaning as an objective entity requiring us to describe one way rather than other will be in danger. Besides, the skepticism would make us believe that our language system is chaotic and unjustified.

What is skeptical about rules is that, as Kripke would say, "we follow the rules as we do without reason or justification."[19] "Plus" as we understand it forces us to say that "68+57" equals to "125", but the rule of plus function has nothing to identify the plus-rule as distinct from *quus-rule*. "Any finite set of examples, mathematical or otherwise, can be extrapolated in an infinite number of ways; equivalently, any finite set of examples instantiates an infinite number of rules."[20]

Why Paradox?

The mathematical function of 'plus' which is defined by the symbol '+' is used for discussion. This is the well known rule of addition. It appears that we learn to use rules and identify the applications of rules on the basis of our successful use of rules in the past. One important point to be noted is that although, one has only computed limited number of cases, the rule determines infinitely many new sums which one has never previously considered. This is what is called grasping the rule.[21]

When we speak of the rules with reference to past and present use, we are speaking of the descriptive function of rules. However, there are also normative component to rules. Rules do not help us to simply identify objects fall under their scope, but they also compel us to adhere to the norms set by them in our future use. The meaning of "plus" should "determine my answer for indefinably many new sums that I have never previously considered... my past intention/use determines a unique answer for indefinably many new cases in the future".[22] Thus, directions for future use must be contained in the criterion of meaning. The criterion of meaning should incorporate the justification as to why a word signifies this and not other object. As Kripke would say: "It must give an account of what fact it is that constitute meaning "plus" and not any other thing and a condition that a putative candidate must satisfy".[23]

When we grasp the meaning of a word, for example "plus" in the metalinguistic sense or mathematical sense as the function of "+", by examples of actual addition, we put ourselves in touch with a rule which we are then in a position to honour in future cases of addition. Each calculation of addition based on the rule of plus, e.g. 1+1 = 2,

2+1 = 3, 3+1 = 4 and so on are the applications of the rule of addition. The applications of rules we have performed so far are finite. But the applications of rules are infinite, which not only covers all cases of addition we have calculated so far, but also infinite cases yet to be performed. Further each application of the rule is a new and unique application. Though we follow the same rule of "+2", each of its application is different from each other and are unique. In the series of "+2", the step 1002 is different from both of its previous step and next step, i.e., 1000 and 1004. Thus, the present step is the unique application of the *plus-rule*. The application of the plus is determinable independently of any particular cases. This is what constitutes the meaning of the word plus.

There are two basic requirements for the theory of meaning. First, the theory of meaning should provide the criterion for right and wrong use of words or criterion for warranted use of words. This requirement not only takes care of the question of what a word means but also why the word does not have different meanings. This condition can be called as a criterion of *correctness* of rules. The other requirement is that meaning should be universal in the sense that the criterion of meaning should be applicable to indefinably many instances of word used both in the past and future. This characteristic of the rule can be called as the *adequate* use of the rules.[24]

Thus, to follow the rule, we should be in a position to say that the rule that we have followed uptill now correctly is the same that we will be following in future cases also. Secondly, we should have some mechanism to determine the future applications of rules which are yet to take place. That is to say we have to identify cases infinitely independent of the actual application.

This is apparently an impossible job on the part of followers to determine the infinite applications of a rule. The object of infinite requirement does not affect our sense experience like a physical object and we are not causally connected to the object in the ordinary way.[25] For example, as Kripke says, "The infinitely many cases of the table are not in my mind for my future self to consult."[26] The user or the follower cannot identify the appropriate rule under whose scope the activity falls, with his limited cognitive abilities.

There are three interrelated problems in fulfilling the condition of rules. First, there is the problem of identification of the unlimited applications of the rules. Since, the followers have limited cognitive resources; it is very difficult to bring all the applications of the rules under the purview of the rule. Second, the followers do not grasp the extensions of the rules on the basis of limited past experiences or given experiences of the following the rules since, they have no control over the applications of the rules. There is a problem because the past experiences are always finite and the rule-following is going beyond what is given in the past. Third, if our accumulated practice of the rule-following is not enough to keep track of the future applications of the rules, and if we do not have the control over the future operation of the rule, it is quite possible that the follower may not be following the same rule which he used to follow in earlier cases to justify the same action. Now, this possibility will give rise to the problem of multiple interpretations of the rules. On the one hand, there may be more than one contradictory behaviours fitting to the same given set of rules and on the other hand, the same behaviour can be accounted for using two contradictory rules.

Kripke's formulation of the skeptical paradox is based on the presupposition that a theory of meaning is descriptive and truth-conditional. The truth-conditional theory of meaning holds that words get their norms from the facts outside; words are meaningful if their correspondence with the fact can be established. The truth-conditional theory of meaning can never account for the "normativity" of meaning, given the fact that our cognitive abilities are limited. We cannot know all the extensions of a rule in order to know the meaning of a word. Consequently, we have the freedom to think of a situation where our past usage of a word may not conform to our present use and at times may mean exactly the opposite. There would not be any contradiction, for example, in thinking that by plus we meant "*quus*" in the past according to which 56+68 would amount to 5 and not 125.

The issue of meaning and justification are essentially normative in nature. Kripke holds that, "the relation of meaning and intention to future action is normative, but not descriptive".[27] The issue is normative for, the criterion of meaning, like the ethical norms, is *prescriptive* and *prohibitive*; positively prescribing how a word should be used and prohibiting wrong uses of words. As Kripke himself writes: "Meaning is that which instructs me what I *ought* to do in all future cases. I do not predict that I will do..., but instruct myself what I *ought* to do to conform the meaning."[28] The normativity condition of meaning only puts certain constraints on usages over an indefinitely varieties of cases and determines the meaning independently of any particular use.[29]

Assertive *Versus* Truth Conditions

One of the reasons why Kripke thought that Wittgenstein has accepted what he called "skeptical solution to the skeptical problem" is the adoption of the assertive conditions in place of truth conditions of meaning. Kripke rightly points out that Wittgenstenian changed his priorities. Speaking of reversal, Kripke points out that the later Wittgenstein likes to first speak of the use of sentences as against the correspondence of sentences with fact. Thus, it is the assertive condition that is given priority over the truth conditions. Thus, Kripke says that the question "What must be the case for this sentence to be true?" is replaced by two questions: first, under what conditions these words can appropriately be used in asserting or denying something?; second, "What is the role played by such assertions in our practical life?"[30]

In this context, Kripke draws our attention to the Wittgensteinian suggestion of actual context in which certain uses are made of certain sentences. Kripke, following Wittgenstein, advices us to not to look for facts and entities, but look for the utterances and their uses in that context.[31]

Kripke was right when he said if facts and truth conditions are essences of meaningful assertions, then stating that anyone meant anything would have been senseless. In the changed perspective, if the circumstance is such that we can assert that someone means something by certain expression, we are asserting appropriate sentence provided the circumstance does permit us to have that belief about others. Thus, the speaker must have the linguistic license to have certain belief about others in order to have the belief according to the new theory.[32]

Kripke manages to speak of past use of rules and how our present use matches with that of past by invoking the concept of community. He writes "Wittgenstein finds a useful role in our lives for a 'language game' that licenses, under certain conditions, assertions that someone 'means' such-and-such and that his present application of a word 'accords' with what he 'meant' in the past."[33] He points out that rules are not applicable to single individual.

But if community has the right to assert that the person has followed the same rule in the past in certain circumstances, why the individual who uses the rule presently cannot know that he had used the same rule in similar manner in the past? Granted that the notion of rule cannot be applicable if only one individual uses applies it. But an individual could judge of others that they have followed the same rule in the past, what bars the same individual speaking of himself that he followed the same rule earlier. We do not think that an individual is wrong in thinking that he has followed the same rule in the past. An individual being the member of society does not lack any information about his own behaviour which is accessible to others so that they judge that the person in question is following the same rule which he has used in the past. If the context is appropriate, then the person can assert about himself that he has followed the same rule in the past. For this assertion, it would not be required to introspect and know his secret data about himself and declare that he has followed the same rule. The ground on which the others use for declaring that he has followed the same rule, would be enough even for the person who follows the rule to know that he has followed the same old rule even in his own case. This works exactly the way self-pity works for instance.

Our understanding of what Wittgenstein holds regarding the theory of truth seems to be different than what Kripke writes. Kripke writes "Like many others, Wittgenstein accepts the 'redundancy' theory of truth: to affirm that a statement is true is simply to affirm the statement itself, and to say it is not true is to deny it. ('p' is true = p)"[34]. This understanding seems to be wrong. Wittgenstein claims that truth is not a concept,[35] which means it is not governed by rules. Wittgenstein is of the opinion that there is no one way of determining the truth of a proposition. He speaks of the decision about the truth value of a proposition. When we say that a proposition is true or false, we are in a position to decide the truth value. Also if we notice that he has replaced truth condition by assertive condition, it is quite important to notice that he would not have spoken of redundancy theory after having spoken in favour of assertive conditions. This is because even to speak of redundancy theory one needs to speak of, "necessary and sufficient truth conditions". We are inclined to think that the redundancy theory of truth is rejected by Wittgenstein of *Investigation.*

The application of distinction between the assertive condition and the truth condition to our philosophical discussions would have important consequences. In fact, the assertive condition is wider than the truth condition and therefore, in *Investigation* Wittgenstein has accepted the assertive condition. Moreover, in any context, all that we can do is to establish assertive conditions. Truth condition cannot be spoken of in the context of epistemology, though we do speak of verification. Verification does not give us the truth conditions, it makes use of our knowledge of truth conditions. Grammar gives us the truth conditions,[36] it tells us which sentence is sensible and which is not. And because of grammar we know even to verify what to verify.

Given the above, Kripke' attempted skeptical-solution to the skepticism does not consist of providing necessary and sufficient truth condition for following a rule, rather it would consist in providing assertive condition. That is to say that one should justify one's use in terms of rule of language. If one is able to justify the use, then the use of the words is legitimate. There would be no question of the use being defective. The problem of truth might remain, but Wittgenstein seems to have *inversed* the process. He does not want to raise the issue of truth first and then the use, he would do the other way round. If certain sentences lack truth value, that is not a serious concern for Wittgenstein. In fact while describing what is sensation, he declares clearly that neither one can assert nor deny it within the language.[37]

The Presuppositions of Skeptical-Solution

Kripke argues that there is no possibility of attempting, what he calls a "straight solution" to skeptical paradox. We cannot offer a definite solution to skepticism by producing a mental fact or a disposition the description of which would answer skepticism once and for all, i.e., the truth-condition of meaning. One cannot answer skepticism on its own terms opines Kripke, because skepticism expects the cogniser to be a logically perfect and cognitively complete human being. Only an omniscient person can see all cases of addition or table, both past and future, to grasp the meaning of plus or table.

Without assuming the three basic concepts in Wittgenstein's conception of social life, it would not be possible to place the above discussion of skeptical solution. The language game works basically because we have (a) agreement, (b) form of life, and (c) criteria.[38] The community attributes certain concepts to rule governed behaviour of its members. This agreement of the members on practice allows them to use language as a tool, in the form of communication by issuing orders, requesting for something, promising and so on. It is not that disagreements are not there, but they are within the limits.

Agreement in the use of language is essential for the normal use of language is asserted by Wittgenstein.[39]

The other notion which is constitutive of the language game is that of the *form of life*. Form of life is the basis of our norms of life. We respond to the agreements that we have in rule governed behaviour and in action. Wittgenstein never admitted any language without being adopted by some community or the other. Not that one cannot formulate a language game for a specific purpose, but that language game derives its larger significance only when that is linked to our actual life. Thus, it is possible to speak of different forms of lives as we do speak of different language games. Yet, one cannot think of a language without there being the users of language. The form of life gives the base to any natural language.

Yet, another notion that is constitutive of language is the notion of the criterion. The term 'criterion' has been used by Wittgenstein in various ways. Sometimes, it is called symptom and sometimes it is the same as the rules for the use of words. However, either in the form of symptom or in the form of rule, criteria are inseparable aspect of any language game. Without this notion, one cannot conceive of language.

The skeptical solution of Kripke can be advanced only by granting these basic components of language. Once having assumed the full functioning of language that we can give an account of the skeptical solution. It is not possible, for instance to imagine the skeptical solution if it is thought to be some form of foundation of language. The skeptic visualized here would not allow us to have first philosophy at all. He needs to be comforted by saying that we have already conceded to his points, yet we would like to draw his attention to the attitude that we have about each other in the use of our language. We all live together, share our beliefs and have agreement in action.

The Skeptical-Solution

Kripke took the approach of granting the validity of skeptical argument at the logical level, but nevertheless trying to give a proper explanation of the fact that we are able to have meaning and justification. He has offered a solution to the skeptical paradox which he calls "the skeptical solution to skepticism". The skeptical solution "begins by agreeing with skeptic that there is no "stipulative fact" about my mind that constitutes my "plus" about and determines in advance what I should do to accord with this meaning."[40] The solution offered is called a skeptical one because, it concedes skeptic's claim that skepticism is unanswerable, "nevertheless our ordinary practice or belief is justified because it need not require the justification the skeptic has shown to be untenable".[41] Moreover, there is no need of an *a priori* justification of having meaning. The demand for an *a priori* justification is based on a "philosophical misconstruel".[42] He has termed his solution "skeptical, solution" by comparing his solution with that of Hume's classic sense. In this method, we first give up the attempt to find any fact about me in virtue of which I mean '*plus*' rather than '*quus*'. Instead, we must consider the actual use, the way we use words: (i) the categorical assertion that an individual is following a given rule; (ii) the conditional assertion that 'if an individual follows such-and-such a rule, he must do so-and-so on a given occasion". That is to say, we must look into the circumstances in which these assertions are made and their role in our lives.[43]

The "skeptical-solution" to skepticism has three aspects: First, it argues that there is no need of an *a priori* justification for our ordinary concept of meaning. The demand for an *a priori* justification is a "philosophical misconstruel". Second, we need a non-logical justification for our having meaning. And third, the non-logical justification for meaning must have its base on the social and community view of meaning. All these conditions of the skeptical solution lead to what Kripke has called the "assertability-condition" of meaning which, as we noted, argues that the meaning of the word does not depend on the truth or falsity of the external condition. The assertability condition asks the question: Under what circumstances can the meaning of a word be asserted or denied?

When it is the matter of our behaviour as the members of society or of an institution, again what we get to know is the behaviour of other people. From the behaviour, we attribute certain concepts to them. In other words, given the behaviour of a person within the social institution, we express our attitude towards him. It would not be truly Wittgestenian to say that we attribute concepts to him on the basis of his behaviour, rather we form our attitude towards him on the basis of his behaviour would be more appropriate. There is no institutional fact to which we refer to when we form our attitude towards the others, but what we can verify if any, it would be whether we are justified in forming our attitude towards others the way we form the attitude towards others. When someone sincerely utters the sentence "I am in pain", even without other signs of pain is sufficient to induce in us the feeling of pity for him, make attempts to help him and the like, and if we are sadists, the opposite behaviour towards him. That is to say, we do not, as a matter of fact find out whether the sentence is true or false first and then form the attitude towards others, it is the reversal of it.[44]

Making use of the distinction between truth condition and assertive condition, Kripke makes it clear that to ask for truth-conditions of certain statements, especially the ones which involve mental states, would be wrong. This distinction helps us to draw the line as to where can one ask for truth-conditions and where one should not. This has the advantage of overcoming the problem of knowing the mental facts about others. Like certain form of behaviourism, this theory can also boost itself by claiming that it has not only overcome the difficulty of knowing the mental facts, it has also overcome the difficulty of expressing the meaning of certain statements in terms of truth-conditions. As openly admitted by Kripke, this theory of meaning too is descriptive in its general approach. This is the reason why the skeptic is demanding for a normative theory of meaning.[45]

Descriptive Theories of Meaning

If we are to say that the skeptic is false, we must be in a position to produce some facts about my past usage to refute him. The challenge the skeptic takes has two forms: first, whether there is any fact that I meant *plus*, and not *quus* in the past, second, whether I have any reason to be so confident that now I should answer '125' rather than '5'. An answer to rule-following skepticism must satisfy two conditions. First, it must give an account of what fact it is that constitute my meaning *plus*, not *quus*. Second, it must provide the justification for such rules. Two traditional theories can be examined which have been proposed to account for meaning and consequently to answer skepticism. The common theory prevailing about meaning believes that the meaning is engraved in the mind of the user as an image or a mental state.[46] The meaning of the word "table" is the representation of the physical object table or an image of it in the mind called "table in the mind". This theory is known as the occurant theory of meaning, i.e., that meaning is a mental state existing constantly in the user's mind. According to this theory, grasping the meaning of a word means possessing such a fact which guides us to identify indefinite many new cases. To grasp the meaning of a word, for example "table" is to refer to our mind and associate it with a mental state "table" which guides for indefinite cases even though we have encountered only a few cases of that kind so for. Our present usage also conforms to our past usage, for we are referring to the same mental state when we speak of it.

Contrary to the common-sensical view, we may note that there is nothing like a mental state or a psycho-physical state which looks like an image of a table. Even if there were such a mental state, it cannot fulfill the requirement of the normativity of meaning and justification. The mental state called "table" is, on this assumption, a finite state and it cannot cover infinite cases. So, far my application of the word "table" might have been correct, but this fact cannot ensure that the mental-state can direct me to use the word correctly to all cases of tables in future. Even if one suggests that the mental state or image is like a sample which we carry all the time with us to compare and contrast and finally decide whether the word "table" should be applied to the instance at all, it would not be a satisfactory theory. The question is deeper than this. We are in fact searching for the mechanism by which one compares the mental state or image with that of an instance having no resemblance with one another. However, this theory cannot provide this crucial insight to us by invoking the concept of an image or a mental state.

We shall now turn to the second theory of meaning which argues that meaning is not an occurant state in the mind, but a dispositional state. Having a disposition of a word is to display a pattern of applying it to new cases. The dispositional account of meaning runs as follow: the fact that determines what, in the past, I meant by a word is a dispositional fact about how I would have used that term. For example, what determines that I meant the standard function plus by my past utterances of "plus" is how I would have responded to queries about addition. To mean addition by "plus" is to be disposed of its meaning i.e., when asked for any sum *"x+y"* is to give the sum of *x* and *y*. Meaning is dispositional in the sense that grasping of the meaning is a propositional attitude or a bent of mind based on which I point out the right answer when asked to. Propositional attitude is not a mental state; rather it is a hypothetical state. When we are asked the sum of say, 68+57 and when our answer is 125, the meaning of the word plus is said to have been grasped.

One variant of the theory is behaviourism which holds that meaning is understood and expressible in terms of the behaviour of the person. Behaviourism as a descriptive theory would fail to predict the rule-governed behaviour of an individual, though it might be able to do a good analysis of the past and present behaviour. There are some philosophers who argue that a criterion of justification is inherently proposed in the description of physico-chemical processes of how we justify our meaning. But here the proposal is off the target. The question is not "whether there is a causal mechanism inside the speaker's head responsible for speech and whether science can theorize about it"[47] rather can we theorize about meaning by plain description of overt behaviours.

Kripke criticises the dispositional theory of meaning by arguing that it admits of the ordinary view of meaning "whatever is going to seem to right is right",[48] because it simply equates meaning with correct performance. Since, our total disposition is always finite and our total past performance is also finite, therefore, using limited experience one cannot possibly provide the basis of meaning which has infinite applications claims Kripke.[49]

Not all reading of a dispositional theory need to be rejected as incompetent. It is possible to read a dispositional theory to be normative. Since, certain versions of dispositional theories, especially the ones which provide a competent account of evaluative and moral terms in terms of dispositions are not merely descriptive theories. In describing the dispositions, it is possible to indicate the possession of certain values which are indicative of the future behaviour of the person. For instance, a person who has the disposition to tell the truth under any circumstance would be following the rule of "tell the truth" and behaving in accordance with this rule. The behaviour of this person is perfectly understood by the members of the society and they would be in a comfortable position to predict his rule governed behaviour in the future by observing his past and present behaviour. However, we are concerned here with the dispositional theory only as a descriptive theory of meaning.

Remarks on the Rule-Following Skepticism

It is generally argued that the problem of not being able to decide which is being followed for a given action is a problem of failure of memory. Baker and Hacker argue that the problem rests on an exaggerated skepticism about memory.[50] But this argument does not seem to affect the core problem of skepticism. The problem of the rule-following skepticism arises very much even with sound memory. We may ask the basis of our interpretation of the rule especially when both the rules, *plus* and *quus* are equally applicable. One of the suggestions may be that two languages are different, one using the *plus* and the other using the *quus*. However, even this suggestion is not a very sound one. Just because there is a difference of one word, we cannot call a language a different one. Kripke has invoked this example of *quus* just demonstrates that there can be two rules which are similar having common instances within the same language. The rule-following skepticism is a problem if and only if several interpretations can fit the same behaviour within the language. Thus, the solution that the skeptic is using the word '*plus*' in a different sense or using a different language all together to express the meaning of '*quus*' is not very attractive. What should be noted is that the skeptic does not question that "68+57" denotes "125". He merely questions whether my present usage agrees with my past usage, whether I am presently confirming to my previous linguistic usages. The question is how do I know 68+57 as I meant plus in the past denoted the *plus* function, not the *quus* function. Collin McGinn[51] argues that the rule-following skeptical problem cannot be extended to cover thought/ concept/mental content. She says that we cannot make sense of employing the concept from that of originally intended, it would be just a different concept. Since, "*quus*" is a different concept and is in no way related to the concept of *plus*, there does not arise any paradox of rule. In contract, Boghossian rightly points out that though we cannot directly apply such skeptical thinking to meaning and other mental contents, but they can be expressed in some semantic ways. We do not have access to these mental contents directly; we cannot refer to and discuss them independently of the semantic properties. Thus, the problem of rule-following equally applies to the mental content as expressed in semantic way.[52]

It is also felt that the paradox of rule-following can be ignored on the pragmatic ground. So, long as a person is able to follow the rule properly and has not committed any serious and repeated mistakes, the skeptic does not pose a serious problem. Be that as it is, the problem is serious problem theoretically and those who are concerned with conceptual problem, they cannot simply ignore this problem on such pragmatic grounds.

Norman Malcolm[53] argues that, though following a rule is a practice, it does not necessarily mean "social practice" as Kripke seems to be arguing for in his skeptical-solution. The rule-following is a practice that presupposes regularity, repetitive and recurring way of acting is very much possible in the life of solitary individual. That is why we say that even Robinson Crusoe was also following the rules in his deserted island all alone. He argues that the rule-following presupposes a community in that sense that it is embedded in an environment of teaching, testing and correcting may be individually or in a group.

Kripke remarks that when we speak on Robinson Crusoe following rule, we speak of him as "taking him into our community and applying our criteria for rule following to him."[54] Irrespective of the fact whether he follows a rule or not, meaning and standard to apply to himself and behave.

Note that we cannot discuss the issue of rule-following without applying our own notion of rule-following. There is no way, we cannot disassociate ourselves using our language and rules in judgeing the behaviour of Crusoe. If we do that, our behaviour would no be in any sense different from the behaviour of Crusoe. The point of solitary language follower is an ontological one. Whether there can be solitary rule-follower independent of the person who judges whether the person in question is following the rule. Kripke gives an epistemic and linguistic twist to this question. When we judge the solitary rule-follower, we judge from our point of view using our criterion of rule-following. A critic of Kripke might agree with this point and yet insist that the issue of solitary follower remains unresolved.

Immediate Response to Kripke's Skeptic

Let us analyse the situation and examine the genesis of the skeptical paradox. Among other things, the paradox is based on the assumption that one ought to know the rule-governed behaviour of one's own past so that one can judge whether one has accorded with the same rule at present. But this is an impossible condition to be met holds the skeptic, because first, one cannot be sure of one's own past intentions; second, one cannot read off the rule from the behaviour of a person since, in any context multiple rules fit the behaviour equally.

Contrary to our normal belief, Wittgenstein and following Wittgenstein, Kripke believed that one cannot know one's past intentions. And the argument in support of this is the following: intention is always in the present. This being so, when one speaks of the intentions of one's past actions, it is the same whether one speaks of one's own intentions of past behaviour or some one else speaks of the same. One does not have any added advantage in being the agent of the action while identifying the intentions of one's past behaviour opines Wittgenstein. According to him, what one normally does while identifying the intention of one's own past behaviour is that one recollects one's past behaviour and assigns what one now thinks *appropriate intention* to it. And one's present act of *assigning a particular intention* to one's past behaviour is one's *present intention*, and there is no way one can circumvent the role played by one's present intention. Therefore, in a manner of speaking, all my descriptions and explanations of my past intentions are in true sense my present conceived intentions of my past behaviours.

On the above interpretation, it is impossible to know the intention of our past behaviour and that is the reason why Kripke's skeptic asks: How do I know that I followed the same rule in the past? And the same question is reformulated with reference to meaning: How do I know that I used the word with the same meaning in the past?

Intention of a person is not an event in time, whereas, mental events of taking decisions are. Nothing happens whether in the mental world, or in the physical just because I intend to give a lecture on Wittgenstein. But if this intention is executed in the form of action, i.e., I actually gave a lecture on Wittgenstein, then it is an event in time and it can be stored and retrieved from my memory.

It is possible to know whether I followed the same rule in the past and now, but not in the manner Kripke's skeptic wants us to do, but in an entirely different manner. For instance, we need to remind ourselves the Wittgensteinian thesis that if a rule is given its application is given, i.e., the rules determine their extension. However, this thesis should not be interpreted in the manner in which the thesis is obviously false, i.e., all the contexts of the application of rules are given when the rules are given. The thesis rightly asserts that given a context with necessary details, we would be able to know whether the rule applies or not if we know the rule. This thesis of internal relation between a rule and its application can be fruitfully made use of in assessing our past and present actions in terms of rules.

All that we need to do is to re-assess our past and present behaviour in the light of the rule in question. I remember what I did in the past and I also know what I should do if I were to follow the same rule again by simply knowing what are the two situations in which I would apply the same rule. If rule determines its extension, it is possible for me to know whether I followed the same rule then and now if they are the instances of following the same rule. Kripke's skeptic assumes that the rules and their extensions are not necessarily related (internally) and therefore, he needs to know whether present rule is the same rule which he has followed in the past. This is one like putting the cart before the horse. The right way of knowing whether one has followed the same rule then and now is by raising the issue: If last occasion where I behaved in a certain manner is an appropriate context where one can say that I followed a certain rule, can my present behaviour too be a right context where the same rule be applied? Or can a rule have past and present correct applications? And every one knows that the answer is clearly "Yes".

Similar analysis can be offered in the context of meaning. "Meaning" like "intention" can only be spoken of in the mode of present. This can be demonstrated with an example. When I say "By democracy I meant....", my use of past tense does not refer to anything that was past. It indicates my continued use of the word in a particular manner. The issue of identity of meaning across time rests on a mistake. Even when I say that I meant "such and such" it is only with reference to present that I mean such and such. That is to say, one cannot attach temporal dimension to meaning.

There can be no history to meaning, however there can be history of words. There is no sense in which we can speak that meaning has changed, though we do often speak of the change of meaning of words. When we speak of change of meaning, it is only in the contexts of words changing the meaning: being associated with different meanings with certain interval of time. Instances of an unequivocal term becoming equivocal and an equivocal term becoming unequivocal etc. are many. This is a unique feature of meaning that it never changes; while the words do undergo changes, and most importantly words are associated with different meanings which we call change of meaning in the common parlance.

Another common belief which is questionable is that intention is the meaning of the word. Consider the example: I wanted to warn my friend by saying "you are irresponsible". Here, intention is not the part of the meaning of the sentence. "You are irresponsible" is a value judgement and my intention to warn my friend is not part of it at all. A descriptive sentence might coincide with the intention of the speaker provided the sentence is used for asserting something. And similarly, "be careful!" can be a warning provided it is used in the right context to warn someone. But multiple uses of these sentences are possible and multiple intentions cannot be embedded in the sentence. Thus, meaning of the sentence is unquestionably different and is distinguishable from the intention of the one who uses the sentence.

If this is so, how do we speak of our past at all? What is not noted is that we do remember events that have happened in the past. And this includes any event that has happened to me as a person including my experiences and feelings, and the events that have happened which I have witnessed or heard of. Memory stores an experience which is an event which has a temporal dimension.

It is not absurd to refer to yesterday with regard to our decisions and commitments. When we say "yesterday I decided to work on my research paper, but today I decided not to work on that research paper" is not a contradiction in terms, because there are no two intentions in some way conflicting with one another. It would be a contradiction if and only if I want to work on my research paper and also do not want to work on my research paper just now. But that can never occur-together.

My yesterday's decision to work on my research paper remains in the form of a commitment. In this sense all my lasting promises remain in the form of commitments. And we should not mistake commitments to be our intentions or past intentions. We do remember our commitments and if we have accepted a rule, Wittgenstein claims that we have a commitment to it. Since, commitment can be over a period of time, it is possible to have commitment to a rule across the time. And if rule determines meaning, it is possible to speak of identity of meaning across the time by speaking of commitment to a rule across time. Thus, though we cannot know our past intentions and meaning, we can still know our past commitments and obey the rule as per our old commitment.

The skeptic believed that it is impossible to establish the link between what is known as "private language" and the public, since, we are not in a position to know the intention of others. However, we may note that this again rests on a mistake. We are told that the early stage of our economy depended largely on the barter system where people exchanged their commodities for one another. That is to say, even though their commodities are different, they have valued them equally. This analogy is applicable to our problem of interpersonal meaning. Even if the physical feeling and the physical impact the sound makes on our ear drums are different, the value attached to what is heard in the form of meaning for different people is often the same.

When I have the so-called private experience of fire, I say "fire!" and I have a certain visual experience. When someone else looks at it and says "Oh! fire" he also has some visual experience. We both meant fire when we said "fire", i.e., there are two experiences which are spatio-temporally separated, yet the meaning of the word uttered by both of us is the same. The word "fire" which is used ostensively is functioning like a demonstrative pronoun. There is the meaning equivalence[55] even though the personal experiences of the fire are different since, our personal experiences depend on various factors such as the distance between the person and the fire, the angle, the shape of the eye and so on. No two persons have the same handwriting, yet what is written can be the same.

Since, perception is dependent on various conditions such as attention, sense organ of the perceiver and physical conditions such as the distance between the subject and the object of perception and other conditions like the adequate light in the case of visual perception and so on, it is quite difficult to achieve identical physical conditions to use an expression with the same meaning. If one has to create identical physical condition in order to use an expression with identical meaning in language, we would have never developed our language beyond a traffic language. Meaning communicated does not normally depend on such physical features of mode of communication unless it is in a special kind of context such as shouting at someone.

Language is recognized as a social institution, and all social institutions are built on agreement. Agreement is nothing but agreement in intention on various constitutive components of the institution. In the case of native speakers of a language, there is general agreement on the vocabulary of language, what is grammatical and what is not grammatical in the context of sentences, what is formal and what is colloquial and so on. Once, we have the institution of language which is based on agreement it is possible to have expressions having meaning independent of the personal factors of the members of that institution.

For instance, we can consider the institution of telegraph services. There are certain rules and regulations in availing telegraph services and as a member of the society, one can avail of these services by adhering to the rules and regulations. However, the institution of telegraph services will not be concerned with individual intentions and feelings at a given point of time. For instance, a member of the society sends a telegram to someone wishing him a happy and married life by writing a number on the prescribed telegraph form and paying prescribed fee. The telegram would be delivered at the other end to the addressee by decoding the coded number into the text form following the rules by the telegraph department. The telegram communicates certain intention which is institutionally recognized; but this communicated intention may not match with the intention of the person at this end. The intention of the person might not have been to actually wish the person but to acknowledge the receipt of marriage invitation card. The meaning of a sentence and the intention of the speaker may not match always. For instance, "Who are you?" is a sentence which indicates that the speaker is making certain query, but in some context the speaker might use the sentence to question the authority of someone else. And this intention of the speaker may not be obvious if the meaning of the sentence is different from the intention of the speaker.

Communication failure occurs if the meaning intended and the meaning of the sentence do not match, and occasionally the meaning of the sentence is not obvious because of ambiguity. However, what is obvious is that one can communicate one's intention through language and that is what we do when we write letters and declare our intentions through an affidavit etc.

Can we mean something else than what the words mean? is a sensible question within a framework and is a non-sensical question in another framework. Those who believe that we cannot are the ones who believe that language is an institution and we need to be a member of the institution even to make an attempt to change the institution. i.e., this group does not believe that you can be an outsider and still change the meaning of the words in a language. Those who claim that it is possible to mean something different than what the words mean, are the ones who do not believe in the institution of language as given and eventually face the paradox of rule-following as the following analysis shows.

If intention can be different than the meaning of a sentence, how is it that we are able to assign new meanings to words and sentences even by arbitrarily defining them? It is possible because, normally we take the term to have the normal meaning in ordinary usage and whenever we assign new meanings, we define these terms; and in the written form we indicate this difference by putting the word which is used as a technical term deviating from the normal usage by putting the word into inverted commas. In the context of verbal communication, there are various ways that one can communicate this fact that one is using a term in a unique manner. A hermeneutician or for that matter everyone who claims that intention is the meaning of the sentence or word should put each and every word into inverted commas and thus, make the language an impossible one. That is to say, only while arbitrarily defining a word, or assigning the meaning to a word, our intention and the meaning are the same. However, subsequently, we can separate our intention and meaning. If we want to abide by ourselves by the rules of the society, we can continue using the words without any special meaning and if we do not want to abide by the norms of the society, we can use the terms in our own way. The thesis that intention is the meaning of the term or the sentence has, to fail. And it is demonstrated by the following example.

Let us assume that two of us are familiar with English and one holds the view that intention is the meaning of the words and sentences and the other holds the view that intention is independent of the meanings. The former, is well within his scheme to use each and every word the way he wants, as there is no social constraints that he should care for; while the latter who believes in the social theory of meaning cannot do that. However, it is well within the scheme of things for an intentionalist to imagine a situation where he for a moment is willing to take the social theorist seriously and abide by the rules within a certain context of say, playing chess. If both of them agree on rules, it is possible to play several games of chess where one wins and the other looses. Let us now introduce an element in this chess game from the intentionalist's point of view. What is checkmate is decided by the player. It is possible to imagine a context where one willfully looses, and if a person willfully looses, he wins. For instance while teaching chess to one's own child, one may willfully loose the game just to encourage the child and by loosing one has succeeded in what one wanted to achieve. Thus, in this modified context, if intentional theory of meaning is correct, then no one can loose the game of chess unless the player himself wanted to loose. For the meaning of what is to win is offered by the person concerned. The player might decide to give up, which is in his own scheme of things winning.

Let us further stretch the example and imagine that both the intentionalist and the proponent of the social theory converse on a mundane topic for sometime. Let us also assume that intentionalist being considerate would speak words with normal meaning most of the time yet he fails because of the influence of his theory and uses one word in his own peculiar way in every sentence he utters. The social theorist asks for clarification to which the intentionalist responds in his usual manner. However, being consistent with his own theory the intentionalist uses a term in his own unique manner while explaining the peculiar use of the sentence in his previous utterance. If the intentionalist continues with his own style of speaking, there is no way that the social theorist would ever understand anything that is uttered by intentionalist.

Intentionalist can produce a sample or two only to argue that his theory is correct. He cannot practice his own theory while demonstrating the validity of his theory. If one thinks that every time one utters a sentence one offers a definition, it would be a gross mistake. Kripke's skeptic believes in the validity of this intentional theory and demands the demonstration of the type which we have indicated is impossible. The skeptic's demand rests on a mistaken theory of meaning that meaning lies in intention.

If our understanding is correct, it is possible to imitate someone else, and learn the meaning of an expression simply by imitating others. Since, intention is not part of the rule and part of the meaning of a word, it is possible to imitate the behaviour of others without knowing the intention of the other person. As a consequence what happens is that one learns the use of words and the meaning of those words. Thus, we have understood the meaning of the word "week" without knowing what the intention of the speaker is.

NOTES AND REFERENCES

1. Kripke, S.A., (1982) Wittgenstein on Rules and Private Language, (hence, forth WRPL) Blackwell, Oxford.
2. However, there are some philosophers who have supported Kripke in this regard. For example, Byrne, Alex, ("On Misunderstanding Kripke's

Wittgenstein", *Philosophy and Phenomenological Research*, 1996) supports this view by arguing that, "On my reading of Kripke's text Kripke's Wittgenstein begins to look recognisably like Wittgenstein himself", p. 339.

3. *WRPL*, p. 5.
4. *Ibid.*, p. 7.
5. *Ibid.*, p. 4.
6. *Ibid.*, pp. 8-9.
7. *Ibid.*, p. 21.
8. *Ibid.*, p. 60.
9. *Ibid.*, p. 62.
10. Mulhall, S. (1989) "No Smoke without Fire: The Meaning of 'Grue", *Philosophical Quarterly*, 39, p. 185.
11. *WRPL*, p. 21.
12. *Ibid.*, p. 55.
13. *Ibid.*, p. 3.
14. *Ibid.*, p. 17. Compare this with the comment "I obey the rule blindly." by Wittgenstein, (Wittgenstein, L, *Philosophical Investigation* (henceforth *PI*) (ed.), G.E.M. Anscombe, Blackwell, Oxford, 1958. *PI*, § 219. The sense Wittgenstein wants to communicate is different here. He wants to indicate that once we accept a rule, we have no freedom to revise it in every case of applying it. It seems to us that applying the rule blindly would not be acceptable to Wittgenstein.
15. *PI*, § 151.
16. *WRPL*, p. 13.
17. *Ibid.*, p. 21.
18. Kripke claims that the indeterminacy of meaning held by skeptical paradox is similar to Quine's thesis of Indeterminacy of Translation and Inscrutability of Reference and Goodman's New Riddle of Induction. For a comparative study see, *WRPL*, pp. 55-59.
19. *WRPL*, p.viii.
20. Pettit, 1990, "The Reality of Rule-Following", *Mind*, Vol. 99, 1990, p. 4.
21. *WRPL*, pp. 7-8.
22. *Ibid.*, p. 11.
23. *Ibid.*, p. 14.
24. Boghossian, P.A., (1989) "The Rule-Following Consideration", *Mind*, Vol. 98, pp. 509-515.
25. Pettit, pp. 7-8.
26. *WRPL*, p. 22.
27. *Ibid.*, p. 37.
28. *Ibid.*, pp. 22-24.
29. Pettit, p. 3.
30. *Ibid.*, pp. 73-75.
31. *Ibid.*, p. 77.
32. *Ibid.*, pp 77-78.

33. *Ibid.*, p. 79.
34. *Ibid.*, p. 86.
35. *PI*, § 136.
36. Wittgenstein, L., *Philosophical Grammar* (henceforth PG) (ed.), R. Rhees, trans. A.J.P. Kenny, Blackwell, Oxford, 1974. He remarks: "What belongs to grammar are all the conditions (the method) necessary for comparing the proposition with reality. That is, all the conditions necessary for the understanding (of the sense), pp. 88/45.
37. Thus, he remarks about sensation of pain "It is not a *something*, but not a *nothing* either! The conclusion was only that a nothing would serve just as well as a something about which nothing could be said. We have only rejected the grammar which tries to force itself on us here." *PI,* § 304.
38. *WRPL*, pp. 96-107.
39. *PI*, § 240.
40. *WRPL,* p. 65.
41. *Ibid.,* p. 66.
42. *Ibid.,* p. 65.
43. *Ibid.*, p. 109.
44. *Ibid.*, p. 105.
45. *Ibid.*, p. 37. See section 2.3 of this chapter.
46. Basically the conceptualists defend this theory. For example, see Peacoke, C., "What are Concepts?", *Midwest Studies in Philosophy*, 1989, pp. 1-28.
47. Kartz, Jerrold J., *The Metaphysics of Meaning*, The MIT Press, Cambridge, *Mass*, 1990, p. 168.
48. *WRPL,* p. 24.
49. This kind of criticism of the dispositional theory of meaning is called "The Normative Objection" by Coats. See Coates, P., (1986) "Kripke's Skeptical Paradox: Normativeness and Meaning", *Mind*, pp. 77-80.
50. Baker, G.P. and Hacker, P.M.S. (1984) *Skepticism, Rule and Language*, Blackwell, Oxford, preface.
51. McGinn, Collin, (1984) *Wittgenstein on Meaning*, Oxford, Blackwell, p. 144.
52. Boghossian, *The Rule-Following Consideration*, p. 512.
53. Malcolm, Noman, (1989) "Wittgenstein on Language and Rules", *Philosophy*, Vol. 64, pp. 5 *ff.*
54. *WRPL,* p. 110.
55. This view is different from Quine's stimulus theory of meaning, but is comparable to his notion of similarity of 1981. For Quine's view, (1981) see his *Theories and Things*, Harvard University Press, Cambridge.

3

Goodman: The New Riddle of Induction

Introduction

Our purpose in this chapter is to present and understand Goodman's new riddle of induction[1] as a form of rule-following skepticism. Some scholars have taken the new riddle of induction as a problem in induction but not a problem in skepticism. Many others have, like us, believe that this is a problem in skepticism anything else it may be. The new riddle of induction on the face of it may not appear to be a version of rule-following skepticism. We believe that Goodman had anticipated the rule-following skepticism of Kripkean kind and has formulated the paradox of rule-following pertaining to induction.

What we consider the core of the skeptical issue is: given certain data or behaviour, how does one determine which rule is being followed if more than one rule fits the data equally? The uncertainty due to the multiplicity of rules which fit the context or given behaviour is the essence of the rule-following skepticism. Even the doubt about the past use of words *vis-à-vis* the present use of words is the question about the applicability of multiple rules to the same or similar context. Even if one knows all the facts about our past behaviour for sure, the skeptical question remains according to Kripke. To be brief, even if we know that we wrote 68 + 57 = 125 in the past, that would not in itself be a justification to conclude that one followed the rule of addition in the past, it could as well be another rule similar to the rule of addition which behaves exactly the same way till one reached the number say 100 as its one of the components of summation and changes its behaviour thereafter.[2] Thus, the skeptical issue does not depend so much on the fact that we do not know which rule we followed in the *past*, or we do not *remember* or know our *past intentions*, but it is regarding the uncertainty that prevails due to the failure of the mechanism which could help us to precisely say which rule is being followed.

Goodman in his formulation of the paradox makes use of the rule-following consideration in generalising un-observed from observed. He uses the word "hypothesis" in the place of the term "rule" and speaks of the observed data supporting two incompatible hypotheses. The hypothesis proposed would be simple and non-controversial in the sense that the next observation is expected to match the previous one provided everything else remains the same.

What should be noted is the different ways in which this problem of induction can be looked at. Critics are of divided opinion. Some thinkers have taken this problem to be involving the problem of probability since, they view this to be the problem of moving from limited observation of narrow universe to the observation of universal domain on the basis of induction by simple enumeration.[3] There are others who have not taken this line of thinking at all, but have taken the new riddle of induction to be a skeptical problem involving not probability, but uncertainty of predication.[4]

The process of induction by simple enumeration and the process of rule-formulation are similar. Induction moves from one example of a kind to anotner and finally to the generalized form of the sentence. For example, the inference is from this emerald is green, that emerald is green to all emeralds are green. Often rule formation takes place in similar manner. A figure with three straight lines is a triangle, and another figure with three straight lines is a triangle... all figures with three straight lines is triangles.[5] One cannot conclude merely from the structure of the inference from particulars to general that the process is induction by simple enumeration. This is because the basis on which the inference is made could be different. Let us outline these two basic types of inferences below:

(1) ***Empirical basis***: When Hume tried to find the basis for generalization, what he found was psychological basis. If we simply compare an event with another at the level of perception, what we get is mere sequence of events may be often repeated in that order. The assumption of this process is that what we experience of an object is a quality of that object. A quality of an object, as everyone knows, is conditioned by spatio-temporal factors. A mango is green could be true of a mango and it is yellow could also be true

of the same mango, but at different points in time. Normally, the qualities of objects are known to be accidents. That is to say, all the qualities of objects are contingent attributes of those things. Given this broad view of what a quality of object is, the inductive generalization based on the perception of qualities or predicates would remain probabilistic only.

(2) ***Rule based induction***: As against the above view, one can have generalization from simple enumeration. This time it is not the generalization on the basis of an accidental quality of an object, but generalization of the quality itself. For instance, in understanding what greenness is, one may examine several objects possessing the quality of green. After examining several green objects ranging from light green to dark green, one may conclude that one has learnt what green is. That is to say, one is in a comfortable position to identify all green objects given the chance to identify them and one is in a position to assess if someone else has claimed that an object is green etc. without much difficulty.

This process of generalization is different from the empirical enumeration in a crucial sense. The examples that we have examined in order to form the rule for the use of the word "green" serve only as instances or paradigms and do not add up to increase the probability of the generalized statement like in the case of simple enumeration. For instance, in the first type mentioned above, the validity of the statement "apples are red" is enhanced if supporting evidences are increased. But when we speak of generalization of the second type which is linguistic rules including some laws of nature are different from the probablistic generalized statement of the first type.[6] For example, water boils at 100°C at sea level or triangles are figures formed with three straight lines. Whether one has noted two examples of figures formed with three straight lines or whether one has noted ten figures of this kind, the validity of the statement that "all triangles are figures with three straight lines" would remain the same. Moreover, there is uncertainty attached to the generalized statement based on induction by simple enumeration because we find the empirical relationship between two perceptual qualities observed again and again. That is to say, in induction of this kind we infer the presence of a quality on the basis of the observation of another quality in an object. This does not happen always in the case of rule governed generalization. It is one and the same quality or predicate with respect to which we form the rule and once we form the rule, we know that the rule can have infinite applications. We can say that we generalize not on the basis of an accidental property of an object, but with respect to the very property that is under consideration. This is the reason why generalization does not have the uncertainty attached to it in the case of rule based generalization. This is the reason why one need not know all the cases of applications in order to learn the rule at all.[7]

The New Riddle of Induction

Goodman formulates his new riddle of induction by making use of three predicates, namely, green, *grue* and blue. All these three predicates are attributed to emeralds in such a manner that there clearly arises a paradox. The predicates green and blue are used the way we are familiar with them, whereas the predicate "*grue*" is used in a special way. Making use of the linguistic liberty, Goodman defines the term "*grue*" in an unusual way. He combines in this predicate green as well as blue predicate but with a special condition. He explains it in the following words:

Now, let me introduce another predicate less familiar than "green". It is the predicate "*grue*" and it applies to all things examined before *t* just in case they are green but to other things just in case they are blue. Then at time *t* we have, for each evidence statement asserting that a given emerald is green, a parallel evidence statement asserting that the emerald is *grue*. And the statements that emerald *a* is *grue*, *b* is *grue*, and so on, will each conform the general hypothesis that all emeralds are *grue*. Thus, according to our definition, the prediction that all emerald subsequently examined will be green and the prediction that all will be *grue* are alike confirmed by evidence describing the same observations. But if an emerald subsequently examined is *grue*, it is blue and hence, not green. Thus although, we are well aware which of the two incompatible predictions is genuinely confirmed, they are equally well confirmed according to our present definition.[8]

Thus, the peculiarity of the predicate *grue* is: (1) *grue* applies to all the objects which are green as well as which are blue before a chosen time *t*, (2) *grue* applies to all the objects that are only blue after time *t* and not to green objects. That is to say, *grue* is a predicate that applies to all blue things before and after time *t*, but only to be examined green things before *t*. The paradox works out this way:

Each and every observation of emerald before time *t* supports the two hypotheses equally:

(1) All emeralds are green.
(2) All emeralds are *grue*.

This is so because all emeralds so far observed are green and the predicate *grue* includes the predicate green till time *t*. However, at time *t*, an incompatible situation would arise. Since, we have no counter instance against both green hypothesis and the *grue* hypothesis, we have to claim that all emeralds are green as well as *grue*. Going by the green hypothesis, if we have to predict the colour of emeralds after *t*, then we are committed to say that the emerald observed would be green, and going by the *grue* hypothesis, if we have to predict the colour of emeralds after *t*, then we are committed to say that the emeralds observed would be blue. However, it is not possible that the emeralds observed after time *t* would be both green as well as blue as green and blue are incompatible predicates. How did we have the incompatible hypothesis and how do we resolve the paradox is the question that Goodman is interested in understanding.

Let us try to understand the issues involved in the above paradox. At the outset what can be said to be obvious is that Goodman's supposition that our past observations are considered to be ground of our future expectations. No one would deny the expectation that emeralds observed after time *t* would be green if emeralds observed before time *t* are all green and none are non-green. This is quite a reasonable thing to happen though logically one cannot deny the possibility of emeralds changing their colour enmass at time *t* due to some global factors. If such global factors are known to us in advance, then we may doubt the predications we make on the basis of observations so far about emeralds. It is equally reasonable to believe that the next emerald observed would be *grue* on the basis of the observation that all emeralds observed so far are green and all green emeralds observed are *grue*. Our *grue* hypothesis so far is identical to our green hypothesis. But the trouble begins the very moment one reaches the specific time *t*. At *t*, both the hypotheses are equally justified so far as the number of evidences that have supported the hypotheses. Of course, if we are to speak of their probability, they would have had different probabilities, the green hypothesis would have had higher probability and the *grue* hypothesis would have had lesser probability. This point we shall discuss little later.

Note that our *grue* concept has two criteria both are mutually exclusive. It is important to note this because, our green predicate involves only one criterion and the *grue* predicate involves two. The criteria or the rules for the use of the predicate *grue* are: (1) an object if it is green before *t*; and (2) an object if it is blue it is *grue* irrespective of time constraint. These two criteria (rules) for the use of the predicate *grue* are incompatible since, they are criteria based on colour concepts which are themselves incompatible. Moreover, a predicate is normally considered to be an atemporal predicate. No predicate is a natural predicate if time is a dimension of the predicate. This is because the laws of nature are also atemporal. That being so, atemporal law cannot be captured by temporal predicates. If anyone makes an attempt in this direction it would be something like claiming that 2 + 2 = 4 is true only in the twentieth Century.

When there are two criteria for the use of a word and when each one is a sufficient criterion for the use of the word, all the objects fall under each of the criteria would be the part of the extension of the predicate. That is the reason why all observed green emeralds till time *t* and all blue emeralds are the part of the extension of the predicate *grue*. It is not clear whether unexamined green emeralds before time *t* are also part of the extension of *grue* given the definition of *grue*.[9] However, we may note that the term "*grue*" need not be taken to be ambiguous or equivocal. We have several examples of predicates having multiple rules. For instance Wittgenstein has indicated that the predicate "game" has various rules for its use. There are board games, card games, ball games and so on having the feature of winning and loosing, two parties, and sometimes lacking even these features. The word "game" thus, can be considered to be a more general term having large scope rather than a narrow term. Generality is opposed to specificity and ambiguity is opposed non-equivocality. The term "bat" can be considered to be equivocal not general. It has two distinct sense, one refers to the mammal and the other refers to the instrument used in games. One may consider "bat" as a mammal is very narrow and more precise in comparison to "bat" in the context of games. Since, the criteria (rules) for the use of the term "bat" are distinct and separate, the two senses of the term are also felt distinctly. Taking hint from this example, we may say that Goodman's *grue* is an equivocal term.

Please note that the term "coloured" is not equivocal even though it is very general. We can say safely "all green objects are coloured" and "all blue objects are coloured". We can also say "all red objects are coloured" and "all yellow objects are coloured". The term "coloured" is a more general term including all colours as part of its extension and yet the term does not seem to be equivocal. However, the term "*grue*" is not a term like "red" which includes pink, deep-red and so on as part of its extension. "*Grue*" is more general in comparison to "green" or "blue" since, it includes some green objects and all blue objects as part of its extension. Hence, it is necessarily more general than blue, but with regard to green nothing conclusively be said. All green objects after the time *t* are not part of the extension of *grue* as per the definition. Therefore, though it behaves relatively like a general term till time *t* since, it includes all observed cases of green and blue, it includes only blue things after time *t* and this condition makes, we suspect, the *grue* term to be equivocal. In other words, if *grue* had included all the green and blue objects as part of its extension without attaching any time restriction to its application, then the predicate would have been one like red or any other colour with wider scope. Since, one of the criteria for the use of the term "*grue*" is limited by time factor, we suspect the term "*grue*" is equivocal.

If we are wrong in our supposition that *grue* is an equivocal term, then it is due to the very nature of the problematic criterion for the use of the predicate *grue*. No doubt that every user of a natural language has the license to introduce a new term by declaring the rules for the use of a word in terms of exemplification or definition. Goodman's *grue* is one such predicate which is introduced as part of our philosophical vocabulary in the context of induction. However, where *grue* deviates from the norm of introducing a new term is that the criteria offered as rules for the use the word are limited by time. When we introduce a term we make a commitment to the use of that term unconditionally thereafter. This is one of the implicit assumptions within which all natural languages work and Goodman's *grue* violates this implicit assumption of language.[10]

A predicate does not have time restricted rule is clear from the fact that a temporal predicate also is atemporal. For instance, consider the predicate a day, or for that matter a week. The notion of duration is required to have both these concepts. Duration is something that stretches in time, has a beginning and an end. Thus, a day begins immediately when a previous day ends. Conventionally, after midnight a day begins and stretches up to the next midnight. The duration between one midnight and another midnight is a day. Thus, one can consider the duration between any one midnight and the next one in an absolute time series to obtain a day. That is to say, a day has 24 hours but it is not fixed which 24 hours. Similar is the notion of a week, month and so on. What must be noted is that even a temporal predicate does not have a date or a particular time as part of its rule. The interesting question would be: why can not time dimension be attached to a rule? For instance, 1997 B.C. or the first century A.D. etc. are predicates having time as part of their component. Of course, this is so with certain concepts of duration. For instance, "Gandhi was born in nineteenth century" is true of Gandhi and it would not be true of Gandhi if we say "Gandhi was born in twentieth century". There are only a particular number of people who are born in nineteenth century and others are not born in that century. People who are born in nineteenth century would include only certain individuals and not others and yet the predicate is quite sound. There are individuals who are quite like nineteenth century people yet they are not born in nineteenth century and are not included in the predicate of nineteenth century people. Therefore, there can be any restriction to a predicate one like this: individuals who are born between eighteenth century and twentieth century.

A duration can be named and that duration can be used as a predicate. This is the contention of Goodman, and the predicate *grue* is such that it has one of the criteria as time restricted, i.e., till time *t* all green objects are *grue*, of course it incidentally happens that all emeralds observed so far are green. If a nineteenth century man can be similar to twentieth century man and yet nineteenth century man is not twentieth century man, why can not this happen with respect to green emeralds which are *grue* till time *t* and are not *grue* then after? Is it because *grue* has two criteria, one time restricted and the other atemporal?

When particulars are made part of the criterion of a rule, then the criterion also behaves like a particular. By invoking time *t* as part of one of the criteria for the use of the word *grue*, Goodman has restricted the use of the term "*grue*" on this basis. Normally, rules are always provided in general terms and no particular would occur in the specification of the rule. There can be very special situation where a rule may be defined with respect to a particular context. For instance, the rule of inheritance of certain Privy Purse could be defined in terms of particular family. But this is a special case and this does not apply to most of the natural kind terms or terms in science and philosophy of science.

Notice that when we speak of scope or extension of a predicate we claim that all objects in the past, all objects that exist today and all objects that would come into existence constitute the extension of the predicate. For instance, the predicate red would include even the apples of twenty first century. However, nineteenth century man does not include anyone else except those who are born in the nineteenth century. That is to say, its extension is time-restricted. *Grue* is not a colour concept if it is time restricted like nineteenth century. Both the concepts of green and blue are not time restricted yet the predicate *grue* is defined in that manner in the new riddle.

We suspect, the above is the reason why *grue* is an equivocal predicate. On one criterion, it is a time-restricted predicate and on another criterion it is a colour predicate like green or blue. Let us identify these two senses of *grue* so that clarity in discussion is maintained. We prefer to call the two senses to be temporal notion of *grue* and the colour notion of *grue*. And when we generalize, we suspect that the process involved with reference to each sense of the term *grue* is different. Temporal predicate of *grue* would involve induction by simple enumeration and the colour predicate *grue* would involve rule-based induction.

Let us now turn to the issues of probability attached to the generalized statement and the inductive support by the evidence statements. We suspect that it would not be appropriate to believe that the two hypotheses namely all emeralds are green and all emeralds are *grue* are equally supported by the evidence statements at time t when taken in the probabilistic sense. If there are 100 emeralds totally which are green in the world and if we have examined only 10 of them before time t, then 10 out of 100 would put the probability at .10. Now, consider all the *grue* objects. All the 10 green objects that are observed out of 100 emeralds are *grue*, and if we assume that there are n number of blue emeralds un-observed which are *grue*, then the probability is 10 for $100 + n$. Thus, we notice that the first hypothesis, i.e., all emeralds are green is more probable in comparison to all emeralds are *grue*. An extension of a predicate includes all the objects that existed in the past, all the objects that fall within its scope presently and all the objects that would fall within its scope in the future.

The Skepticism and Induction

The new riddle of induction presents a paradox similar to the problem of rule-following skepticism. The evidence statement that all emeralds observed so far are green fits the supposition that the next emerald that we are likely to observe would be green as well as *grue*. This is what leads to uncertainty of the rule that is being followed. Not only had that if one has to speak of an instance of emerald after time *t*, the situation is further complicated. At the linguistic level the supposition is perfectly fitting, i.e., the emerald obsessed would be green following the green hypothesis and the emerald observed would be *grue* following the definition of *grue* following the second criterion of *grue,* i.e., it is blue after time *t*. Kripke's formulation of the rule-following skepticism raises the issue of identifying our present use of word with that of our past use. Since, there is no fact mental or physical to indicate the identity of meaning between our present use of word and the past use of word, one cannot certainly claim that there is some justification to our present use in terms of the past usages. Kripke in his formulation of "*grue*" problem states:

Perhaps by "green" in the past I meant *grue*, and the colour image, which indeed was *grue*, was meant to direct me to apply the word "green" to *grue* objects always. If the *blue* object before me now is *grue*, then it falls in the extension of "green", as I meant it in the past. It is no help to suppose that in the past I stipulated "green" was to apply to all and only those things "of the same colour as" the sample.[11]

However, if both these predicates are predicated of all the observations of emeralds and every instance of emeralds, then at no time we know for sure which predicate is being ascribed to the emerald, green-*grue* or blue-*grue*. Moreover, how do we know that we have followed the rule of predicate green to claim that all emeralds observed so far are green rather than the temporally restricted rule of *grue,* i.e., all green objects are *grue* till time *t*? Thus, all emeralds observed till time *t* fit two hypotheses and thus, one is not in a position to precisely determine the meaning of the observations. This skepticism is essentially the same as rule-following skepticism where multiple rules fit the given evidence or behaviour and hence, the uncertainty.

Sharing our sentiment, Barker and Achinstein propose that a single picture or representation can be given for all instances of application of a non-positional predicate, while at least two different representations are needed to cover all instances of application of a positional predicate. For example, a single patch of green paint will represent the colour of all green things irrespective of their dates; but two present patches will be needed to represent all *grue* things: a green one for cases up to time *t* and a blue one for cases thereafter.[12]

Against this objection, Goodman has tried to defend that his concept of *grue* is not positional. Since, till time *t*, anything which is green is also *grue* and therefore a sample of green would also be a sample of *grue*. Moreover, Goodman is of the view that a sample green would not represent different shades of green. And thus, Goodman does not accept the analysis of Barker and Achinstein that blue is not positional whereas *grue* is.

However, there seems to be some truth in the argument of Barker and Achinstein. May be the objection has to be re-formulated. Aristotle said that each particular has the universal in equal measure. The spirit of the thesis is that every man is a human being in equal measure whether he is healthy or unhealthy, whether he is rich or poor, white or black. That is to say, an instance of a rule is equally an instance irrespective of other factors. In the same vain, a green patch of colour is equally green with respect to any other patch of colour. But this may not be true of the predicate *grue*. It would not be possible to claim that a patch of green colour is *grue* in equal measure in comparison to any other piece of colour of green. This is because there is the constraint of time *t* on green patches of colours to be *grue* and moreover, it would be quite difficult to say that a green patch of colour which is *grue* before time *t* is equally *grue* in comparison to a blue patch of colour after time *t*. Of course, in a sense it ought to be exactly the way both a teaching and a non-teaching staff are employees of the same institution. But in all contexts it may not be all right to say so. For instance, if one is searching for a person to give a talk on the concept of freedom, either of them may not do.

Goodman adds further clarification in response to the objection raised by Barker and Achinstein[13] that *grue* is a temporal concept as it involves temporal term in defining the concept. He writes:

True enough, if we start with "blue" and "green", then "*grue*" and "*bleen*" will be explained in terms of "blue" and "green" and a temporal term. But equally truly, if we start with "*grue*" and "*bleen*", then "blue" and green" will be explained in terms of "*grue*" and "*bleen*" and a temporal term; "green", for example, applies to emeralds examined before time *t* just in case they are *grue*, and to other emeralds just in case they are *bleen*.[14]

A normal reply to the above comment is the following: Having had the concept of green and blue, one is in a position to define the term "*grue*" and "*bleen*" making use of the predicates green and glue and a temporal criterion. And having achieved to have the predicate *grue* and *bleen*, he is in a position to re-define "blue" and "green" as temporal predicates. This is possible apparently because language permits re-defining the terms or changing the use of words. Let us make an attempt to see what would happen if one since,rely makes this attempt.

To begin with one needs to suppose that *grue* and *bleen* are not temporal predicates. If they are not temporal predicates, one of the following things would happen: either *grue* is a predicate which has at least one non-temporal rule for its use and the same is true of *bleen*. They would be colour terms one like red or yellow. They would be perfectly projectible and positional etc. On this supposition, our language lacks the terms "green", "blue" from the stock of colour terms. Let us now suppose that we define the terms "green" and "blue" as temporal predicates. We begin by saying "green" applies to emeralds examined before time *t* just in case they are *grue*, and to other emeralds just in case they are *bleen*.

Goodman has proved nothing here by stating that if *grue* and *bleen* are introduced first then the terminologies of "green" and "blue" would turn out to be relative. This is nothing but the reversal of the roles of two sets of pair of predicates, green and blue on the one hand *grue* and *bleen* on the other. What he has demonstrated is nothing but the reversal of terminologies and not of the concepts or predicates. He only asks us to use the symbol "*grue*" in the place of "green" and "*bleen*" in the place of "blue". This is one like making Thursday come first and Wednesday come later in a week by interchanging the names of the days. This makes no change to the substance of the argument that his predicate *grue* is temporal and the predicate green and blue are not. There is nothing in a name, after all names are arbitrary! What Goodman fails to notice is the fact that an atemporal predicate can be restricted and shown as a temporal predicate; however the reversal is not possible. A temporal predicate cannot be converted into a non-temporal. For instance, if we remove all restrictions on a day, a week etc. then there is no difference between a day and a week, all end at infinity. The day also began at midnight and goes up to infinity, and the week also began at the same time and goes up to infinity. The apt comparison is from logic. some from all, but not always all from some. One can derive existential quantifier from universal quantifier but not the other way around. Given the rules of green and blue which are unrestricted, Goodman could derive a restricted rule of *grue*, i.e., if something is green before time *t*, then it is *grue* because the rule all emeralds are green is a atemporal.

What follows from this analysis is that a temporal predicate cannot be considered as projectible and not that blue and green are predicates which are relative. The above analysis conclusively shows only one thing: given the natural predicates of colour, one can define an arbitrary predicate using a temporal term. But this is a thesis about the linguistic ability of man or at best a point about language rather than a thesis about predicate itself.

Moreover, a colour predicate if it is made into a temporal predicate one like *grue*, then we suspect that predicate turns out to be a relative one. The predicate becomes relative because one of its criteria is relative. For instance, one of the criteria makes use of the contingent fact of number of observations that have been made of emeralds before time *t*. Of course, the definition does not include the number of green emeralds which are not observed before time *t* as part of extension of *grue*. No need to say that the criterion is imprecise because it does not make it obvious who has examined these emeralds. Whether, the set of "examined emeralds" would also include the observation made by Berkeley's God is not clear.

Lawlike Statements

Goodman is of the opinion that a general statement is lawlike if and only if it is acceptable prior to the determination of all its instances.[15] Here Goodman seems to be quite right though he does not accept this very statement on the basis that "acceptable" is a dispositional predicate. We have very good reason to believe that the statement is very right despite the qualification, the general statement is acceptable. In fact, one could go a step ahead and make the condition mandatory by claiming that only if the statement is "accepted". Goodman believes that acceptable is a dispositional term and this needs to be replaced by a non-dispositional term eventually. We have two questions to address to: first, is acceptance a dispositional term? and the second what is wrong with a dispositional term as the condition of generalization? Our first impression is that acceptance is a dispositional term if and only if when it is taken in the sense of approval or as a value and all values are dispositions. And it is highly improbable that we will have a theory whether scientific or otherwise which we do not value and yet it is desirable or acceptable to us. Secondly, what would be wrong if we value generalization, i.e., if the rules in the form of generalizations are normative?

Goodman seems to say something very basic: The laws of nature can only be descriptive and no dispositional term such as "acceptable" can figure in its formulation. In other words, no law of nature is normative. This contention of Goodman is shared by most thinkers in the field of philosophy of science. However, we would like to examine this supposition later.

Let us begin with the supposition that a law of nature must have the explanatory power, otherwise it is not a law. This supposition is often supported by all those thinkers who support Goodman on the point that a law should be descriptive. We need to know how the law acquires this explanatory power if the law has to remain explanatory. A point of caution here. Explanation is not the same as description. We can describe the process that is taking place, and we can describe what has happened in the past. Of course, we can even describe the events that are likely to take place tomorrow. Normally, describing the future events is called predicting, yet predicting as an activity can be distinguished from describing.

One likely suggestion (as is the case with Goodman) would be that the strength of the generalized statement is derived from the positive instances that have gone in support of the statement. Of course, more the instances of the law observed, more the strength of the law. Hume thought that this kind of strength of the law is derived from psychological association in the form of habit and others might call this to be due to the rational inductive process. But this is not the strength of the law at all. Neither the psychological association nor the rational inductive reasoning is the part of the world as it is and therefore it would be quite odd to say that the world has the inductive process. If the world has the inductive process it would have completed its process of reasoning long before the first human being came into existence on this planet. Thus, it would be quite appropriate to state that our formulation of the law of nature is our understanding of the nature and the process of our formulation of the law is not to be confused with the nature having the law.

Though said in some other context, we find much truth in the statement of Wittgenstein that the process of justification should come to an end somewhere. No doubt, the process of justifying should begin somewhere as well. Thus, if we are alert, we notice that the law of nature existed and we started formulating the law at a particular juncture. The strength of the law cannot depend on the number of observations that we have made. The laws had to have this explanatory power even before formulating our law. Once we discover or formulate the law of nature, we can even explain the pre-historic stage of this world. How did we manage that? Not because we existed before any man existed on this planet, but because our present formulation about the evolution of Earth gives us the strength to explain how the world would have evolved.

It is our contention that no descriptive theory could have the explanatory power in the above sense In the strict sense, a description is a true description if and only if the description corresponds to the fact. However, if I have to describe something that was in the past, there is no fact that can correspond to the past. In this sense, we cannot describe our past! Wittgenstein remarked once that we cannot claim that Mr. N.N. is dead because if Mr. N.N. is dead on the reference theory of meaning soon after he is dead the expression Mr. N.N. became meaningless.[16] In a similar vain, we may say that if a true statement describes the fact, then all the statements that refer to past events cannot describe the events any more and similarly we have no right to describe the events in future which have not yet become the realities!

We tend to reject the above supposition that we cannot describe what has happened in the past and we cannot describe the possible events in the future. However, note that there is immense difficulty in overcoming the problems raised. Even if we admit the indirect verification method, verification does not constitute the facts and hence, there is no reason to say that the statement "I visited the library yesterday" corresponded to the facts since, the facts about myself and the facts about library have changed so drastically that there is no way we can rebuild the facts. Yet, we believe that there is something that helps us to describe the past events and the descriptions if true correspond to the facts in the past.

Our memory or record of any kind cannot help unless the situation is viewed in the manner in which we did in concluding the last chapter. A sample of this is already examined by Kripke in his formulation of the rule-following skepticism. There is no way that one can be sure that one has used the word with the same meaning in the past. The same is applicable again in the context of laws and their application in the past. If the strength of the explanatory power of the law is derived from the observation made by individual scientists in the twentieth Century, then the same law cannot be used to explain the birth of the planets and evolution of different species since, those events have occurred long before the law is even in its infancy.

If the above discussion has some merit, then the strength of the law is not derived from human psychology or from inductive inference that human beings use, but the very nature of laws that are constitutive of nature. These laws can be discovered at any stage of human civilization. If one were to give an analogy, it is like a tribal man discovering the two railway lines passing through his forest discovering neither the beginning nor the end. Yet, by some process of reasoning he can possibly predict where the trains come from and what is their destiny provided he is aware of the towns in these two directions. The laws of nature are operating long before we have known them and they may continue to operate for quite some time even after we vanish as humans, yet we can examine the instances of their applications beginning somewhere and terminating our process of induction somewhere by accepting the laws as given in the form of general statements. We would prefer to call the laws "general statements" rather than "generalized statements".

An explanation is possible only if there is a rule or the basis on which one provides an explanation. Why the house was on fire? can be answered by saying that there was sparking due to some short-circuit in the house which lead to the fire. This is to say that an explanation can be advanced if and only if something lawlike is accepted by the people. Therefore, the explanation would not be an explanation if the lawlike principle is not accepted at all. Say if someone says that God was angry and he set the house on fire, it would not be an explanation to those who do not believe in the authority of God. Therefore, acceptance of a law is prior to the explanation that can be offered by using that principle or law.

One could distinguish between natural laws and cultural laws. Both are used in explaining events natural or cultural. We use natural laws to explain the events in nature and we use cultural rules or laws to explain human behaviour. Why was he reprimanded by the traffic police? is explained by referring to a cultural rule: Because he did not obey the road rules.

We may draw the attention to the distinction between "brute facts" and "institutional facts" made by John Searle.[17] This of course is related to the two senses of the term law. Moritz Schlick also distinguishes between two senses of the term law. "Law" is a rule by which the state prescribes certain behaviour to its citizens. These rules often contradict the natural desires of the citizens. In natural science, Schlick observes, the word "law" means something quite different. The natural law is not a prescription as to how something should behave, but a formula, a description of how something does in fact behave. The two forms of "laws" have only this in common: both tend to be expressed in formulae. He further opines that since, natural laws are only descriptions of what happens, there can be in regard to them no talk of "compulsion".[18] Thus, corresponding to the two senses of laws one may draw the distinction between brute facts and institutional facts. Brute facts would be something like the fact that the table exists just in front of me, whereas I am an employee of an organization can be considered to be an institutional fact. We could readily apply this distinction to our discussion above, namely, the laws of nature formulated by human beings are institutional facts and the observations made by using these laws could be called brute facts. The house is on fire, but what set the house on fire? The first part of the question states a brute fact and its justification or explanation is sought in terms of a law, i.e., the cause of the fire in the second part. Moritz Schlick, for example, writes "To explain means to refer back to laws: every science, including psychology, is possible only in so far as there are such laws to which the events can be referred."[19]

Commenting on compulsion and necessity Schlick writes that to apply the word "necessity" to natural laws is senseless, since, the word "necessity" is derived from the word "need" and the presupposition of an opposing desire in the case of natural laws is lacking. It is of the essence of natural laws to be universally valid claims Schlick and opines that it is only when we have found a rule which holds of events without exception do we call the rule a law of nature. Universal validity is different from compulsion claims Schlick.[20]

This trait of universal validity is applicable to cultural laws as well. Schlick fails to note this, though the word compulsion is used in one case, the word disposition may be used in another case. If brittleness of a glass can exist in the glass, the disposition to attract iron files exists in the magnets. We are somehow mistaken in thinking that natural laws are not dispositional. In fact, if natural laws only describe and do not explain, then it is not possible to predict any future events using those laws. Therefore, we may opine that all those philosophers who took natural laws to be descriptive as opposed to dispositional or normative would have sever shortcomings in their explanations. For instance, they have no means to explain: why there was firc in the building. Of course, they can describe how the fire lit up. But that is not an explanation in the sense that if one were to take precautionary measures what one were to do cannot be explained. Someone who believes only in the descriptive nature of laws might say, yes the electric short circuit has led to fire in that house, but why should one worry about that since, our house does not have that problem? This person fails to understand the connection between old electric wires lead to short circuits. Without knowing the underlying law, one cannot understand the explanation offered, i.e., if you do not replace old electric wires in your house, it might lead to short circuit and eventually your house would in fire. "It has never happened in our house" is an appropriate answer following descriptive theory.

One tends to think that the descriptive theory has the power to describe the future events as well. Following this line of thinking one might say that using the laws of nature one can describe the future events such as old electrical wires leading to short circuit and the house being in fire. But a truly descriptive theorist can also describe the opposite of this. In future the house with old electrical wires are not leading to any short circuits. There is nothing compelling for a descriptive theorist to choose one instead of the other. Both of these are the projections or predictions and in order to make predictions we need laws which are more than mere descriptions and a descriptive theory cannot speak of a law in the strict sense is evident from the above example.

Contingent Lawlike Statements

Goodman also speaks of the contingent lawlike statements and the lawlike statements which express laws and he feels that there is no syntactic or semantic criterion which can be used to distinguish between these two types of statements. For instance, he cites the example of "All the coins in my pocket are silver" and claims it to be contingent lawlike statements.[21] He opines further that there is no syntactic and semantic criterion for distinguishing lawlike statements from contingent generalizations.[22]

Let us ask the question: What are the types of contingent generalizations possible? There seems to be only three types of contingent generalizations possible:

(a) A generalization is contingent because the subject term is artificially restricted. For example, all coins in my pocket are silver.
(b) A generalization is contingent because the predicate is restricted. For example, all *grue* objects include all observed emeralds examined before *t* and all blue emeralds after *t*.
(c) A generalization is contingent because it is between two predicates and there is no logical relation between the two predicates. For example, creatures with heart are the creatures with kidneys.[23]

The first two types are contingent generalizations which are restricted by the arbitrarily defining a term in terms of particulars. They cannot be lawlike. The last one, is a contingent statement, i.e., it is an induction by simple enumeration and yet is contingent. This is because it relates two predicates empirically. It is a contingent fact that we have not found a single counter instance for this generalization. And we have not found a single logical reason why heart and kidneys should go-together. It is one thing to say that in future we may understand the basic function of heart which would include pumping the blood to different parts of the body at the same time purifying the blood by sending the blood to lungs and to kidneys as essential feature of our conception of heart. Even if this happens at a future date, yet it is possible to imagine creatures with only heart and not kidneys and even then one could say that the relation between a heart and a kidney at the logical level is contingent. This is an example of a lawlike statement without it being a law.

Ask the question: how did we know that there is no logical relationship between these two predicates? Since, logic is based on human convention, we can know that there exists no convention regarding the use of these two predicates, namely, heart and kidney in such a manner that they are logically related. One does not discover a logical relationship between any two predicates by observing something external to language. Wittgenstein has said that there is nothing hidden in a language and since, logical relationship between two predicates are within language, one always knows that there is no logical relationship between two predicates if there is absence of any convention which relates these two predicates. Therefore, we do not need to look for any outside factor to know if there existed any logical relationship among predicates. However, we need to look out for an empirical relationship. By looking into the use of the terms in language one cannot conclude whether an empirical relation would obtain between creatures with heart and creatures with kidneys. Therefore, the third statement is an empirical generalization and is not lawlike is evident because the relationship is not one of logical type is known to all those who are familiar with the two predicates "heart" and "kidney" adequately.

Let us ask a counter question: How does one come to know that creatures with heart are the creatures with kidneys, is a contingent generalization and not a law? Speaking of ourselves, we have never even noticed two instances of there being such a relationship or lack of such a relationship. Yet, we know on the basis of our linguistic competence we can assert that there exists no such logical relation between these two predicates. That is to say, it is enough for us to know these predicates to conclude that there exists or does not exist any logical relationship between these two predicates. This is the reason why we readily accepted the words of Quine that the statement "creatures with hearts are creatures with kidneys" is an empirical generalization.

We have the linguistic competence to identify or differentiate a general term against a specific term, a synonym from an antonym; an ambiguous sentence from an unambiguous sentence, an imprecise sentence from a precise sentence and so on. But how do we succeed in drawing these distinctions? How do we know where to begin even to start the linguistic analysis to make the distinctions evident? For instance, how does one distinguish a dispositional term from a non-dispositional term? Normally, we are satisfied if an analyst points out to us that certain terms are dispositional even if the dispositional property is not evident in the object cited. For instance, the glass is brittle we admit, but the brittleness of the glass cannot be found in the glass that we are presently examining. The glass is brittle meant that the glass would break if we drop it. In contrast to this, redness of the glass is not a dispositional property. We are able to observe the quality of redness of the glass immediately. Descriptive predicate red is essentially different from the dispositional property like brittleness.

But how this brittleness is different from that of being ancient? The same glass could be a piece in a museum and the attribute of being ancient may be attributed to the piece. Both dispositional property and the piece being ancient cannot be directly observed. Why is this analysis convincing? It is nothing but our linguistic competence that gives us the clue that this distinction between a predicate that is dispositional and a predicate that is not dispositional is tenable. Thus, any distinction drawn in a language would be acceptable or not acceptable to us on the basis of our linguistic practice and intuition.

Ask the question how do we know that the term "table" is an equivocal term? One tends to answer this question by pointing out that the word has at least two uses. But what made us count them as two uses why not many more or only one? For instance, one may indicate, the word is used in the context of mathematics and that use is different from the use of the word in the context of furnitures. But one may indicate that in the context of mathematics, there are tables, but there are also tables in the context of logic say truth-tables. There are also tables in the context of railways time-table and in the context of books the table of contents and so on. But why should we treat the table of contents in the context of books has different meaning in comparison to the railway time table? How railway time table is different from truth table in logic? Just by indicating the extension of the term, we may not be able to show that the term has different meaning. Each instance that is different from another can be shown to be different from another instance. Each entry in the railway time table is different from the other entry, and the same is true of a truth table in logic. And it is not difficult to imagine that mathematical table and truth table are put in one table. Yet, that would not make truth table a part of mathematical table or *vice-versa*. Those who believe that by indicating that the extensions are different one has succeeded in indicating that the two uses are different and hence, there are two senses to the term would not be able to satisfy a nominalist like

Goodman. He would say, there is nothing in the object that makes it the part of the extension of a term except the convention that we have adopted.

We do not need to test our extensions to know whether a term is equivocal or univocal. Though we normally point out that a term is equivocal by indicating that it has two types of objects as part of its extension. It would be misleading to believe in this type of reasoning. Just because the term "animal" would have cows and cats as part of its extension, the term would not be equivocal. In fact the term is univocal is obvious to us. War is not univocal but equivocal. Thus, we move from meaning to extension rather than extension to meaning when we speak of ambiguity, equivocality etc.

Answer to the issue lies in the following. If nominalists are right, there should not have been any equivocal terms. Since, all uses of the terms are legitimate uses if they are based on convention and even if they are not based on conventions, one can always invoke a new convention by defining that way (e.g. *grue* of Goodman) in an arbitrary manner. Therefore, the question is why are there equivocal terms and what makes them equivocal when the same term is used to refer to multiple things of various groups? A nominalist cannot answer this linguistic fact satisfactorily by maintaining the thesis that universals are mere names. And the realist answers this question always with reference to the nature of objects that fall as part of its scope, but he has no reason to offer to the question why these varied things should fall under the scope of the same predicate.

We can conduct a thought experiment to demonstrate that an arbitrary definition when offered to the terms already having some meaning can make the term equivocal. For instance, we know the expression "lady's finger" in the literal sense. When for the first time this expression was used to identify a vegetable grown in Asian countries, it was an extension of the use of the expression based on some superficial look of the vegetable. But the expression now has acquired independent meaning of its own and is equivocal by any standard. But there can be no concept of extension of the use of an expression in nominalistic framework. Now, consider compound words. Both the terms "war" and "cold" having their conventional meaning. But when we combine these two terms to form a phrase "cold war" the expression has a new meaning. And similarly, we have obtained the expression "civil war" by combining the terms "civil" and "war". But in these combined expressions, there is an attempt to extend the use of the term "war" to cover the political phenomena which were not considered to be war-like phenomena. If nominalists were right, there were no need to even combine the two expressions to obtain a compound expression. Simply start calling civil wars also simply wars, star wars also simply wars and that would have done the job. But even if we had followed this method, the subtle difference in these uses of the expression "war" would have remained. Thus, even if one extends the use of a term beyond its normal scope, the sense of the term does not remain the same. And this indicates why nominalism is wrong.

The Myth of Induction

It would be unfair if we do not give due credit to Popper who has said many pertinent points about induction and related issues. The basic position of Popper as against all those who believe that induction is respectable and rewarding is this:

Hume's psychological explanation of induction is both factually and logically incorrect. Because there are many psychological repetition of experience in the nature without giving rise to regularities. That does not compel us to expect a lawlike succession of events.[24] Logically, it is incorrect because the kind of similarity it tries to establish among the objects or events are similar from a certain point of view.[25] The kind of repetition envisaged by Hume can never be perfect; the cases he has in mind cannot be cases of perfect sameness. Thirdly, instead of explaining our disposition to expect regularities as the result of repetition, he proposed to explain repetition *for us* instead of finding the repetition in nature. We try to discover similarities in nature, but what we land up with is our own invention of similarity of nature.[26] Bold conjectures are made to be eliminated if they clashed with observations.

The following points are found in Popper's summary of his position on induction:

(1) *Induction is a myth.* It is neither a psychological fact, nor a fact of ordinary life, nor one of scientific procedure.
(2) The actual procedure of science is to operate with conjectures: to jump to conclusions often after one single observation.

(3) The mistaken belief in induction is fortified by the need for a criterion of demarcation which, it is traditionally but wrongly believed, only the inductive method can provide.
(4) None of these is altered in the least if we say that induction makes theories only probable rather than certain.[27]

The first point makes an overstatement as we know that rule formulation takes place after certain observations. However, it is also possible that we define a term and find whether there are fitting objects. We also, as is noted by Quine, discover empirical facts about creatures having hearts and kidneys which by any standard an inductive generalization by simple enumeration. However, if the induction is spoken about in this fashion, Popper would not deny them as the last point mentioned above indicates. Though there are examples of jumping from one observation to the generalized conclusions, this does not happen always. It often happens where it is evident what we observe is a natural kind. But certain fields of science where one does not deal with direct observables, such generalizations are not often made on one observation. Sometimes, we need to control various factors before formulating clearer ideas or hypothesis.

Quite often one feels the need to formulate clear criterion in order to determine the scope of the predicate: what falls within the scope of the generalized statement. This is where sometimes there is difference of opinion: Whether a rule determines its extension?[28]

Popper has rightly recognized that if the induction that one speaks about is induction by simple enumeration, then a theory in science would only be probable. If we want to ascribe certainty to our theories in science, then the process needed is different inductive generalization based on empirical observation opine Popper. We have identified this process in the beginning of this chapter as rule based induction and not induction by simple enumeration.

We agree with Popper largely that the law like statements are not often observed by simple enumeration of the kind Quine talks about. However, we see the regularity, it strikes us as a rule and formulate the rule so that the future instances are also determined. In other words, the regularity found in nature is conventionalized by accepting them as a rule. Next step would be to refute the accepted generalization. We do not believe that scientists formulate the generalized statements in order to refute. But if there are counter evidences, then that would be noted. Now the question would be to explain the counter evidence which might take one of the following course of actions: (1) Counter evidence is accepted as an exception to the law. That is to say, the evidence even though goes against the law, the law is not believed to be false. This happens because we do not have any further refinement of the law to replace the present law. (2) Counter evidence is taken seriously and the theory is suspect. Efforts to build new theory is hastened. There is no reason to believe that the scientific community would choose one method or the other stated above. As Popper points out the success or failure of a theory depends much on luck, ingenuity and the deductive rules of critical argument.[29]

But it is not as futile exercise as it might look on Popper's treatment. There is much difference between animals using trial and error method and intelligent beings using this method. We do make intelligent guess work and most of the time our hypotheses are confirmed rather than refuted. Yet, it is true that if a hypothesis is rejected, then the repeating the wasteful exercise is very remote. We attempt to formulate rule based generalizations for pragmatic reasons because rule based generalizations help us to project, i.e., allow us to estimate the future on the basis of the past and present codified observations. This process of jumping from observed to unobserved is possible if and only if we formulated a rule for the use of a predicate in language.[30]

The Theory of Projection

Hypotheses form a good part of a scientific attempt to build the knowledge system. Goodman speaks of projecting a hypothesis and it will be said to be *actually projected,* when it is adopted after some of its instance have been examined and determined to be true, and before the rest have been examined. He speaks of projection both in the future and of the past cases. Projection is of the undetermined cases and if it is of future cases it is called prediction and if it is of past cases it is still projection although it is not called prediction.[31] Of course, Goodman also speaks of "the twofold problem of projected unprojectable and unprojected projectable."[32] But this should not concern us here as we are not keen on eliminating all the possible errors in projection here. What is worth nothing is Goodman's projection makes use of the hypothesis, i.e., the rule that has been proposed.

The difficulty arises if projection depends on the hypothesis. Until the proposed hypothesis is accepted, it would not be possible to make projections at all. However, accepting a hypothesis would be to get into the problem of disposition for Goodman, and dispositions have to be explained in terms of manifest predicate. In order to explain the dispositional predicates and projections of undetermined case of a hypothesis, Goodman banks on the concept of possibles.

The concept of possibles is invoked not as something fictitious, but as something actual. Exactly the way, he spoke of dispositions as the actual predicates of things, he tries to include possibles as part of the actuals.[33] Something that is actual could not have been actual if it were not possible.[34] He makes use of this notion of possible in order to explain what is actual. Goodman opines that what we often mistake for the actual world is one particular description of it. And what we mistake for possible worlds are just equally true descriptions in other terms. Goodman further remarks that we have come to think of the actual as one among many possible worlds. All possible worlds lie within the actual one.[35]

It is the last sentence of the above paragraph which is intriguing. How can a possible world lie within the actual one, and in what sense? It is one thing to say that a possibility is dependent on the actuality, and another thing to say that the possibility is exhausted by the actuality. The sentence in question gives the impression that if one lists all the actuals, one has also included all the possibles within it. However, Goodman certainly does not mean to suggest this is obvious from the following passage.

Possible processes and possible entities vanish. Predicates supposedly pertaining to them are seen to apply to actual things, but to have extensions related in peculiar way to, and usually broader than, the extensions of certain manifest predicates. A predicate ostensibly of possibles as compared to a correlative manifest predicate, like an open umbrella as compared to a closed one, simply covers more of the same earthly stuff.[36]

No doubt that the stuff a predicate covers is earthly, otherwise, it could not have been identified as the part of the extension of the predicate. For instance, a possible pen should be one which can be compared and identified as pen when actualized. However, a possible pen is not the one which I can use for writing a letter today. What is the meaning of the claim that possibles are part of the extensions of the manifest predicates and the manifest predicates are wider?

Certainly, there is lack of clarity on the issue of what constitutes an extension of a predicate. Elsewhere while explaining the dispositional predicate he opines that the predicate in question applies to only actuals not non-actuals in its extension.[37]

In the present context of hypothesis and their projections, it is not obvious whether the hypothesis on its own is capable of determining undetermined cases. If that should happen then the distinction among the class of positive cases, negative cases and undetermined cases would not have been required for Goodman.[38] One would have said that all those cases which are not examined would have been determined cases, i.e., they positively fall within the scope of the predicate, nevertheless have not been actuals yet. But this mode of speaking is not acceptable to Goodman for, he does not seem to be permitting us to speak of future events as something that has not yet occurred, even the possibles are part of the actual world for him.

Apart from the above difficulty of subsuming the future possibilities as part of the actuals in some peculiar manner, we have the difficulty of speaking of the distinction between the hypotheses which are exhausted and the hypotheses which are not exhausted so that we can use unexhausted hypothesis to project.[39] However, we seem to again depend heavily on the notion of extension to find out whether an hypothesis is exhausted at all. At a given point of time, one would not be in a position to claim whether one has exhausted all the cases unless the hypothesis determines all its extensions, even the ones which are not examined or yet have not come into being. If we were to go by what we have observed so far, there is no reason to believe at a given time *t* that one has exhausted all the cases of that kind unless a predicate is arbitrarily restricted to certain time or place. For instance, the presidents of India before 1995 A.D. would be a predicate if it occurs as the consequent of a hypothesis, then one could possibly know whether one has exhausted all the cases if the question is raised in twenty first century. Though one might agree with Goodman in substance that the exhausted hypotheses are not projectible, not on the ground that we know whether a hypothesis is exhausted, but on the ground that the hypothesis itself is restricted.

Now, we may note that Goodman's position on projection that "the *determination* of an undetermined case is always later than the projection in question"[40] is problematic. Goodman has no way of speaking of undetermined cases since, he cannot even theoretically identify them. He would even entertain the talk of all the emeralds having the same essences. Having rejected the ground for grouping emeralds on the basis of their similarity, he has no way to speak of unactualized emeralds at all.[41] Coming to speak of the extension of a predicate, he needs to constantly update his predicates since, cases that have not manifest the property so far might do so in due course. Thus, the extension of a predicate changes its size for Goodman if he is to count only actuals as part of the extension of the predicate. If he has to count possibles, as there are sufficient indications that he would like to include them, then one has to speak of the predicates having constant number of cases, observes and unobserved.

However, further difficulty would arise. How does one identify a negative case of a hypothesis. This would not be possible unless one has thought of two predicates being associated with one another. There could be basically two ways of relating to two predicates, one empirically and another logically. The empirical way of relating two predicates are outdated according to Goodman. If so, the other relationship is the logical one. Can we speak of logical relationship of what is discovered empirically? Yes is the answer. Let us sketch such a situation.

We are aware of the rules for the use of the word "copper". We are also aware of the rules for the use of the word "electricity". What one does while forming a hypothesis is to form a third rule making use of the extensions of these two rules. We do declare as a law that "copper conducts electricity" after making some initial examination. This law, like the rules that we have generalized, is the one conventionally excepted till we reach a situation where there are negative instances. That is to say, one comes across a situation where something is called a piece of copper for sure and yet the predicate "conducts electricity" cannot be ascribed to it. Thus, we have negative instance to the hypothesis (rule) that copper conducts electricity.

If rules determine extension, one might opine, how is it that there are counter instances falsifying the hypothesis if hypotheses are proposed rules? The answer is not so simple. It is not possible to find how an instance falls outside the extension of a rule. It is either part of the extension of a rule or is not. There is no reason why an instance does not fall under a rule. There is no justification further. However, an instance can be justified in terms of rules. Going by this, there is no reason to say an instance is not an instance of a rule at all. However, a hypothesis which makes use of at least two predicates, if the rule claims that there exists some logical relationship among the predicates, a counter instance can be produced to show that such a logical relationship has led to a situation where one of the following things have to be done: either modify one of the predicates and their criteria to identify their extensions, or do not recognize the problematic instance as the part of the extension and call it to be an exception.

Credit should go to Goodman for having rightly recognized projection as an important aspect of induction and law like statements. However, he has been misled by his own thesis of nominalism that the projection is based on practice and standards of the society. We believe that it is the logical projection[42] that is important and prediction in science making use of the laws of nature are law governed projections rather than a form of psychological expectations.

We can say that a projection is possible when we have some evidence statements confirming to rules and we make a leap into unobserved on the basis of rules. However, projection is different from induction in this sense. In the beginning of the chapter we have noted the difference between induction through simple enumeration leading to generalized statements with probability attached to it, and the rule based induction leading to certainty of the generalized statement. Projection is the function of rule based generalization where on the basis of the rule, one can predict the future instances of the rule. For instance, on the basis of the rule of what a triangle is, one can project what would be the characteristic of a triangle in future. That is to say, a rule-governed predicate permits us to take a logical leap from observed cases to unobserved whereas a contingent predicate can help us to take a psychological leap from observed to unobserved with less certainty. From the look of the mango, I cannot predict the taste of the mango for certain since, this projection is based on contingent, but repeated experience the uncertainty is always attached to it. Certainty attached to projection based on habit, is always less than the one attached to the logical projection based on rules.

Goodman defines the term "entrenched" in terms of our linguistic habits. How often a predicate is projected goes in favour of the predicate being more entrenched. If a predicate is more entrenched, it has the better prospects to be law like.[43] In addition to this, Goodman pleads for simplicity criterion when we are not in a position to decide which conflicting hypothesis to be chosen among competing hypotheses. He opines that entrenchment is perhaps simplicity criterion itself.[44]

Entrenched predicate may not be simple all the time. For instance, the concept of mind that is entrenched in a section of Hindu society, say those who believe in *Advaita* philosophy or that of *Sankhya* philosophy, the concept of mind is quite complex in comparison to the materialist concept of mind which is also available to the Indian people. Similarly, the concept of mind that is entrenched in German is more complex than the one that you may find in the followers of empiricism. Of course, the followers of Goodman might reply by saying that everything being equal between two hypotheses, one that is simple should be chosen against the complex. In practice, this would amount to saying that the simplicity criterion is theoretically the best one to adopt, however, there is no real situation where one will find any two competing hypotheses being equal to compare them on the parameters of safety and strength since, their explanatory power would always vary as they involve different predicates. Thus, simplicity criterion is made useless as there can be no two hypotheses which are equal!

Science needs to make progress and at times no progress would be made if one does not put a step forward. Simplicity would be a pragmatic criterion to put a step forward. May be, it is clear to many scientists that the first bold step is often inadequate, nevertheless it may be adopted with the hope that new facts would emerge and make way for further modification in the hypothesis or help us formulate more accurate hypothesis in the light of further discovery.

Apart from the fact that the concept of entrenchment is quite vague and unproductive, Goodman's concept of projectibility is also not philosophically very rewarding since, Goodman does not believe in the rule-governed behaviour of the predicates. For example, Ian Hacking, claims by summarizing Goodman's position: things are of a kind and in a class *not because* they resemble each other. They do resemble each other, but that is not *why* they are of a kind. And Hacking recognizes the importance of a predicate when he writes, "To use a name for any kind is to be willing to make generalizations and form expectations about individuals of that kind. To use a common noun to classify is to use it, and to use it is to be willing to project it."[45] Because of these reasons Goodman's projectibility has to heavily depend on the empirical experience of past which he identifies as "entrenched". Since, projectibility is strongly dependent on the history of the predicate, he cannot project any predicate newly introduced due to the development of a branch in science for instance unless one takes all the pain to show that there are competing hypotheses which somehow are less acceptable on simplicity criterion or some other parameter. However, Goodman is aware of this problem and perhaps is not in a position to incorporate it in his work given his general stand on nominalism. He writes, for instance, "Merely to reject unfamiliar predicates wholesale in favour of familiar ones would be to disallow the introduction of the needed new terms into scientific language."[46]

Goodman rightly recognizes counterfactual conditional and semifactual conditional as important for our understanding the problem of induction or law like statements. One is able to build a counterfactual conditional as well as semifactual conditional if and only if a clear notion of a law emerges apart from the knowledge of other relevant conditions. Goodman speaks of the relation between the antecedent and the consequent in a counterfactual conditional. Let us consider his favourite example:

If that piece of butter had been heated at 150° F, it would have melted.

Here, the antecedent puts a condition and the consequent speaks of a possible perspective in the Goodmanian sense. That is to say, this counterfactual conditional states something true of the world only in a different perspective. However, if one has to determine the truth of the counterfactual conditional, it is never necessary since, the antecedent of the conditional is false, the conditional is anyway true. Thus, the negation of the above counterfactual conditional also would be true for the same reason. Thus,

If that piece of butter had been heated at 150°F, it would not have melted.

Also would be true for the same reason. This of course makes us critically reflect on the meaning of counterfactual conditional statement. If we carefully analyse our intuitions about such counterfactual statements, we realise that what is said is not fully expressed by the hypothetical conditional. We would assert the counterfactual conditional which claims that the piece of butter would have melted and do not subscribe to the second counterfactual conditional that the butter would not have melted even if it had been heated at 150° F.

Also note that we would subscribe to the view that the following semifactual is true:

Even if the match had been scratched, it still would not have lighted.

and yet we would not have thought the following counterfactual conditional to be the opposite of "*Had the match been scratched, it would have lighted*"[47] as Goodman believes. The reason being that the conditions that needs to be fulfilled for a law to apply are several. For instance, when someone asserts that even if the match had been scratched, he could be sure that the match would not light for the reason that he knows (1) that the adequate oxygen is not present; or (2) the friction would not be adequate because the surface of the matchbox is smooth or is wet; or (3) the match is of a very inferior quality etc. Under such varied circumstances, we would have asserted the semifactual conditional without much hesitation. If we were to accept semifactual conditional as negation of a counterfactual conditional, then we need to say that a negation of an unambiguous sentence can turn out to be ambiguous if it is negated.

It is our considered opinion that semifactual and the counterfactual are different ways of stating the same law of nature as is the case with possible worlds. We have noted the view of a possible world which is taken to be another competing perspective about the same world, and a counterfactual conditional and semifactual conditional are all different ways of expressing the law. If the law holds, one expects to obtain certain relationship between an antecedent and a consequent of a counterfactual conditional. The relation is not, as we have pointed out already, one of a conditional statement in logic, i.e., the conditional statement is true if the antecedent of the conditional is false.

The counterfactual conditionals and semifactual conditionals are obtainable simply because, they are nothing, but projections. All the instances of the predicate "melting of butter" would have included even the above counterfactual instances. Since, an extension of a predicate does not include the actual cases alone, all the cases of melting of butter are included under the scope of the predicate. Moreover, having known what would be the extension of the predicate "melting of butter", one could also know what does not fall within the scope of the predicate if the rules determine their extensions. We tend to believe that rules do determine their extensions at least to the extent that what properties the instances should possess should they be of a certain type. Therefore, we do not need any separate analysis to show that how semifactual conditionals are also asserted or denied on the basis of our conception of laws.

It is worth noting that Goodman and Popper agree on one point. A lawlike statement would not have a negative instance. If there is any negative instance, it would be considered to have been falsified for Popper. However, a statement having negative instance cannot be considered valid lawlike statement.[48] Wittgenstein, in similar vain speaks of contradictions, and claims that it is an easy thing to resolve a contradiction. All that we need to do is to invoke a new rule. Similar is the situation of our scientists. When they are confronted with challenges by the counter instances to their laws, they either modify the law or consider the counter instance to be an exception or illusion. However, it is a fact that some new decisions have to be taken and any decision would modify the language of science to that extent. And these modifications and changes are called progress in science and both Goodman and Popper would agree with us on this.

When a counter instance is provided, we do not agree that the rule is rejected in toto. What may be required is to modify our criterion in a minor way so that the exception is taken care. In fact we could ask the question: Why is it that our formulation of the law are still defective? We cannot show that the world is irregular. If the world is irregular, it could only mean that the regularity has not been captured by us. Or, we are trying to find the law between two predicates which are not related at all. If it is true that the language and reality are in harmony, then the failure to formulate a consistent system of laws only indicates our inefficiency. And therefore, if a counter instance is found to a law, instead of rejecting the law as falsified, we would suggest that the law needs careful modification of its criteria or the law itself. However, there is no denying of the fact that a counter instance is the indication that our formulation of scientific concepts need further refinements.

A point of clarification may be added here. It may be suggested that one should look at the issue of the new riddle of induction should be re-examined following the distinctions among three types of rules explained by Blackburn. Blackburn calls these three rules the right-rule, bent-rule and no-rule. When the follower is able to continue a series correctly as per the mathematical rule, for example the rule of addition, or is able to identify the extension of a given predicate "red", and is able to exclude all non-extension of the given predicate, then the case is of a right-rule. In the case of the bent-rule, if the follower is not able to distinguish the correct application of rule from the incorrect one, or is not in a position to give justification to the deviant application of the rule, the case is that of a bent-rule. He cites the example of *quus* of Kripke and *grue* of Goodman as examples to illustrate this type of rule.[49] The third case is the no-rule case where the applications of the rule are followed correctly, but the follower is not following the rules intentionally. In this case the following of the rule, though correct, is not a case of rule-following. He cites the example of the possibility of a lunatic writing the series of numbers correctly as a case of no-rule.[50] Having made the distinction between these three types of rules, Blackburn argues that there is no satisfactory way to distinguish these three cases of following the rules. The problem is that the applications of the rules are not given or are not contained in the given rule in any case of the rule-following. What makes the right-rule view the correct view and not the bent-rule and the no-rule view cannot be explained.[51]

Blackburn's distinction among these three rules is not relevant to Goodman as we see it. First, Blackburn makes the assumption that bent rules are the rules that have flexible extension. That is to say, the use of the term is the extended use and is for the same reason temporary. Goodman does not believe that his conception of *grue* is a temporary one, though time is mentioned in the very criterion. Secondly, Goodman positively believes that extension is logically contained in the rule itself. This is the basis on which he speaks of projectibility of hypothesis. Thus, for these two important reasons, the Blackburn's understanding of *grue* as having the bent-rule does not seem to go well with Goodman's formulation.

In conclusion, we might say that Goodman's new riddle of induction clearly indicates the problem of rule-following which Kripke has elaborated in his own way. Goodman's attempt to answer the skeptic in terms of entrenchment of a predicate is a good step towards answering the skeptic. But, unless the normative aspect is built into the concept of predicate or rule, one cannot show why the projection made is binding on a skeptic. This is the reason why despite making every attempt to answer the skeptic, Goodman fails to satisfy the skeptic.

NOTES AND REFERENCES

1. Goodman, Nelson, (1965): *Fact, Fiction and Forecast* (henceforth *FFF*), 2nd edition, Bobbs-Merrill Co. Inc., Indianpolis, pp. 59-122.
2. More details on this problem is already discussed as *quus* problem in Chapter 2.
3. For instance Sober, Elliott, ("No Model, No Inference: A Bayesian Primer on the *Grue* Problem" and Skyrms, Brian, ("Bayesian Projectibility", in *Grue*, pp. 241-262) hold this stand on induction.
4. Please note that human beings do not encounter Goodman's type of riddle in the areas of non-verbal learning. See Suppes, P., "Learning and Projectibility" in *Grue*, pp. 263-272.
5. Please note that all entrenched natural predicates would permit this rule-based induction, but all the cases of mere psychological association between one predicate and another would not permit this rule-based generalization. All generalization on the basis of association or co-relation leads to what is known as social science and all rule-based generalization leads to laws of natural sciences.
6. See Chapter 6 for the detailed discussion.
7. Inductive generalization on simple enumeration does not lead to the paradox of *grue* because it would only have the element of probability attached to it, but not uncertainty of rules that apply to it. One does not get surprised if a paradox is resolved. However, if one confronts a paradox, there would be a surprise. The *grue* problem having apparent rule based generalization is the source of the paradox. If one realizes the error involved in this generalization, we believe that the paradox is resolved, not solved.
   Basically, there are two readings of the new riddle. One, those who go in the Humean line that this induction both in the case of blue and *grue* involves probability. And hence, there is lack of certainty. Of course, the problem of incompatible hypothesis is acknowledged as an additional issue. There is the other reading which does not recognize probability as the serious issue at all. This group recognizes blue and *grue* as two distinct predicates of colour. Having identified them as predicates and having known that green and blue are incompatible concepts, how is it that both the hypothesis are confirmed by the same evidence statements? The issue is one of predication of incompatible attributes to the same objects. Of course, all of them seem to be concerned with the issue of entrenchment and projectability of predicate as a step towards gaining scientific knowledge.
8. *FFF*, p. 74.
9. Goodman seems to use the word "extension" only to cover the existing objects that fall within a predicate. However, this would be not an acceptable explication of the term extension. The question is: if the non-existent objects are not in principle part of the extension, what made one identify them to be belonging to the kind which we have in question. If one identifies certain

properties as the criterion and when the object manifests that property alone belongs to such kind, then every predicate should be reduced to perceptual field. Thus, all predicates have to be defined in such a situation in terms of sensations. This process is not tenable since, this leads to all the problems which empiricism would face. *See FFF*, p. 41.

10. Please see "commitment to rules" in Wittgenstein in Chapter 6 for further details.
11. *WRPL*, p. 20.
12. Barker, S.F. and Achinstein, P., (1968) "On the New Riddle of Induction", in P. Nidditch (ed.), *Philosophy of Science*, Oxford University Press, London, p. 162.
13. *On the New Riddle of Induction*, p. 165. Also see C.A. Hooker, (1968) "Goodman, '*Grue*' and Hempel", *Philosophy of Science*, 35, pp. 232-247 for the discussion of temporal predicate.
14. *FFF*, pp. 79-80.
15. *Ibid.*, p. 22
16. *PI*, § 40.
17. Searle, J.R., (1969) "How to derive 'ought' from 'is'", in W.D. Hudson (ed.), *The Is-Ought Question*, The MacMillan Press, London, pp. 130-131.
18. Schlick, Moritz, (1973) "When Is a Man Responsible" in P. Edwards and A. Pap (eds.), *A Modern introduction to Philosophy*, The Free Press, New York, pp. 60-61
19. *When Is a Man Responsible*, p. 59.
20. *When Is a Man Responsible*, pp. 61-62.
21. *FFF*, p. 20.
22. *Ibid.*, p. 83. Also see Goodman's article (1967) "Two Replies", *Journal of Philosophy*, 64, pp. 286-287.
23. Creatures with heart are the creature with kidneys is simply an empirical generalization. So far we have not found any contrary evidence. See, Quine, W.V.O., (1969) "Two Dogmas of Empiricism" in T.M. Olshewsky (ed.) *Problems in Philosophy of Language*, Holt, Rienchart and Winston Inc., p. 399.
24. Popper, K., (1963) *Conjectures and Refutations*, Routledge and Kegan Paul, London. p. 43.
25. *Conjectures and Refutations*, p. 44.
26. *Ibid.*, p. 46.
27. *Ibid.*
28. For the discussion of the debate, *see* Chapter 5.
29. *Conjectures and Refutations*, p. 53. The same line of thinking is also adopted by Feyerabend in his book (*Against Method*, NLB, London, 1975). Feyerabend believes that in science the principle of any thing goes provides the conducive factors are conducive for the hypothesis, pp. 23ff.
30. Goodman points out that the valid and invalid predictions, i.e., inductions or projections are drawn upon the basis of how the world is and has been described and anticipated in words. *FFF.* p. 119.

31. *FFF*, pp. 91-92.
32. *Ibid.*, p. 92.
33. Goodman believes that "what we want is a criterion in terms of actual occurrences–that is, in terms of manifest predicates–for the correct assignment of dispositional predicates to things." *See FFF* p. 42.
34. *FFF*, p. 55.
35. *Ibid.*, pp. 56-57.
36. *Ibid.*, p. 57.
37. *Ibid.*, p. 42.
38. *Ibid.*, pp. 89-90.
39. "A hypothesis without any remaining undetermined cases is said to be *exhausted*." See *FFF*, p. 90.
40. *FFF*, p. 91.
41. *See FFF*, p. 44, where Goodman rejects any ground to group things in terms of shared properties. See his remarks on the rejection of dispositional properties as essential. *FFF*, pp. 44-45. Also see Hacking, *Grue*, p. 221.
42. Projection has to be distinguished from psychological expectation of the Humean type.
43. *FFF*, pp. 95, 118-19.
44. Goodman, N., "Safety, Strength, Simplicity", in P. Nidditch (ed.), (1968) *Philosophy of Science*, Oxford University Press, London, p. 123.
45. Hacking, Ian, "Entrenchment", in *Grue*, p. 221.
46. Goodman, *Safety, Strength, Simplicity*, p. 122.
47. *FFF*, pp. 5-6.
48. Talking about the hypothesis and the manner in which we accept and reject the hypothesis Goodman writes, "Hume thought of the mind as being set in motion making prediction by, and in accordance with, regularities in what it observed.... We on the contrary, regard the mind as in motion from the start, striking out with spontaneous predictions in dozens of directions, and gradually rectifying and channeling its predictive processes. We ask not how predictions come to be made, but how-granting they are made-they come to be sorted out as valid and invalid." *FFF*, p. 87.
49. Blackburn, S., 1984, *Spreading the Word: Grounding in the Philosophy of Language*, Clarendon Press, Oxford, pp. 74 ff.
50. Blackburn, *Spreading the Word*, pp. 70-71.
51. *Ibid.*, pp. 73-74.

4

Quine: Three Indeterminacies

Introduction

Two strategies that are normally adopted by philosophers to overcome the gap between language and reality are the following: empiricists and realists claim that language is derived from reality and therefore, language ought to match with reality. The others, phenomenologists and the idealists, assert just the opposite thesis. They claim that since, our notion of reality is constructed partially at least by our language and mind, the reality would match with the concept of reality that we have in advance. And therefore, there would not be much gap between language and reality. Both the camps think that they are in a comfortable position to give an objective account of induction, science and other important philosophical aspects of epistemology. Quine is one whom no one can clearly classify as belonging to either group. He has the advantages of both, and he has the disadvantages of both the groups too.

No doubt that Quine ingeniously manages to carve his way through the intellectual debates siding sometimes one group and some times the other. What we need to notice is that, despite all his attempts to make room for his methodology, his philosophical arguments do not satisfy the skeptic. What he does not seem to admit is this failure of his arguments especially in the context of objectivity of knowledge. Wherever he seems to see some difficulty, he seems to claim it to be unresolvable and hence, there is no point in pursuing them and settle for the best available alternative. This has been his general approach to epistemic issues in philosophy in answering skeptics.

Three main skeptical issues, all interconnected to one another in one way or the other, are being entertained by Quine. They are, first, indeterminacy or inscrutability of reference,[1] second, indeterminacy of translation and third, underdetermination of scientific theory. The first two skeptical problem, involve the notion of observation sentences and the third involves the issue of the truth of empirically equivalent theories.[2]

All the three skeptical issues mentioned above are in one respect similar to Kripke's formulation of rule-following skeptical issues. They are all skeptical issues because of the applicability of multiplicity of interpretations. They share the same feelings: Given the behaviour or data which rule or theory do I fit to the context? Let us be more specific. In the context of indeterminacy of reference, the issue is: how do we interpret the quantified sentence if the predicate term refers to different ontologies or different perspectives? In the context of translation, the issue is that of finding the exact translation from one language to another given the verbal behaviour in addition to the individual's sense perception. How does one claim a particular translation to be the authentic one when there seem to be several equally fitting ones available? And the third issue is regarding the underdetermination of scientific theory where if a theory is never deduced from the data and if the theory is transcending the observations, and if two theories are empirically equivalent, how do we choose one theory against another? In this context, the problem of induction and natural kind emerge equally even though Quine does not show much interest in them.

Quine has claimed that he has dealt with three uncertainties. He addresses all the three uncertainties and tries to resolve these in terms of objectivity of knowledge. He would like to achieve the objectivity of knowledge by naturalizing epistemology. The earlier formulation of epistemology within empirical framework was to construct epistemology from sense data. The attempt did not succeed. Quine feels that it is better to discover how science is in fact developed and learned then to construct a theory. This is what is naturalizing epistemology. Epistemology in its new form, would be a chapter in natural science; as a chapter of psychology. But the goal of the old epistemology would remain valid too in its own way. It is important to study how humans posit bodies and project their knowledge from the given empirical data. And it is equally important to know how and why we grant the status to other human beings who are like ourselves as it is important to know how we develop physical and social sciences. All this is our construction, or projection from stimulations from our sense data opines Quine. It is the mutual give and take; epistemology helps natural science and natural science lends itself to epistemology.[3]

Quine is a unique philosopher who attempts to combine the traditional virtues with that of modern. Having merged epistemology with natural science, he would concede that the naturalized epistemology has the traditional virtue of being normative. The fear that by naturalizing epistemology, we lose the vital component of normativity of epistemology is unfounded. Quine points out that when epistemology is naturalized and becomes a chapter of theoretical science, normative epistemology gets naturalized into a chapter of engineering: "the technology of anticipating sensory stimulation."[4] We know our external world only through sense impressions. Yet, the normative role of the epistemology cannot be denied. Epistemology has the role of warning us against telepathies and soothsayers, says Quine.

Yet, on Quine's own admission, given the conventions as they are, the rival theories describe one and the same world. Limited to our vocabulary and abilities, we grasp the world in different ways. Quine gives the analogy of someone trying to measure the diameter of an impenetrable sphere. There are different ways of finding the diameter of the sphere without getting inside.[5] This indicates that Quine would admit multiple understandings of the same world given our conventions and theories. Therefore, this is comparable to the concept of possible worlds i.e., the competing accounts of the same world mentioned both by Goodman and Kripke.

Indeterminacy of Reference

The main function of reference is to relate a name to its object. But there are some names without referring to any object, for example terms used in scientific theories and quantified sentences. If we must go by the empirical evidence alone, it is not possible to fix the quantification. This is not a serious problem for Quine. It seems that Quine is convinced of the idea that if we can have well developed two valued predicate logic that would be conducive to naturalizing epistemology and unification of science. Once we are able to develop predicate calculus to fit our ordinary language, we will be able to do away with singular terms altogether keeping variables as the only link to objects. Variables take all objects as values irrespective of the fact whether they are specifiable or no. Singular terms can still be obtained as and when required.[6]

Our behaviour is the result of the values that we hold and the aims that we express.[7] Therefore, Quine is of the opinion that the difference in our world-view would bring in the difference in ontological commitments. For instance, believing that whales are fishes leads to one kind of ontological commitment and believing that whales are mammals leads one to have different ontological commitments. When we quantify (*x*)(Fx....) whales are included in the former case and they are not included in the latter case where *F* stands for fish. Thus, the range of objects over which we quantify depends on the world-view we adopt. The world-view could be a scientific one or could be any other, but certainly ontology is relative to the perspective. This of course leads to the problem of deciding as to what we mean by a sentence if its scope is different when perspectives are different.

While discussing problem of the ontological relativity, Quine opines that there is no empirical ground to choose one ontology instead of another. He gives the following example:

> What is empirically significant in an ontology is just its, contribution of neutral nodes to the structure of the theory. We could reinterpret 'Tabitha' as designating no longer the cat, but the whole cosmos minus the cat; or, again, as designating the cat's singleton, or unit class.[8]

The theories differ from one another in their ontologies, i.e., the ranges of their variables.[9] The quantifiers used in a theory are to be considered as restricted by that predicate to be operated within the theory.[10] He remarks "It is interesting, then, that a theory can thus, vary its ontology."[11]

What is true of theory is also true of common predicates. Quine has held that to be is to be the value of a variable. However, it is not possible to determine all the values of a variable, i.e., all the objects that exist. This is what appears as the main problem of the rule following skepticism where Kripke points out that we have no way to determine the next step in the application of a rule. There is nothing that guides our future use of words even if we know all the applications of the rule till today.

Indeterminacy of Translation

Indeterminacy of reference and indeterminacy of translation are interrelated philosophical issues in Quine. We have noted that indeterminacy of reference has the difficulty of fixing the ontology of a sentence. The indeterminacy of translation has problems at two levels, one at the level of words and the other at the level of sentences. In order to make the issue focused and directed, let us take Quine's two examples to formulate the problem, one is that of a child, and the other is that of a field linguist learning the language. The child has no language to go by, and the field linguist has the knowledge of his own mother-tongue, and is trying to master an alien language.

When compared to translation, indeterminacy of reference occurs at the level of words, and the translation occurs at the level of a sentence as a whole. Indeterminacy of reference works within the limits of a single sentence, whereas indeterminacy of translation needs to care for the language and reality relationship as well as facts outside the language.[12] It is easy to mistake one with the other. Indeterminacy of reference has to do with the word and its indeterminable reference, whereas ontological relativity has something to do with the translation. When different manuals of translations are used, we obtain different ontologies. To say that 'gavagai' denotes rabbits is to opt for a manual of translation in which 'gavagai' is translated as 'rabbit', instead of opting for any of the alternative manuals remarks Quine.[13]

There would be some difference between translating a word and translating a sentence. While making the distinction between translation of sentences as wholes and translation of expressions or terms, Quine says that translation of expressions or terms can lead to ontological relativity.[14] Viewed as a term, the word "gavagai" is an example of indeterminacy of reference. Seen as a sentence, the word is one word observation sentence, translatable as "rabbit".[15]

Quine believes that the philosophical journey from the talk about observable objects to the talk about the observable qualities such as "it is cold" is natural for a child. And from this one word observation sentence, one generally moves to predicate sentences of the form "This pebble is blue". One could have a compound predicate sentence as the next step. For instance "The sun is rising and birds are singing". Of course, they do learn commands, questions, exclamations etc. in addition to these.

Quine speaks of behaviourism approvingly. He opines that behaviourism in the context of linguistics is mandatory whereas a psychologist may choose not to be a behaviourist. Describing the situation where a child and a field-linguist learn the language not familiar to them, he opines that only scientific method available is that of observation of the behaviour of the native speakers. The language is learnt whether it is the case of a child or the case of a field-linguist, in a systematic manner. There is no way that one can know the usage of a word without observing the behaviour of the members of the community. Both in the case of child and the field-linguist, it is the observation of the linguistic behaviour of the other person that gives one the first hint. Of course, this has to be combined by the effort on the part of the learner by making adequate hypothesis and the possible use of the word and checking it against the assent or dissent by the competent speaker of that language. Quine writes:

> The field-linguist assumes that the native's attitude and ways of thinking are like his own, up to the point where there is contrary evidence. He accordingly imposes his own ontology and linguistic patterns on the native speakers wherever compatible with the native's speech and behaviour.[16]

Along with this, empathy is required for further understanding of the language. In the case of child, the parents must show empathy and in the case of the field-linguist, he should show empathy towards himself. When the speech behaviour of the members of the linguistic community matches with the speech behaviour of the child or the field-linguist one could conclude that the child or the field-linguist have understood the language in question. For instance, the field-linguist makes his first conjecture about 'gavagai' on the strength of the native's utterance, and again he requests 'gavagai' for the native's assent in a subsequent exercise and confirms his hypothesis.[17] The field-linguist tentatively associates the native's utterance with the observed situation with the hope that it is simply an observation sentence linked to that situation. He checks this in the very next opportunity. He makes attempts to use the sentence himself and notices the native's assent or dissent.[18] Thus, observation is important for translation.

Since, Quine holds the thesis that translation has to be done according to a manual of translation, it follows that there can be difference in translation if the manual used are different. Moreover, he seems to discount the difference due to the very nature of syntactic structure even though certain syntactic structures seem to be conducive for expressing certain type of ideas, whereas certain syntactic structures do not seem to allow certain construction of sentences. Somehow Quine does not seem to regard this difference important in the context of translation.[19]

If it is not possible to arrive at a satisfactory contextual translation of what there is given in the form of an existential quantification, we are at loss to assess the ontology of the speakers of that language. The language they spoke must be so different than ours that we are not able to translate their existential quantifiers into ours.[20] Commenting on two indeterminacies, namely, indeterminacy of reference and indeterminacy of translation, Quine expresses his opinion that the problem of translation is going to remain because it does not depend on facts as well as human inability. No effort is going to solve this problem. What the indeterminacy of translation shows is that the notion of propositions as sentence meaning is untenable concludes Quine.

One of the reasons for which Kripke claims the paradox of rule-following is genuine is that the meaning is indeterminate. The meaning is indeterminate because several interpretations of the rule is possible in a given context. Since, Quine believes that translation is not on the basis of facts or of human ability, there is bound to be the problem of interpretation. Hence, it remains a rule-following problem.

Observation and Theory

The epistemological significance of observation sentences lies in their ability to link our sensory stimulation with that of our theories about the world.[21] Quine opines that observation sentences are not reports of sense data but they are reports of external circumstances. Early stage in language learning involves association of words with a range of stimulation and conditioning. Observation sentences consisting of these terms are theory free. These very observation sentences can be viewed from the point of view of a theory as well. Thus, these observation sentences logically connect observation on the one hand, and theory on the other. Now, the observation sentences have become theory-laden indeed. An observation sentence containing an ordinary word like 'water' can join theoretical sentences containing terms as technical as 'H_2O'. Quine writes: "Seen holophrastically, as conditioned to stimulatory situations, the sentence is theory-free; seen analytically, word by word, it is theory-laden."[22]

Quine is of the opinion that any knowledge can be considered to be theory free or theory-laden. In the context of language, when a child learns one word sentence, the observation sentence is not theory-laden at all. However, the simple term like heat may join the realm of science and become theory-laden. Therefore, it of course, depends at what level one does speak about the matter. At the level of linguistic behaviour, all the behaviours are observational and to that extent they are not theory-bound.

The scientist has a backlog of accepted theory and a theory is constituted of sentences having logical connections among them.[23] He considers a hypothesis for possible incorporation into it. The theory tells him that if the hypothesis under consideration is true, then, whenever, a certain observable situation arises, a certain effect could be observed. So, he sets-up the situation in question. If the predicted effect fails to appear, he abandons his hypothesis. If the effect does appear, then his hypothesis may be said to be true and can be tentatively added to his backlog theory.

The theory and the hypothesis put together are said to imply an observation categorical. That is to say, a predicted observational sentence is called observation categorical. The observation categorical is compounded of two or more occasion sentences. Thus, observation categorical is itself an independent sentence though implied by the scientific theory and the hypothesis put together. As we have noted above, we can treat them theory free if we so desire. It thus, solves the problem of linking theory to observation, as well as epitomizing the experimental situation says Quine.[24]

A scientist is prepared to reject an observation categorical, if need arises, as they are occasion sentences. The occasion sentences are observation sentences which are true or false in a given context. They can be observed without the help of the theory. Sometimes, progress in science takes place without prior planning. The scientist has no hypothesis even, he happens to note an anomalous phenomenon points out Quine. He happens to chance on a counter-instance of an observation categorical which ought to have been true on the current theory as a whole, he opines.[25]

Prediction is the back-bone of the scientific endeavour. If prediction succeeds, the theory is said to be justified, if the prediction fails, then the issue of the validity of the theory arises. This leads to the problem of holism in philosophy.[26] Some theories are there in a given society and we need to modify those theories if necessary. Quine differs from Grunbaum who held the view that if observation statement falsifies the theory, the theory needs to be rejected.

Quine describes the process of adding a hypothesis to a theory in the following manner. Always we have something that is given as the established backlog theory and we want to add a component to the backlog theory in the form of a hypothesis. We derive observation categorical from the backlog theory and the hypothesis making use of other statements which are not controversial ones. After deriving the observation categorical which we use for verification, we wait for the right occasion to know the truth value of the observation categorical. A theory is tested on the basis of synthetic observation categoricals. If our observation categoricals are true, then the theory is verified.

And if the occasion sentence is false, it does not prove that the theory is false.[27] However, on this matter there is disagreement. Popper and Grunbaum have thought that the theory is falsified with single observation statement. Quine believes that there are different possibilities that are open. The falsity of the observation categorical refutes sometimes only the conjunction of sentences that was needed to imply the observation categorical. In order to withdraw that conjunction, one need not always withdraw the hypothesis itself.[28] By making appropriate modifications in the auxiliary sentences, we can save the hypothesis. Sometimes, we may make changes in both the hypothesis and the auxiliary sentences to save the accepted theory if the prediction fails. Only in the event of having no option, do we recommend the modification of the theory. Quine is of the opinion that this is the way work in science progresses.

Quine is of the firm opinion that at the level of theory, the distinction between language and theory fades away once we go beyond observational sentences.[29] This is the reason why Quine believes that certain changes are easily permitted and certain other changes are not so easily permitted by the society. When it is the case of the belief in the occasion sentences, Quine is of the opinion that we are willing to readily change our opinions, but when it is a matter of more serious kind, for instance the change in the vocabulary, we resist such change.

The observation sentences or occasion sentences are neither true nor false Quine opines. However, what bears the truth-values are their utterances. Quine is of the opinion that time and place are enough to identify the occasions in order to find whether an occasion sentence is true or false. That is to say, using Strawson's terminology, it is only the use of the sentence that is true or false not the sentence itself. How can the same occasion sentence can be true or false gets answered by this remark of Quine. He further remarks: "What enter the web of the belief as protocol are their records, as dated eternal sentences. These depend for their credibility on whatever theory attests to the fixity of records or memory."[30]

Empirical Equivalence and Underdeterminacy of Theories

Having noted the relationship between an observation sentence and a theory, we may now consider what is known as the problem of choice of theory. Quine speaks of empirically equivalence of theory in the context of the relationship between the theory and observation. This relation is best exhibited in the context of experiment and prediction he opines.[31] Quine feels that two theories can have the same empirical content and the problem of theory choice arises when the totality of possible evidence is insufficient to clinch the system uniquely.[32]

We have the familiar example of Riemannian and Euclidean geometry as applied to the surface of a sphere. Riemannian geometry says that straight lines always meet and Euclidean geometry says that some do and some do not. The conflict is resolved by reinterpreting 'straight line' in Riemannian geometry as 'great circle'. Quine gives yet another example from Poincare to support his claim. We have on the one hand our commonsense conception of infinite space and rigid bodies that move freely without shrinking or stretching, and on the other hand the conception of a finite spherical space in which those bodies shrink uniformly as they move away from centre. Both conceptions can be reconciled with all possible observations; they are empirically equivalent says Quine.[33]

Quine considers four alternatives to resolve this problem of incompatible empirically equivalent theories. One, the hard-line adopted in *Theories and Things*[34], i.e., we should believe that our own theory is true and the other false, even while believing them empirically equivalent. The argument is that the truth predicate itself makes sense only within our theory. However, the difficulty would arise how to choose if both empirically equivalent theories are equally elegant as well.

The second alternative is to hold the view that both theories as true. The above difficulty about the truth predicate is then met by fusing the empirically equivalent theories as a single tandem theory. The core thesis of the two theories remains the same they differ on trivial matters which can be dropped without loss of empirical content. However, this is not to the taste of the scientists since, their ideal of economy and the empiricists' standard of meaningfulness is not respected in this tandem model.[35] This theory may be accepted as good one, opines Quine, provided neither of the given empirically equivalent theories contain terms irreducible to the other.

The third alternative is that if the sentences in the other theory are irreducible to our own theory. If this is the situation, then the sentences that are neither true nor false since, they are alien terms, we are to reject them as meaningless.

The fourth alternative is that empirically equivalent and logically compatible theories can be accepted as true descriptions of the world even if one of them uses terms irreducibly alien to the other. There is no attempt to combine them into a single redundant theory. The economy one spoke of while rejecting the tandem theory is that of conceptions and not of vocabulary. Meaningful application of the truth predicate extends to the whole language and is not limited to any theory formation. Our language can embrace the full vocabularies of both theories, and our truth predicate can then apply to each on its separate merits.[36]

Quine is of the opinion that theories can have different objects over which their variables of quantification range and still the two theories can be empirically equivalent.[37] Instead of counting them to be two theories, we could as well call them to be two interpretations of one and the same theory.

The question may arise as to when to count theories as distinct and when to count them as merely different formulations of a single theory. If two empirically equivalent theory formulations are interconvertible sentence by sentence through reinterpretation of terms, surely we should regard them as formulating a single theory opines Quine. If we just interchange the words 'proton' and 'electron' in a physics treatise, that may not be considered two theories at all.[38] While discussing the issue of theory choice, Quine makes it evident that two theories can be empirically equal yet have affinity to two different theories which he calls the underdetermination of theories. Thus, Quine concludes by saying "What the empirical under-determination of global science shows is that there are various defensible ways of conceiving the world".[39] If we settle upon one of the empirically equivalent systems of the world, we still have the underdetermination of the theory, since, the theory does not fit the observation data uniquely.

What the thesis of empirically equivalent theories shows is that we are not warranted in a position to assert any theory as objectively superior to another, or that the evidence and arguments in favour of one theory are stronger than the others.[40] In other words, the underdetermination of the theory from the given data shows that there is no rational ground to choose between the empirically equivalent theories or the rival theories. The underdetermination of theories from the given data also implies the thesis that all theories are evidentially at par. Putting the same fact negatively, it can be said that a theory can never encounter evidence which forces a scientist to abandon one theory in favour of the other. If the underdetermination of theory is correct, the much discussed criterion of the falsification as a rational method to refute theory and thus, choose theory on the basis of the alleged 'crucial argument'[41] faces serious problem. The Duhem-Quine thesis argues that when a theory is refuted, we are not sure whether the auxiliary or background hypothesis is falsified, because "our statements about the external world face the tribunal of sense experience not individually but only as a corporate body" as Quine would say.[42] Thus, what the underdetermination of theory-choice from the given data shows is that there is total hopelessness in searching for a methodology.[43]

The problem of choosing the theory on the basis of some logical principle, deductive or inductive, remains because there are no deductive rules to justify the derivation of the theories from the relevant data. The data is always less than the theory and therefore, it cannot determine the theories. In this sense, the theories are not only underdetermined by the observation but also positively contribute to the confusion where the same observation, supports two rival theories as Quine's thesis of empirical equivalence of theories suggests. The attempt to justify the derivation of the theories from the data through the rules of enumerative inductive rules will not only leave the theories underdetermined but also it will lead to competing empirically equivalent theories.

As we have shown in the previous chapter, the new riddle of induction presents a paradox by proving that the same observed cases give rise to two contradictory claims. The new riddle of induction, similar to the problem of undertermination of the theory-choice, shows there are no rules of enumerative inductive rules which can allow us to choose between the claim that "All emeralds are green" and the claim that "All emeralds are *grue*".[44] Some methodological rules usually applied for choosing between the rival theories in the context of their empirically being equivalent, are the principle of simplicity, consistency, universality and making surprising predictions etc. But these so-called methodological principles cannot be accepted as the standards to choose theory because of their ambiguity. As Kuhn,[45] has enumerated a number of multiplicity of the meaning simplicity so that virtually any theory can be said to be "simple" in some sense or other. The same can be said about other methodological rules also. It is possible to imagine that two theories are consistent and at the same time empirically equivalent in Quianian sense, then these principles do not help us much to select one theory instead of other. Moreover, if we look at the history of science, we can see that the so-called scientific rules are constantly being violated in building a theory and choosing theories. Thus, the indeterminacies which Quine talks about remain unresolved.

Speaking of the debate on theory choice, Quine thinks that he has wasted his time and energy. As long as the theories are empirically equivalent and when there is no advantage in adopting one theory against another, the issue can be dropped altogether from our discussion. It would not matter at all which theory we adopt. Of course, simplicity, elegance and other pragmatic and aesthetic factors can be taken into consideration but eventually what succeeds is our predictable scientific theory.

Naturalization of Epistemology

Observation sentence is the objective ground of knowledge. In *Word and Object* Quine had thought that there is similarity in the sense-data which results in the similarity of perception and ultimately becomes the base of objective knowledge. But this 1963 version is replaced by 1981 version of observational statements. In this version

Quine adopts the mechanism of defining objectivity for only one individual if the perceptual response is the same irrespective of the difference in the sense stimuli. This is comparable to something that is called 'specious present' in psychology. Using this kind of notion Quine defines the identity of the perceptual objects. This is the same object which I have perceived earlier. Having achieved objectivity at the individual level, he moves to the intersubjectivity. Even here, he says that the individual differences drop out. This is because, he is no more speaking of the stimulus meaning. The notion of stimulus meaning is replaced by the notion of linguistic meaning. Here, he invokes the concept of speech community where people belonging to one community have the same language and use their language in an intersubjective manner despite there being some differences at the individual level while perceiving the individual level. He says that the differences drop out. We adopt conventions that are given within the language and thus, language filters the difference in perception.[46]

The concept of kind, in Quine's philosophy, is fundamental to learning language, induction and expectation.[47] It plays a greater role in establishing the truth and objectivity science thus, the unification of sciences or naturalization of epistemology.

Our reasonable expectations depend on similarity. Therefore, it would be right to say that projection depends on expectations and expectation depends largely on similarity or natural kinds and natural kinds are in some sense innate.[48] Animal expectation and habit formation leads to induction opines Quine. Ostensive learning of words for instance is an implicit case of induction he says. Those who learn the term "yellow" ostensively are learning about the rules of the English word in an inductive manner through observing the verbal behaviour by noticing the instances where a competent speaker of English assenting to the use of the word and dissenting from it.[49]

Notice that Quine considers that similarity is perceived by different individuals in similar manner. Speaking of yellow and how people might acquire this word by observing the linguistic behaviour he believes that one could generalize his yellow samples by similarity considerations and his neighbours have themselves acquired the use of the word "yellow," by the same similarity considerations. "The uniformity of people's quality spaces virtually assures that similarity will elicit similar verdicts",[50] Quine writes.

What is worth noting is that the above linguistic induction is primarily based on the prior perception of similarity. That is to say, the person has the concept already in order to generalize. It is not possible to have the concept of yellow first and then generalize it in order to have the concept of yellow. Quine thus, explains that a word is attached to a natural kind by inductive generalization. If this is taken to be true, then it is one like the rule based induction.[51] From simple examples, one conventionalizes the use of the word yellow and thus, it is inductively accepted.

However, the linguistic inductive process is one thing and the impersonal world is another, claims Quine. It is reasonable to think that our ostensive definition of a word would match with the inductive process of our neighbours because we are birds of the same feather. But what is more striking is that our inductive generalization about the world too matches. The world we have is not our creation, whereas our language is. Yet, we see that striking similarity exists between our language and that of universe. Thus, the interesting question Quine asks is this: why does our innate subjective spacing of qualities accord so well with functionally relevant grouping in nature as to make our inductions tend to come out right?[52]

Quine is of the opinion that language and reality are in harmony not because they were in harmony all the time, but the evolution of the species is such that only those species which were in harmony with nature have survived and others have vanished. This is the reason why our present linguistic categories into different kind have perfect match with different natural kinds in reality.[53] Speaking of the innateness of natural kinds, Quine claims that animal behaviour can be interpreted in behavioural terms. At the level of behaviour, we can notice that animals too distinguish between different natural kinds; they salivate for instance, in similar fashion.[54]

Quine opines that his sense of innate similarity can be helpful in one sector, but can be a hindrance in the other. Human beings have found more regularities in nature rather than in their perception of the regularity in colour. Thus, the man has learnt to re-classify by modifying the systems of natural kinds. By the trial-and-error process of theorizing, man has regrouped things into new kinds which prove prudentially advantageous in lending themselves to many more inductions than the old ones says Quine.[55] Moreover, one's sense of similarity changes and even becomes multiple, making increasingly dependable predictions. This improvement is a welcome development in man different from animal sense of similarity. Things are similar in the theoretical sense, once we have adopted theoretical kinds.

Thus, one finds the relevance of the distinction between the natural kinds and the theoretical kinds. As we noted above, the natural kinds are the results of the innate ability that man has got by birth. In this level of food gathering, man makes use of colours and learns how to distinguish something that is food and something that is not. But this level of knowledge needs to be revised when we progress a little further. We felt, for instance, the need to reorganize the concept of fish and exclude whales from this list. This need was a theoretical one. Though at the perceptual level, we tend to treat whales as fish, when we consider the same at a second order level of organization, we feel the need to consider whales under the category of mammal. This has the theoretical advantage of studying the features of group of animals and thus, we adopted that. Quine also speaks of yet another example of kangaroos and certain type of mice being put under the same genetic group at the same time excluding some other mice from the group. Thus, we might have to speak of theoretical kinds and these theoretical kinds do a better job of providing good and elegant classification for us.

What is a natural gift of man is that he is able to have a sense of comparative similarity.[56] Insofar as it fits in with regularities of nature with reasonable success in our inductions and expectations, this comparative similarity is appreciated. It is presumably an evolutionary product of natural selection claims Quine. Basing similarity in regularity in nature and evolution, he argues that we are bound by our innate nervous system. Our expectation is built on the similarity in experience. The similarity at this level is subjective and the standard of similarity is innate. And this innate subjective standard is changeable in due course of experience. Quine remarks thus: "Natural selection has favoured in us a similarity standard that has made for largely successful induction by meshing pretty well with the regularities of nature over the past few dozen millenia."[57]

Quine's position in induction and similarity is based on the evolutionary principle of Darwin. We cannot wipe all our prior knowledge, because we have the innate ability to distinguish between kinds and degrees of kinds. Quine is of the opinion that we are born in the society having its own linguistic and other conventions. We use our linguistic ability in building theoretical kinds by modifying our categories of natural kind. For this reason, there is no possibility of first philosophy which would serve as the basis for building the system of scientific knowledge. Philosophy is not an *a priori* groundwork for science. He opines that philosophy and science are at the same level like the Neurath's boat. We can rebuild philosophy as well as science being only at sea while staying afloat in it. "There is no external vantage point, no first philosophy"[58] and "there is no higher court of appeal."[59] He prefers to wipe the boundary of philosophy and psychology on the one hand and philosophy and linguistics on the other and blend them together.

Having had no hope in the possibility of first philosophy, Quine shifts his philosophical base to science. If knowledge acquisition is a natural phenomenon commonly found in human and animal world, it is his firm conviction that acquisition and justification of knowledge can be studied in a scientific manner. Philosophical enquiry is to be conducted with the aim of establishing unified science where epistemology becomes a chapter in science. In order to achieve this end, he adopts the behaviouristic psychology as the method of studying language and concepts in philosophy and science. Proposing new hypothesis, deriving observation categorical, falsifying or verifying the occasion sentences, experimentation, prediction, modifying the backlog theory, etc. are all part of the scientific activities leading to advancement in knowledge. When philosophy and science are merged indistinguishably that is called epistemology naturalized.

When epistemology is naturalized, it studies a natural phenomenon as well as a physical human subject. This human subject can be studied experimentally by controlling certain parameters like any other natural object. The relation between the meager input and the torrential output would remain the same as is the case with natural science. That is to say, the issue of how evidence relates to a theory and how theory of nature transcends any available evidence remains the same.[60]

Speaking of his theory of truth, Quine states that he is a realist when it is the matter of truth. In Quine's programme of naturalism truth becomes immanent. It is not transcendental; there is no higher tribunal for truth he says. However, that does not reduce truth to merely redundant and disquotational in nature. Because, truth is always purposive. Thus, speaking of truth, Quine says "we choose to pursue truth conducive to our well-being and that of other deserving people, and truths that gratify our curiosity about the world."[61] He says that in his naturalism 'true' is accepted as a second order predicate within science. He says "when we find to our surprise an accepted sentence was not true, this is on a par with finding our surprise that light rays are not straight. I am a realist about truth in whatever sense I am realist about light rays and straightness."[62]

Quine draws our attention to a remarkable feature of our use of truth predicate. When a scientific theory is displaced by further research, we do not say that it had been true but became false. We say that it was false, all the way. This is the kind of realism he subscribes to. Quine remarks; "Such is the scientific method: interrogation of nature in a cosmic true-false test. Man proposes, nature disposes."[63]

Quine's naturalism is criticised on the ground that it robs off the normative aspect of epistemology and philosophy. The naturalism, which is so heavily dependent on the evolutionary principle of similarity and the immanence theory of truth cannot but be the mere description of the process in which knowledge is *in fact* acquired and sustained then the prescriptive activity of how knowledge *should* be acquired and justified. However, Quine says that this fear is unfounded because normativity can be preserved in naturalized epistemology. He elaborated three main normative characteristics of naturalized epistemology. First, he claims that the principle of empiricism itself provides the normativity to naturalized epistemology by "counselling us to mistrust soothsayers and telepathists," because "empiricism is both a rule of scientific method and a scientific discovery."[64] It is natural science that tells us that our information about the world comes only through impacts on our sense organs. As it grows, understanding and deriving technology have become the goal of science though prediction retains its importance. Test of a good science would still be checkpoints in sensory prediction.[65] However, prediction is not considered to be normative by Quine.[66] He mentions that in *The Web of Beliefs* he has listed five virtues of a scientific hypothesis: conservatism, generality, simplicity, refutability and modesty. He says:

> A hypothesis may appeal to us by virtue of some analogy or symmetry, or linking up some known laws. I see all this as the domain of normative naturalist epistemology: the norms of plausibility or subjective probability. It is the domain of statistical theory and, at a less technical level, the homely percepts of conservatism and simplicity.[67]

Secondly, he says that his elaboration of natural sciences provides the natural setting to study epistemology only. The study of the relationship between evidence and theory still remains the primary goal of epistemology. Quine says that it is possible to address epistemic issues without getting into the details of neural mechanism and other details which belong to the naturalistic setting. "For epistemology remains centred as always on evidence, and meaning remains centred as always on verification; and evidence is verification."[68] Once we go beyond observation sentences, it ceases to have any clear applicability to any single sentence. Quine does not want to discard non-observational sentences from science as is done by logical positivists.

Thirdly, naturalized epistemology is heavily involved in developing heuristic devices. It has to find rational mechanism to conjecture and frame scientific hypotheses. This is considered to be one of the normative function by Quine. He writes "normative naturalized epistemology tangles with margin of error, random deviation, and whatever else goes into the applied mathematics of statistics."[69] It is part of the language game of science in contrast to other good language games such as fiction and poetry says Quine.

Inadequacy of Naturalism

No doubt that Quine's three indeterminacies are interconnected and he has acknowledged this fact at several places. Even if all the other problems of indeterminacies are resolved, the indeterminacy of translation cannot be resolved on Quine's own admission. This is because, the indeterminacy of translation is not a problem arising due to human factors such as cognitive limitation of man, nor does it arise due to lack of information about the facts.[70] Therefore, the problem of translation is unsolvable in nature. If translation problem cannot be solved completely, can we solve other related problems, i.e., the indeterminacy of reference and underdeterminacy of the theory? This issue is important for us because, whether there is any optimism in the programme of naturalizing epistemology can be assessed only if we are able to assess this situation. What we need to reconsider is the issue of translation.

The issue of translation does not depend totally on the language that one uses. That is to say, the language that one uses could be natural language such as English and Hindi. But the issue of translation could be equally important in the context of one world view to another world view. One may need to translate a sentence from one world view to another world view. We may consider a simple example. A person who is below the poverty line has to be defined keeping the context in mind. One cannot take the simple parameter like the energy consumed by the person per week or the *per capita* income as the criterion. This is because, this criterion is country dependent in the sense that a person having certain per capita income in one country, even if we convert the currency of one country into internationally accepted standard of money, i.e., US dollars, it would still be difficult to speak of poverty line in abstraction. Therefore, depending on the geographical conditions which influence the expenses on food, shelter, health, clothing and education, one has to arrive at a number for a particular country. Thus, we may say that when we speak of poverty line, we need to translate the sentence what it means in another country, not necessarily into another language, but in the same language, say, English. Thus, the issue of translation is applicable even if one has to translate a sentence from one perspective to another within the same linguistic fold.

One may speak of the above situation to be different from the one Quine has been entertaining. For instance, Quine speaks of translation at two levels, one at the level of words, i.e., word to word translation and the other of the translation of sentence to sentence keeping aside the problem of syntax. It is altogether a different matter whether syntax would interfere much with our sentence to sentence translation as some tend to believe. Even if we entertain the idea of translation without considering syntax, translation occurs whether at the word level or at the level of sentence, only means available is through observational sentence. As we have noted earlier, these observational sentences are occasion sentences which can be known to be true or false by anyone by looking into the occasion. Thus, translation are to be carried out at the behaviour level. What we call 'poverty line', no doubt needs to be translated from one language to another, between one country and another may be within the same language for instance, English.[71] But it is possible to argue that this issue is not the one which Quine discusses. True, that it is more difficult to speak of soft sciences and the objective grounds on which the translation can take place. Yet, given the position of Quine, we do not see how this situation is to be overcome, especially when he admits that his naturalized epistemology would cover even the social sciences.

The point that has not been much emphasized by Quine, but much relevant to the discussion of the matter is this. The observation sentences are important, but equally important is the manual of translation. What this manual of translation consists of is not very clear to us. In fact, if controversy emerges it is more due to the manual of translation rather than the observation sentences. As pointed out by Stevenson,[72] if there is disagreement in belief, there is a way of settling it. Therefore, it would not be much of a problem if there is disagreement about the observation sentence. Quine also notices that we do not really get into serious controversies when it is the matter of observation sentences. However, if there is any indeterminacy about the translation it is largely due to the manual of translation since, the observation sentences are not contested at all by both the translators. There would be the question about which manual of translation is the most adequate, and perhaps there are no methods to resolve this issue. Quine rightly recognizes this point but one wonders whether his naturalized epistemology can take care of this problem. Quine cannot overcome the problem of translation within the same language but between different world views or perspectives.[73]

Again, if a predicate is linked to the perspective, i.e., the scope of the predicate is determined by the perspective within which that predicate is considered, we would not be able to settle the issue of even the problem of indeterminacy of the reference as well. Of course, Quine is quite optimistic in this because he assumes that there would be unified science and one day this controversy might vanish. That is to say, each predicate in different sciences when unified would have the same ontological commitment. For instance, what is a planet can be settled within the scientific community and the ontology of the predicate can be fixed firmly. However, this unified science is not to be achieved using Hitler's method of bringing equality in the world by eliminating all others who do not fit our model. Quine simply hopes that there would emerge a situation where all human beings, on their own, submit the creative and imaginative thinking and accept the ontology which the unified science dictates on us. Perhaps, this is too much to expect from mortal human beings. This is because, all possible perspectives on this world is bound to have different ontologies since, their ontological perspectives are different. But Quine would like to see the possible perspectives on the world remains only one when unified science emerges. However, this line of argument is not persuasive and convincing.

And similar ambiguity remains in the Quinean concept of an empirically equivalent theories. It is assumed, and seems a harmless thesis at that, two theories can be empirically equivalent. As Bergstorm has viewed it, this thesis does not seem to have even a single instantiation.[74] However, as noted earlier, Quine provides two non-trivial examples of such kind. He speaks of Poincare's example and that of two geometries, one Reimannian and the other Euclid's. Both these examples are supposed to show that they are empirically equivalent but they differ in their theory. The two theories are not only different, they are said to be incompatible as well.

Two theories are incompatible if and only if they are formulated within the same language is evident. And it seems impossible to have two theories within the same language if the empirical contents are the same. If theoretical terms are different, then the empirical contents are bound to be different if observational statements are theory-laden. But the observational statements which Quine calls observation categorical are occasional sentences and they are not theory-laden. There seems to be some difficulty because Quine uses an observation sentence both as theory-laden and theory free. Therefore, it all depends on the notion of what is empirically equivalent theory.

What does it mean to say that two theories are empirically equal? Would it mean that even the future possible empirical observable statements are also equal? If so, it does not absolutely matter whether the two theories are two theories at all. Since, the theories whatever wherever they differ, that has no consequence to the world. If it meant that till today, whatever observations have been made, the set of all empirical observations fit both the theories equally well, then there is a point of argument. However, it may happen that the two empirically equal theories make predictions which are not the same. Should we include the predicated observation categoricals as part of the theory? Of course, both the theories may be in a position to make same predictions which yield the same observation categoricals, then there is no difference between the two theories at the empirical level. Let us ask the question, then where lies the difference? Certainly not in the empirical slack as spoken by Davidson and approved by Quine and Bergstorm, because if there can be empirical slack, then the two theories are not empirically equal at all. Our supposition that the two theories are empirically equal was wrong. But in case they are having the same empirically equal observational sentences. Still two theories might differ in the possibility of allowing certain hypothesis and the other theory may not be able to permit such an attractive hypothesis. None consider this to be important. In fact, all seem to be silent on this matter.

We need to reject the interpretation that all possible data can simply be identified with the set of all true observation categoricals. This is because, if we claim that it is a thesis in epistemology, then we do not know as a matter of fact, all true observation categoricals since, theories are being modified and new observation categoricals are derived from the backlog theory and new hypotheses put together. Since, we are moving towards unified science and since, we are not yet near to it, it would be useless to speak of the set of all true observation categoricals. Thus, as a thesis in metaphysics, this could be an interesting issue assuming that all true observation categoricals put together form the set and how well this set would fit into a theory. But as an epistemic thesis at this stage of development in science, this would be uninteresting.

What is meant by empirically equivalent does not seem to be whatever observations made so far. It also does not mean all the possible empirical observations put together, for in that case the thesis is uninteresting and useless since, it turns out to be a thesis in metaphysics rather than in epistemology. Given the empirical bent of mind of Quine, it would be quite unfair to attribute this view to him. Therefore, only option that we find is of claiming: two empirically equivalent theories are, as a matter of fact include all the observed statements, all the observation categoricals. It should not matter whether the observation categoricals are occasion sentences. And it should also not matter whether these occasion sentences turn out to be true or false provided they turn out to be true together or false together in both the competing theories.

We need to consider whether the underdetermination thesis is a non-trivial issue. Bergstorm is of the opinion that this thesis is trivial if we consider the history of science. As a matter of fact, there were hardly any two theories which were incompatible and had the same empirical content. But the thesis ought to be non-trivial to have epistemic significance. Since, we do not know all the historical facts, and we are not even expected to know everything about man from the beginning of the evolution. If there is any truth in the statement "history is always a success story", it is likely that the competing theories which have not succeeded have been forgotten. Therefore, arguing from ignorance would not be a better policy.

Quine is of the opinion that any observation sentence can be viewed as theory-laden and the same sentence can be viewed as theory free. All occasional sentences are theory free since, verification of these sentences do not depend on any theory. And since, the economic behaviour of individuals can be observational sentences which are occasion sentences, there is no reason to believe that the situation is different. Quine's theory perfectly applies even to the soft science like economics. And even if what is a poverty line in one country is theory-laden, the human behaviour can be viewed as theory free and so far as the behaviour of human beings are concerned, one can observe the behaviour whether it is in India or in the US. As long as the theory and the observation relationship is concerned, it is the same whether it is India or the US. The economic theory is underdetermined whether it is in India or else where. Therefore, there is nò issue of deriving the theory from the observation and the theory would all the time remain underdetermined.

The point of saying that an observational sentence is theory-bound was quite different than the one which Quine takes it to be. It is one thing to say that an observational sentence that falls within the scope of a theory and another thing to say that the observational sentence is theory bound. To cite an example appropriate to the spirit of those who maintain that a sentence is theory bound would be the following: Given the movement of earth, sun and moon, one could speak of the eclipse as the consequence of the movement of the planets around the sun. Whereas, the concept of eclipse in Indian mythology is quite different. It is believed that *Rahu* and *Ketu* are attacking the moon when lunar eclipse takes place. The observation sentence that emerges as a consequence of these two different conceptions of eclipse are said to be theory bound observations. Another good example is that of the concept of cure in different medical theory. For instance, the concept of what is a disease and what is cure is different in *Ayurveda* and Allopathy system of medicine. And similarly, the theory about how the medicine heals the patient also would be different. This is the point of the view of theory-laden observation statement. It is not possible to conclude, for instance, a patient is healing without knowing what to observe in order to observe healing within a system of medicine. For instance, just before healing, it aggravates the disease in some of the diseases in Homoeopathy, *Ayurveda* and in certain form of Herbal medicine. When it aggravates, medicine is taken to be working well in these systems. And in the case of Allopathy, if the disease aggravates, then the disease is speeding is the view. Thus, it is difficult to say in these situations whether the observation is theory-free.

No doubt that the disease is aggravated is observable, but that the disease is being cured is not. However, after the aggravation of the disease, the disease starts subsiding and the symptoms vanish. Even this is observable. But when the disease aggravates an allopathic doctor would not consider it to be starting point of cure.

Quine's framework is such that there is no question of an observation statement being theory dependent. For him, an observation categorical is predicted from the hypothesis, auxiliary statements and the backlog theory. The observation categorical being the occasion sentence, it is verifiable. The set of all such occasion sentences are observable in a theory independent manner. However, even though observation categorical was predicted from the medical theory that the patient is being cured, but that may not be clearly occasion sentence. For instance, it is not observable that the medicine is healing when the disease aggravates.

If theories are underdetermined, that is to say, if there is no one way of clinching the theory in a unique manner, and if there can be theory-laden sentences, then the skepticism cannot be avoided about the validity of the theory. Quine's discussion on observational statement, natural kinds and theoretical kinds cannot salvage the problem of objectivity. Though the aim was and still is very noble to provide an objective basis for theory choice, there is not one that is emerging.

If the above account of the underdetermination of the theory is reasonable, then one faces the skeptical issue of Kripke. Kripke's formulation is, how do I know that I used the same rule in the past even if I know what I am using today? That is to say, given the theory one and theory two, which of the theory I followed yesterday in making the theory choice cannot be said since, empirically observable for both the theories are equal. Of course, even as a metaphysical thesis, Kripke's skeptic would have the same issue since, there is nothing mental and there is nothing physical that can distinguish theory one from theory two, there is no ground to say that we have accepted theory one or theory two yesterday, or even today.

But the issue is, if two theories are logically incompatible, can they have two empirically equivalent theories? This question is a fundamental one where one can say, if we accept disquotational theory of truth or if we believe in the harmony of language and reality, there cannot be two theories empirically equivalent yet logical incompatible. This is not because one can work out the Davidsonian device of spelling them differently, but this is because one tends to agree with Wittgenstein's view that, there cannot be any language which does not reflect the reality. Moreover, there is no contradiction in reality, if contradiction exists, it is in language. Therefore, neither disquotational approach nor the harmony between language and reality can permit such incompatible theses. However, there can be conflict between one theory and another at the level of language having no implication to observation categorical. Since, no language can contradict with reality, both the theories would be in harmony with reality though the two theories conflict with one another. Thus, it should not matter whether the language used in the formulation of a theory is one and the same for underdetermination of the theory. As long as sentence to sentence translations are possible, then one is speaking of the same theory, and if such a translation is not possible, then whether they are in the same language or in different languages, they are different theories.

Natural and Theoretical Kinds

Quine sees the notion of natural kind problematic because, the notion is linked to the problem of disposition, subjunctive conditional and the problem of cause. He also finds it a problem because he finds theoretical kinds are more objective than the natural kinds. And further, he finds that different notions of kinds are adopted by different branches of science and he expects unified science to emerge and there would be hopefully compatible concepts of kinds. However, all these are problematic since, what is the basis of kinds in reality itself is not answered by Quine.

Of course, it is not at all clear as to what is the advantage that we see in modifying the natural kinds, e.g., whales. Our linguistic classification does not affect the reality, and to that extent what kind of gain shall we have by classifying or reclassifying is not clear. The second or higher level classification could not have been possible without the first level classification and Quine seems to settle and give more importance to the second level classification which would not have been possible but for the first level. And more over, the second level classification being a parasitic one, we do not think that higher level classification could override the first level classification. The talk of theoretical kind is made possible by natural kind and if natural kind is rejected, then the other one also naturally gets rejected. It will not do to kick the ladder after climbing it, for what we have used as the ladder is the pillar and by kicking the ladder we are causing the building to collapse.

Even if we agree with Quine that naturalized epistemology would take care of the indeterminacies, it is not clear how that can happen given the fact that our base of natural kind and theoretical kind keep changing. Quine seems to believe that natural kind gets replaced by the theoretical kind when we adopt ourselves to the scientific theory. However, there is no observation of any type which is indicative of this adoption; there is no fact, change in the way human beings behave. We are in a position to recognize, and may be able to adopt to the new notion of theoretical kinds, but our old sensibility still works. We do see whales as fishes. This process of distinguishing natural kinds would never cease to exist. If that were so, our children should naturally see whales as mammals, which do not happen. Either Quine has to admit that even theoretical kinds have become innate in addition to natural kind, or has to come to theoretical kind only through natural kinds. Darwin's theory is irrelevant to our philosophical discussion then.

Quine seems to justify induction on the basis of theoretical kinds. Even if we admit the theoretical kinds, what follows is that we admit the ontologies of the theoretical kind. We now speak of, H_2O instead of water, and in our conception of H_2O we could speak of molecules which are made up of Hydrogen and Oxygen atoms in the ratio of two atoms to one. But in many cases of theoretical types, we do not perceive them as such. Theoretical kinds do not yield observational sentences always. Our perception can go only to the extent of H_2O as water which is a natural kind. We do not perceive two molecules to one ratio of Hydrogen and Oxygen compound, or in other words, we do not perceive a Hydroxide as a theoretical kind, but water as the natural kind. We have to invariably fall back on our sensitivity of natural kind when it comes to observation sentences. Our modification of the natural kind has to be reversed when we have to have observation categorical to verify or falsify a theory. Therefore, Quine's hope that modification of the natural kind leads to evolution of theoretical kind seems to be unfounded.

The naturalized epistemology hoped to perform well despite there being the above problems, i.e., indeterminacy of reference, indeterminacy of translation and underdetermination of theory. This hope was built on the ground that natural kinds can eventually evolve into theoretical kind, and predicate logic would take over natural language. Having achieved more or less perfect and all encompassing theory of science by the process of conjectures and refutations using the principle of holism, unified science with soft sciences on the side, would reach the state of naturalized epistemology with all normative character of traditional epistemology of warning against culprits of knowledge. Unfortunately, this does not seem to be possible, whether we speak of theories in science being true or simply restrict ourselves to the issue of only observation categoricals being true or false. By making the issue of truth to be the matter of immanence, Quine has only laid the foundation for theory dependent notion of truth. There is no external vantage point for Quine since, he accepts the analogy of the boat, but there are others who strongly feel that boat cannot be overhauled since, it is sinking due to the holes at the bottom. Rejection of the first philosophy by embracing the innatism of a certain kind may not be the right thing to do since, first philosophy need not require wiping the mind totally. The first philosophy might only require "reformatting the existing data"[75] to rebuild the structure of our knowledge of the world.

However, the above notion of science perhaps is itself problematic. It does not seem to be a simple matter that from the natural kind that we are able to move to theoretical kind. Moreover, if natural kinds are removed, a theory in science would become a self-justifying system and one would not require any verification principle at all. At this rate, no theory can be falsified without the natural kinds. Without banking on natural kinds, we will not be in a position to distinguish a scientific theory from a pseudo-scientific theory. Popper needs to be born again.

Quine and the Kripke's Skeptic

Kripke's skeptic would not be satisfied with Quine's account of objective knowledge. Quine takes shelter in language by claiming that he does not any more count the difference between the nerve endings while speaking of the same perception. We can say that I have perceived the same tree again and again because the individual difference in the manner in which stimulus hits our sense organ drops out at the level of language claims Quine of 1981. Even in the context of translation, the individual difference in stimulus dropout. They dropout since, the linguistic behaviour of 'gavagai' and 'rabbit' turn out to be the same. Once having established that they have the same linguistic behaviour, their linguistic meaning would be the same and one need not have to consider individual stimulus meaning at all. This is the reason why Quine believes that observational sentences can be objective. And they being objective, one can establish the objectivity of knowledge and thus, one can answer the skeptic of Kripke, one naturally thinks.

However, Kripke's skeptic would be unhappy with this answer because he would find every explanation of Quine satisfactory and yet argue that our past behaviour is no indication that the rules followed by the speaker of the Jungle language are the same as ours. Quine's temporary acceptance of the hypothesis is going to remain temporary all through. One cannot conclude for sure 'gavagai' means 'rabbit'. We are not far away from the issue of the skepticism since, neither naturalized epistemology is able to solve the problem of indeterminacies nor there is any hope for it. The reason is simply the one which Kripke's skeptic points out. There is nothing in the past either in the mind or in the nature of the world which can give us the guarantee that we have used the word with the same rules and we have meant the same by those words. This is the reason why we are not in the position to say whether the predicate has the same scope when considered in alternative perspective of the world, claim whether translation is determinate and clinch a theory exactly fitting the empirical data. The problem that Quine's skeptic faces is similar to that of Kripke's skeptic. The sentences have to be appropriately translated, let us try and do that here below:

Given the human behaviour, it is not possible to learn the quantifiers, says Quine. Why should this be so, because, no single behaviour can give the universal relation between any two predicates. Let us consider the case of intention and the intended behaviour. I say, I promise to give you the book you lent me yesterday. The statement made here whether it meant the same yesterday cannot be clarified, because the same behaviour cannot be ensured. The word same cannot be explained here because we do not have any fact physical or mental to identify this behaviour in the past.

In the case of translation also, it is not possible to know the exact translation because we do not know what exactly is the proposition expressed. Since, proposition cannot be known translation is impossible. Thus, even though we know the behaviour of the person, we do not know the meaning of that behaviour. Despite showing empathy to the child and the field linguist, one is not able to give the exact translation leaving aside the problem of syntax and other theoretical or theory-dependent statements.

What Kripke's skeptic speaks of rule can be spoken of theory in the context of Quine. Kripke's skeptic found the rule to be underdetermined. Given the behaviour, he found that two competing rules can fit exactly well with the behaviour. Both *plus* and *quus functions* are applicable to the arithmetic calculations so far performed claims he. Similarly, Quine's skeptic finds that given all the empirical data, two theories equally fit and he does not know how to make a theory choice.

NOTES AND REFERENCES

1. Since, the distinction was not clear to Quine himself and since, Quine prefers the expression indeterminacy of reference to inscrutability of reference, we have used indeterminacy of reference throughout in our discussion. Please see, Quine, W.V., (1992) *Pursuit of Truth*, (hence, forth *PT*) revised edition, Harvard University Press, Cambridge, p. 50. Also Quine, W.V., "Three Indeterminacies" (henceforth *Three Indeterminacies*), in *Perspectives on Quine*, edited by Robert Barrett and Roger Gibson, (1990) Basil Blackwell, USA, p. 6.
2. *Three Indeterminacies*, p. 1. Also see *PT,* pp. 50-52 for the discussion on indeterminacy of reference, see pp. 47-51 for the indeterminacy of translation and pp. 96-102 for underdetermination of theory.
3. Quine, W.V., "Epistemology Naturalized" (hence, forth *Epistemology Naturalized*), in Hilary Kornblith (ed.), 1985, *Naturalising Epistemology*, The MIT Press, Cambridge, Mass. p. 24.
4. *PT,* p. 19.
5. *Ibid.,* p. 101.
6. *Ibid.,* pp. 27-28.
7. Barrett, Robert and Gibson, Roger (eds.), (1990) *Perspectives on Quine*, Basil Blackwell, USA, 1990, p. xxii.
8. *PT*, pp. 33-34.
9. This is where the seed of the skepticism is sown. So far as cases of observed are concerned, there is no disagreement, but the question is: how do we know whether they agree on the unobserved part of the theory?

10. *Three Indeterminacies*, p. 15.
11. *PT*, p. 96. Also see, Quine, W.V., (1995) *From Stimulus to Science* (henceforth *From Stimuls to Science*), Harvard University Press, Cambridge, Mass., 1995, pp. 73-75.
12. *PT*, pp. 50-51.
13. The distinction between 'inscrutability of reference' and 'ontological relativity' was not clear to Quine himself. Now he claims that ontological relativity is relative to a manual of translation. Please see Three Indeterminacies, p. 6. Also see *PT,* p. 50. Also see W.V. Quine, (1994) "Responses", *Inquiry*, 37, p. 498.
14. *Three Indeterminacies*, pp. 7-8.
15. *Three Indeterminacies*, p. 6. Also see *From Stimulus to Science*, p. 79; *PT*, p. 42.
16. *Three Indeterminacies*, p. 5.
17. *PT*, p. 42. For discussion on empathy see, *From Stimulus to Science*, p. 89.
18. *PT,* p. 38. Also see *Three Indeterminacies*, p. 2.
19. While speaking of the rule of pronouns and quantifiers, Quine writes "The translator will accommodate them any way, whatever his translations. He may or may not call them pronouns, plurals, quantifiers. etc. accordingly as he thinks in terms of one or another manual of translation. The difference will be only verbal or, at most, a choice of one syntactic structure rather than another for generating one and the same total output of Jungle strings." Please see *Three Indeterminacies,* p. 5.
20. *PT*, p. 28.
21. *Three Indeterminacies*, p. 2.
22. *PT*, p. 7. For detail discussion on Observation Sentences, also see, *From Stimulus to Science*, pp. 22-24.
23. *PT*, pp. 2-3.
24. *Three Indeterminacies*, p. 8. Also see *PT*, pp. 4-5. Also see *From Stimulus to Science*, pp. 43-45.
25. *Three Indeterminacies*, pp. 10-11.
26. *Ibid.*, pp.11f.
27. However, we must note that Quine says that verification is a difficult process, but falsification can be decisive: "refutation of an observational categorical by an observed counter-instance. This is how some of our false inductions get weeded out, and how science keeps a grip of reality. In principle, a hypothesis can be tested, if at all, by deducing an observational categorical from it in conjunction with auxiliary laws and then testing the categorical." W.V. Quine, (1994) "Responses" (henceforth Responses), *Inquiry*, 37, 1994, p. 503.
28. *Three Indeterminacies*, p. 10.
29. *Responses*, p. 501.
30. *Ibid.*, p. 502.
31. *Three Indeterminacies*, p. 8.

32. *PT*, p. 101.
33. *Ibid.*, pp. 96-97.
34. Quine, W.V., (1981) Theories and Things, Harvard University Press, Cambridge, pp. 21-22.
35. *Three Indeterminacies*, p. 14.
36. *Ibid.*, pp. 14-15.
37. *PT*, See section §12.
38. *Three Indeterminacies*, p. 13. Also see "*Responses*", pp. 500-501 for the discussion on theory formulation.
39. *PT*, p. 102.
40. Laudan, L., "Are All Theories Equally Good?: A Dialogue", in R. Nola (ed.), (1988) *Realativism and Realism in Science*, Kluwer Academic Press, The Netherlands, p. 117.
41. Popper seems to suggest that the criterion of falsification can be applied in the case of choosing the correct theory among the rival. Provided every thing being equal, the unfalsified theories to be retained. See Popper, K.R., (1972) *Objective Knowledge: An Evolutionalry Approach*, The Clarendon Press, Oxford, pp. 8-9.
42. See Harding, G.H. (ed.), (1976) *Can Theories be Refuted? Essays on Duhem-Quine Thesis*, D. Reidel Publishing Company, Boston, USA, p. ix.
43. Feyerabend, P., *Against Method*, NLB, London, pp. 23 ff.
44. Laudan, L., *Are All Theories Equally Good*?, p. 122.
45. Kuhn, T., (1977) *Essential Tensions*, Chicago University Press, Chicago, pp. 321-2.
46. See *PT* pp. 3-4, 40, 44. Also see, *From Stimulus to Science,* pp. 17-21. For discussion on the sameness of meaning. please see *From Stimulus to Science*, pp. 76-77, 81-82. This view is also held by later Wittgenstein. For the detail discussion see chapter 5 of the thesis.
47. Quine, W.V., "Natural Kinds" (henceforth *Natural Kinds*), in Hilary Kornblith (ed.), (1985) *Naturalising Epistemology*, The MIT Press, Cambridge, Mass, p. 40. Also see *From Stimulus to Sciences*, pp. 25, 50.
48. *Natural Kinds*, p. 37. Also see *From Stimulus to Science*, p. 19.
49. *Ibid.*, p. 38. Note that Quine also recognizes that learning words to be one of lawlike statement or hypothesis formation.
50. *Ibid.*, p. 38.
51. The issue has already been discussed in Chapter 3, section 3.1 in detail.
52. *Natural Kinds*, p. 38.
53. *Ibid.*, pp. 38-39.
54. *Ibid.*, p. 37.
55. *Ibid.*, p. 40. The question that would arise now is about the status of the present science itself. Could we ever consider the truth that we have discovered to be final? Could we have a definite method of science so that we are sure that what we concluded is lasting?
56. *Natural Kinds*, p. 43.

57. *Responses*, pp. 502-503.
58. *Natural Kinds*, p. 39.
59. *Responses*, pp. 497-98.
60. *Epistemology Naturalized*, p. 24.
61. *Responses*, p. 498.
62. *Ibid.*, p. 497.
63. *Ibid.*, p. 500.
64. *Perspectives on Quine*, p. 229. Also see *PT*, p. 21.
65. *PT*, p. 21.
66. On the other hand, we do consider this to be one. For our argument see chapter 6.
67. *Responses*, p. 503.
68. *Epistemology Naturalized*, p. 28. Also see *PT*, pp. 1, 21.
69. *PT*, p. 20.
70. *Ibid.*, p. 101.
71. Quine uses the notion of language game of Wittgenstein. One could also think of translation between two language games provided they share the same empirical content.
72. Stevenson, C. L., (1994) *Ethics and Language*, Yale University, New Haven, pp. 1-11, makes the distinction between disagreement in belief and disagreement in attitude. He is of the opinion that this disagreement in attitude cannot be resolved at all by persuading the other person following any scientific method. Only way to resolve disagreement in attitude is to persuade by any means and eventually one may succeed or fail. But in the case of disagreement in beliefs, it is possible to resolve the issue by following the scientific method. For instance, if two people disagree whether someone is in the next room, that could be verified and the issue can be resolved.
73. We suspect that this discussion would lead to another celebrated distinction of transparency and opacity of Quine.
74. Bergstorm, Lars, (1993) "Quine, Underdetermination, and Skepticism", *Journal of Philosophy*, pp. 337ff.
75. Computers make it possible to change the format, *i.e.*, the look of the data in various ways without loosing the content of the passages. This analogy seems to be apt in the context of first philosophy because laying the foundation of philosophy would not amount to removing all existing knowledge.

5

Wittgenstein: Skepticism and Certainty

Introduction

Apart from the general skeptical remarks, we notice two types of skepticism that Wittgenstein refers to in his writings. One may be called the skepticism of the *external world* and the other may be called as the *rule-following* skepticism. It is quite clear that Wittgenstein is not very happy about the proof offered by Moore for proving the existence of the external world. In fact, the very opening sentence of *On Certainty* claims "If you do know that *here is one hand*, we will grant you all the rest."[1] There are several passages in the writings of Wittgenstein which indicate the general helplessness of man due to his philosophical and linguistic habits and limitations. Quite a few remarks indicate that the grammar of the language is responsible for trapping of the philosophers. All the efforts made by the philosophers are in vain, they all fail repeatedly as the philosophical issues are language dependent. Moreover, the philosophical problems remain what they are and no progress in philosophy can be spoken about since, language as the source of philosophical puzzles and language has never changed. The second form of skepticism that we notice is the rule-following skepticism which has been popularized by Kripke. This form of skepticism emerges in the context of language and human behaviour. Of all the types this is unique to Wittgenstein and is most powerful as it pervades other forms of skepticism and logically difficult to refute it as well.

Wittgenstein's method of addressing both the skeptical issues is basically the same. He would first entertain the argument of the skeptic. Develop it to the logical extreme so that every advantage is given to the opponent. Then show how the skeptic's position implies absurd conclusion. The strategy adopted by Wittgenstein is known as the *reductio ad absurdum method* in the philosophical parlance.

In the case of the proof for the external world, Wittgenstein shows that it is not possible to prove that here is a hand using any sense perception, for the one who is questioning this doubt against sense perception cannot be made to be pleased by another sense perception. Thus, the very attempt made by Moore to prove the object of an external world by showing his hand is absurd from this angle. If senses are not trusted, it is absurd to say that they give valid knowledge. In the case of rule-following skepticism, Wittgenstein tries to show that if memory has to be doubted, then no rule can be trusted. Nothing that we remember can be said to be knowledge, and no knowledge can be utilized in our future course of action. Therefore, the skeptic is wrong in assuming if something has happened it will always happen. If memory has failed in some cases does not lead to the logical absurd conclusion that memory cannot be trusted. In the case of rule-following skepticism, Wittgenstein holds that it does not follow that we doubt all the time wherever we can doubt. The skeptic does the same. He concludes from the logical possibility of doubting whether some one is actually suffering from pain, whether it is ever possible to know ever if any one is in pain. Wittgenstein is clear that attitude comes first and then the question of belief.

Skepticism about External World

Wittgenstein poses the problem of the external world in the following line. There is no way that one can find out the real nature of things. It is not possible to move from knowledge to the object of knowledge. If there is a possibility of error, there is nothing that such an error has not occurred. In order to be sure that there is no error in our knowledge of the world, it needs to be *shown* that no mistake was possible. Giving the assurance "I know" does not suffice. For it is after all only an assurance that I can not be making a mistake and it needs to be *objectively* established that I am not making a mistake about *that*.[2] Wittgenstein analyses the term "know"[3] in the following manner: He considers "I know" and "I see" are comparable. Both express the relation between the knower and the known. It speaks of the relation between the knower and the fact.[4] And there does not seem to be a mechanism to move from the knower to the known. No amount of ensuring whether one has satisfied all the correctness conditions of the picture of the world would give us the correct picture of the world. How the world is projected in language cannot be described. But one can imagine how it is done, and the picture of this imagination can be described according to Wittgenstein. One could judge this picture on the basis of the mythology that one accepts.[5] Wittgenstein adds further by saying that this would give us a picture of knowing as the perception of an outer event through visual rays which project it as it is into the eye and the consciousness. Only then the question at once arises whether one can be *certain* of this projection. And this picture does indeed show how our *imagination* presents knowledge, but not what lies at the bottom of this presentation.[6] But accepting a perspective of how the language and reality are related and jumping from the knowledge to the fact would be self-defeating, since we do not have an independent way of knowing the fact then.

What is wrong with Moore's method according to Wittgenstein was that Moore tried to prove the existence of two hands to those who did not trust his observation. When Moore's skeptic is not willing to grant Moore the status of a trustworthy person, then by assuring the critic or by uttering the words in a firm voice does not help at all. Claiming that one has not made a mistake does not increase the degree of certainty of what is being claimed.[7] Meta-statement about once knowledge adds no strength to the initial statement. For example, if I know something, then I also know that I know it. But such claims do not add anything to the certainty of my knowledge. Whether I am so must be objectively establishable. Otherwise, if I claim that I know, it has to be taken as self-evident to every person.[8]

Existence of a physical object cannot be proved, but one could instruct what "A" means, or what "physical object" means[9] Wittgenstein claims that the term "physical object" is a logical one like colour, quantity. In speaking about a physical object one could speak of colour of the object; one could speak of other attributes of the object, but not of a physical object in general. "Physical object" is not an object, it is a concept. When we use the expression "physical object" we do not have any particular object in mind and hence, it cannot refer to any object. Therefore, one cannot say, there are physical objects. If ever we use such sentences, then the meaning of the word "physical object" would be almost the same as a "thing" and instead of our asserting that there are many things we call them physical objects. One could not speak of physical objects in the manner in which Moore spoke of two hands to prove there are physical objects.

After having shown that one cannot prove that there are physical objects in this fashion, he asks whether there are any grounds for disbelief. He writes, "But what about such a proposition as "I know I have a brain"? Can I doubt it? Grounds for *doubt* are lacking! Everything speaks in its favour, nothing against it. Nevertheless it is imaginable that my skull should turn out empty when it was operated on."[10]

Claiming that someone knows something has only significance to those people who take the person to be trustworthy. In such contexts, the person who claims that he knows has made only one point that the person in question has made sure that he has not committed a mistake. Others would believe in the authority under the assumption that it is possible for the person in question to make sure. But those who doubt the existence of any physical objects makes no such provision for making sure of the existence of any physical object.[11]

And "I know that there's a sick man lying here", used in an *unsuitable* situation, seems not to be nonsense but rather seems matter-of-course, only because one can fairly easily imagine a situation to fit it, and one thinks that the words "I know that..." are always in place where there is no doubt, and hence, even where the expression of doubt would be unintelligible.[12] The statement "I know that here is a hand" may then be continued: "for it's *my* hand that I am looking at". Then a reasonable man will not doubt that I know.[13] The propositions presenting what Moore '*knows*' are all of such a kind that it is difficult to imagine *why* anyone should believe the contrary says Wittgenstein. E.g. the proposition that Moore has spent his whole life in close proximity to the earth. Everything that one has seen or heard gives us the conviction that no man has ever been far from the earth. Nothing in my account of the world speaks in favour of the opposite.[14]

Wittgenstein clarifies "There is no subjective sureness that I know something. The certainty is subjective, but not the knowledge. So, if I say "I know that I have two hands", and that is not supposed to express just my subjective certainty, I must be able to satisfy myself that I am right. But I can not do that, for my having two hands is not less certain before I have looked at them than afterwards. But I could say, " "That I have two hands is an irreversible belief." That would express the fact that I am not ready to let anything count as a disproof of this proposition."[15] That is the reason why I am certain about it and my perspective is true to me. Speaking on the foundation of certain beliefs, especially the one that there are two hands here, Wittgenstein says that we proceed according to this belief unconditionally and not let anything confuse me, and every reasonable person does that. He remarks, "At the foundation of well-founded belief lies belief that is not founded."[16]

Doubting is not a normal thing Wittgenstein points out. How does one doubt that one had no parents? This doubt does not seem to naturally arise. Has anyone taught me that I had no parents? he asks. How can a child doubt immediately what it is being taught? If no one has taught me that it is not conceivable that I will have such a doubt.[17] If a child doubts something immediately after it is taught, it only means that the child is incapable of learning certain language-games.

We do not test everything and that does not seem to be possible either. Speaking about the testing of only those things which we doubt and not everything, Wittgenstein writes: "We check the story of Napoleon, but not whether all the reports about him are based on sense-deception, forgery and the like. For whenever we test anything, we are already presupposing something that is not tested. Now am I to say that the experiment which perhaps I make in order to test the truth of a proposition presupposes the truth of the proposition that the apparatus I believe I see is really there (and the like)?"[18]

Wittgenstein concludes by saying that people have killed animals since the earliest times, used the fur, bones etc. for various purposes. They have counted definitely on finding similar parts in any similar beast. "They have always learnt from experience; and we can see from their actions that they believe certain things definitely, whether they express this belief or not." Of course, he hesitates to make a normative judgement and says that "By this I naturally do not want to say that men *should* behave like this, but only that they do behave like this."[19]

Wittgenstein's Paradox of Rules

There is substantial agreement on certain philosophical topics dealt with by Wittgenstein. Use and meaning are linked in a definite manner is not debated any more. But what kind of thing is meaning is yet, to be settled by scholars on Wittgenstein. Given the stance of Wittgenstein on grammar and language in general, it becomes all the more difficult to articulate what is the ontological status of meaning at all in his philosophy. Whether such a question: What is meaning? Can be asked within his philosophical framework is not clear since he seems to direct us to the explanation of meaning or the use of the term.[20] Of course, this suggestion of Wittgenstein is read by different scholars differently. Yet, the functioning of language cannot be understood fully without understanding what ontological place ought to be assigned to the term 'meaning'. Moreover, intention and meaning are normally considered to be related to one another. We express our intention in the form of thought when we request for something, ask for something and when we state something. This again is a problem for philosophers since intention cannot always be read off from the sign language and one cannot directly perceive the intention of others. Behavioural criteria for mental phenomenon is quite a difficult proposition since, one cannot have certainty in this area. Stimulus meaning cannot be spoken of since, we do not share our sensation, and for the same reason one cannot understand the meaning assigned to private experiences such as "pain". All the three, sensation, intention and the human behaviour are fully exploited in the rule-following skepticism by the skeptic in forming his problem.

The Wittgensteinian formulation of the paradox of rule is this: How is it that we can say that we have grasped the meaning of a word when meaning lies in use and use is spread over time? How is it that the whole use of the word till infinity can be grasped in a few seconds? This is the paradox which Wittgenstein's skeptic raises. Wittgenstein's skeptic, rather Wittgenstein as skeptic asks the question: There is no doubt that meaning lies in the use of words; there is no doubt that we grasp the meaning of words in a fraction and rules have infinite applications. It is puzzling that limited mind can grasp infinite rule. He tries to answer the skeptic by looking into the details of what rules are and what rules could do in the following manner.

(1) When I learn a rule, I lean it only through limited applications.
(2) How can I know the infinite applications in a flash?
(3) How can a rule tell me what to do next?
(4) Rules are arbitrary and have no justification.

How we learn a rule is explained by Wittgenstein at several places. In the course of teaching the rules, one show him the same colours, the same lengths, the same shapes, we make him find them and produce them, and so on.[21] A student has learnt to continue on his own writing of the series correctly. But we cannot say up to what extent one should help a student and the student would learn to go on cannot be stated.[22] How does one explain the meaning of regular, uniform or same to someone? asks Wittgenstein. He says that to define rule in terms of regularity, one need to explain what regularity is first. The method of explaining is easier if one teach the person this word. "I do it, he does it after me; and I influence him by expressions of agreement, rejection, expectation, and encouragement."[23] When we teach none of the words would be explained by means of itself. There would not be circular way of explaining.[24] Even the most difficult one like "and so on" or "and so on *ad infinitum*" is also explained in this way.

Wittgenstein speaks of the meaning and use relationship in *PI,* §138. If meaning and use relationship is accepted then, he says that meaning of one word cannot fit the meaning of another. In other words, two words cannot mean the same. This means strict synonyms cannot be found. However, he adds further qualification. Use of a word is extended in time and the meaning of a word we grasp in a flash. Giving the example of the word "cube" Wittgenstein remarks that he knows the meaning of that term. But he doubts whether every use of this word he knows.[25] Though a certain use is suggested by the word "cube" so that we are governed by the rule of this word, it is still possible to deviate from this use suggests Wittgenstein.

Wittgenstein speaks of the mistake that one normally commits. We think that use forces a particular application on us. We are not under logical compulsion to use a word in a particular way, but are under a psychological compulsion. When we hear a word what comes to our mind is different from the application of the word to the context.[26] How can a rule determine my action at a given point? asks Wittgenstein. Can we not interpret the rule according to our actions? Wittgenstein says, that is not possible since both the interpretation and the rule using which the interpretation is made cannot give any support to our action.[27]

While comparing the rules in a cookery book and the rules of grammar, Wittgenstein claims that rules of grammar are arbitrary. The use of language is autonomous. When you do not follow the rule of a grammar, it is not that you are doing something wrong, but you are doing it differently, you are speaking of something else says Wittgenstein.[28]

One might say that a new insight or intuition is needed at every step to carry out the order "+n" correctly. And the right step is the one that accords with the order as it was *meant*. When you gave the order + 2 you meant that he was to write 1002 after 1000. The question is: did you also meant that he should write 1868 after 1866 and so on? Wittgenstein remarks: "No: what I meant was, that he should write the next but one number after *every* number that he wrote; and from this all those propositions follow in turn." Wittgenstein responds to this statement by saying, that is just what is in question: at what stage should we call "being in accord" with that sentence. He further remarks: it would almost be more correct to say, not that an intuition was needed at every stage, but that a new decision was needed at every stage.[29] Wittgenstein wants to use the word 'decision' and not 'intuition' at every stage of our working out of the next number correctly. This is the reason why the Malcom and Hacker and Backer debate becomes more important.[30] Malcom is of the opinion that we have to decide everytime when we apply a particular rule to a context where as Backer and Hacker are of the opinion that the extension is determined when the rule is given. In some sense every step of the rule is given when the rule is given. Yet, all the particular cases of rule-following could not have been given is obvious to everybody.

Kripke's formulation of rule-following skepticism, especially, the discussion of *plus* and *quus* is nothing, but the application of this debate between the rule and the extension. Whether the rule would be in a position to indicate what step to take is the same as whether the rule has determined the next step that is to be taken, and if the extension is already determined by the rule, it is easy to compare the *plus* rule and the *quas* rule and see whether they have the same extension. If they have the same extension, then they are one and the same rule, and if they differ in their extension, then the rules are different. However, it is not quite simple to say that they have the same extension either. Since, each rule has infinite application, no human being is in a position to measure or foresee all the cases of the application of both the rules and conclude that they are identical. Moreover, when it is the matter of actually finding the application of the rule, it would be necessary to take decisions whether the rules are applicable in a context at all. Of course, Wittgenstein points out, it is possible to imagine a skeptic who would refuse to believe that there takes place any concept formation. He may insist that all that he knows is only what is empirical.[31] The knowledge of the rule is different from the application of the rule. One could only know the limited number of applications whereas the rule has infinite applications.[32]

What should be noted is that the paradigm used in learning the rule is different from the application of the rule. The paradigm used in invoking the rule cannot be considered to be its own application. "In one case we make a move in an existent game, in the other we establish a rule of the game. Moving a piece could be conceived in these two ways: as a paradigm for future moves, or as a move in an actual game."[33] This is the reason sometimes we get into problem. Both the cases seem to be similar to the beginners if one does not know the language game at all. Wittgenstein discusses similar difficulty regarding the ostensive definition. The one who does not know what pointing to means, would be in utter confusion whether the direction meant is from finger to the elbow or from the elbow to the finger.[34] The one who knows the convention regarding the manner in which pointing accompanies the ostensive definition, there would be no confusion at all. Therefore, those who know the language or some language games would know which one is a paradigm of the rule and which one is the application of the rule.

Having looked at whether a rule could tell us what I should do, one could ask the question the other way around. Can we interpret every behaviour of mine in such a manner that I am said to be in accordance with the rule? Yes, if we do that then it is possible to show that every behaviour can be so interpreted that it can be shown to be in accordance with one rule and it can be shown to be in conflict with another rule or another interpretation of the same rule. If such things can happen, then neither the word "accord" nor the word "conflict" would have consistent use and hence, the point of our argument is lost.[35] Thus, Wittgenstein concludes by remarking "What this shews is that there is a way of grasping a rule which is not an interpretation, but which is exhibited in what we call "obeying the rule" and "going against it" in actual cases."[36]

The paradox of Wittgenstein can be stated again in the following way: how is it that all applications are determined by the rule and yet, decision has to be taken everytime the application of the rule is sought. Both of them do not go together and hence, the paradox.

Justification Comes to an End

Another frequently used expression in Wittgenstein is "... comes to an end". He speaks of justification, explanation, reasons, doubts coming to an end. This is quite characteristic of Wittgenstein that he does not permit us to go on *ad infinitum* when these processes begin. He gives us the impression that we begin these processes somewhere and we need to end it somewhere. This does not seem to be an isolated incident that Wittgenstein thinks that we have to leave all these processes incomplete. It is not simply the rules lead to skepticism due to their failures, they are not justified further. In other words, nothing seems to be justified eventually. We have several passages that indicate such a skeptical attitude.

Remarking on the justification from experience, arguing from past to future Wittgenstein says, "Justification by experience comes to an end. If it did not it would not be justification".[37] Speaking of explanation of the meaning of terms, he remarks "Explanations come to an end somewhere."[38] And speaking of the process of justification he writes, "If I have exhausted the justifications, I have reached bed-rock, and my spade is turned."[39] He remarks on our foundation of belief by saying "At the foundation of well-founded belief lies belief that is not founded."[40] He adds further the act of "Giving grounds, however, justifying the evidence, comes to an end."[41]

But the remarks are totally misunderstood if we do not consider what Wittgenstein has in mind. The act of justifying is used to facilitate our understanding, if the justification does not come to an end, which would only amount to saying that understanding never takes place. If such a state of affairs is to prevail, then there is no point in trying to justify anything.

The act of justifying is something that we do within the language. Wittgenstein is of the opinion that we use rules for justifying the judgements, i.e., the application of the rules to the context. But rules themselves are not justifiable further. That is the reason that Wittgenstein says that if we have exhausted the justification then we are inclined to say: "This is simply what I do."[42] The act of justifying comes to an end because we cannot infinitely continue to justify one rule in terms of another. We have to terminate this act of justifying by action or by simply indicating what we do, i.e., speak about our convention.[43]

By taking the example of Moses, Wittgenstein raises the question which most of us would have asked: "But then how does an explanation help me to understand, if after all it is not the final one? In that case the explanation is never completed; so I still do not understand what he means, and never shall!" An explanation does not require further explanation and to think in this direction is to miss the point of an explanation. An explanation is supposed to serve to avoid misunderstanding. An explanation cannot serve to avoid all possible misunderstandings, but only the actual ones and hence, it should come to an end somewhere. Indirectly speaking of the Descartes' method of doubt, Wittgenstein thinks, might easily look as if every doubt merely revealed an existing gap in the foundations; so that secure understanding is only possible if we first doubt everything that can be doubted, and then remove all these doubts. Note that our process of justification should come to an end. He remarks: "the end is not certain propositions' striking us immediately as true, i.e. it is not a kind of *seeing* on our part; it is our *acting*, which lies at the bottom of the language-game."[44] Speaking of the obeying of the rule, he remarks, "When I obey a rule, I do not choose. I obey the rule *blindly*."[45] This is because a rule is first conventionally accepted before it is being obeyed. A rule is not a rule if it has no application and if it is not made part of the language and social convention. Therefore, a rule cannot be said to be obeyed as long as the rule is not accepted. If the rule is accepted, we do not have such a freedom to revise the rule everytime we obey it in applying it to the context. Therefore, he thinks that once the rule is chosen we have no freedom to choose any more.[46]

It is clear that the mental processes of others are not accessible to us and similarly the sense-experience of others is not accessible to us. This being so, one would tend to think that meaning and language are essentially private and subjective. What follows from this is that both knowledge and certainty turn out to be individualistic and at best psychological.

Wittgenstein argues against the possibility of such a view in what is normally called "private language argument" which can be found in *PI* from §§243-315. Here, the issue of coherence of the meaning of expressions of sensation words is dealt with.

Wittgenstein gives three majors consequences of holding the view that language is private or learning a language is a matter of associating words with, or ostensively defining words by referring to subjective experience or objective reality. (1) Words refer essentially refer to objects in the world and we could describe the state of affairs finding the relationship among the objects referred. For example, the meaning of the word 'pain' is known to referring to some psychological process one has. Thus, it makes meaning private and subjective. (2) Since, we cannot see the mental processes or experience of others, the meaning of such expression "I have pain" is accessible to the person concerned only. He alone is aware of his mental states. (3) The only way to know what others think, feel etc. are through observable behaviour of others. We would require outward criteria for inner process.

Obviously the above view that language is private leads to skepticism and solipsism. Since, pretending and deceiving are always possible, one can never be sure of the experience of others by observing his behaviour. Similarly, communication is impossible on this account of language. Wittgenstein does not wish to embrace the skeptical position. As we have pointed out, he considers skepticism only to refute it. We shall shortly see how he answers the skeptic by examining what he has to say on sensation and human behaviour.

Sensation

Wittgenstein recognizes the fact that language works at a social level and anything specific and unique to individuals it does not distinguish. Not that one cannot speak of unique and specific things that belong to individuals, but it is only those generalizable aspects, but happens to be individual can be spoken in language. That is to say, the contingent facts about individuals by all means can be described by language, yet, what the language captures is something that in principle be true of any individual. Wittgenstein remarks after the discussion on sensation of pain and considering the possibility of someone saying that he knows what the word 'pain' means and how one can generalize. To the issue of generalizing from one's own experience he writes: "That is to say: if we construe the grammar of the expression of sensation on the model of "object and designation" the object drops out of consideration as irrelevant."[47] Pain behaviour is as much important as the word "pain" in our understanding of pain. Wittgenstein remarks "Pain-behaviour can point to a painful place—but the subject of pain is the person who gives it expression."[48] Without the behavioural aspect of the pain experience, we would not have learnt to use the word "pain".

Speaking of the impossibility of private exhibition of pain Wittgenstein writes "But I can give anyone an exhibition of the difference between a broken and an unbroken tooth." The difference between a broken and an unbroken tooth is knowable by anyone including the person whose teeth they are. He adds further, if it is enough to imagine the pain when it has to be exhibited to oneself; you pretend the pain behaviour let us say, but that is as much a public exhibition as anything else says Wittgenstein. There is no possibility of private exhibition. He remarks "This *private* exhibition is an illusion."[49] He concludes by saying "I can exhibit pain, as I exhibit red, and as I exhibit straight and crooked and trees and stones."[50]

Explaining the sensation and its relation to the notion of pain, Wittgenstein wants to be extremely careful in placing his findings. He would not like to say that sensations are important in understanding what pain is and yet, does not want to say that they are irrelevant either. Thus, he remarks about sensation of pain "It is not a *something*, but not a *nothing* either! The conclusion was only that a nothing would serve just as well as a something about which nothing could be said. We have only rejected the grammar which tries to force itself on us here."[51] We cannot say anything about the sensation of pain, at the same time, it is not absent either. We need to therefore make a radical departure from our usual view of word-object relationship of a certain kind. "Tree" refers to tree we say, but in the same manner one cannot speak of pain. "Pain" does not name the sensation of pain. He remarks, "The paradox disappears only if we make a radical break with the idea that language always functions in one way, always serves the same purpose: to convey thoughts—which may be about houses, pains, good and evil, or anything else you please."[52] This is the reason why Wittgenstein wants us to note that the grammar of such terms "pain" are different from that of other nouns. They cannot be said to be referring to sensations, yet, they are not fictions of our imagination. They have to be given the middle place of linguistically shared observable phenomena. Speaking of behaviourism and its facets, Wittgenstein would like to attribute himself of speaking of fiction of behaviourism which he would prefer to call "grammatical fiction".[53]

If there were not public way of knowing what pain is, perhaps I would not have developed the concept of pain itself. It is not enough to have only vocabulary and pain behaviour in order to have the concept of pain either. Without the observable aspect, what is pain cannot be learnt by any individual and yet, a particular sensation is not required to recognize it as pain. At the level of language all that is unique and individualistic aspect of pain is filter out. What is important in learning the concept of pain is the attitude that goes with it. When I say I am in pain, what immediately follows is the formation of a certain attitude. Wittgenstein remarks: "His attitude to me will then be that of belief; disbelief; suspicion; and so on."[54] One does not check whether someone is in pain or not by trying to find out whether he had such a sensation or no. What we immediately do is to form an attitude. We do not need any justification for forming an attitude. He remarks, "his attitude is a proof of his attitude. Imagine not merely the words 'I am in pain' but also the answer " 'it's not so bad' replaced by instinctive noises and gestures."[55]

Human Behaviour

We understand human behaviour in the light of the collective behaviour of human beings. We do not give account of one individual and his idiosyncratic behaviour in order to determine the human behaviour at large. Wittgenstein writes "What determines our judgement, our concepts and reactions, is not what *one* man is doing *now*, an individual action, but the whole hurly-burly of human actions, the background against which we see any action."[56] He wonders whether unpredictability of human behaviour would come in the way of our understanding other people. If we remove the unpredictable aspect of human behaviour from our account, Wittgenstein finds it very uninteresting because it would not remain the human behaviour.[57]

One could say that we can imagine an human being perceiving colour, but one cannot answer the question what the inner process of the experience of colour for instance. Such questions cannot be answered because the inner process is not something that we can talk about in language since, it is not part of language.[58] We do not observe our own behaviour says Wittgenstein. Only occasionally, a musician might pay close attention to the note he plays and judges it so that it can direct his action accordingly.[59]

What would have been the advantage of knowing the functioning of the nervous system in others can readily be imagined and determine their reaction without their having any reservation about them. And this can be the basis of their attitude towards others and there need not have any doubt claims Wittgenstein.[60] This is quite possible for Wittgenstein because he considers outward criteria to be the basis of the formation of the attitude and the inner process is not required for him at all. However, even if some one insists on having inner process as part of the scheme of his forming the attitude towards others, Wittgenstein allows one to have this without qualms about it. That is to say, whether one imagines or does not imagine the inner process in order to form one's attitude towards others, that does not matter at all since, there is no way one can know the inner process and inner process is not part of our language at all. We tend to treat the wounds of others when they are hurt and are in pain. We do pay attention to the pain-behaviour of others.[61] We hardly pay attention to the pain behaviour of our own claims Wittgenstein.

On the basis of the behaviour of someone, we say that he is sad. Behaviour itself is not the cause of sadness. Behaviour is its symptom says Wittgenstein. If the person in question says that he is sad, he does not point to his sad face and say this. But the more complicated issue would be if someone says that "Experience has taught me that I get sad as soon as I start sitting about sadly, etc."[62] Wittgenstein says that this might have two different meaning. Firstly, it means my pain behaviour caused more pain. It might be that toothache got worse by groaning. Secondly, it might mean that "if you could somehow or other produce certain bodily states, you would make the man sad." But here one should be careful that we do not call someone who looked and acted sad in all circumstances. If one used the expression "I am sad" and acted all the time like that the expression would have lost its normal meaning says Wittgenstein.

In a concluding tone Wittgenstein asks what would be the gain of saying that the child learns the use of the word "pain" on the analogy of my pain sensation. Someone might hold the view that the child learns to associate the feeling it gets when there is pain with the word "pain" and it learns to use the word when the feeling reappears. Wittgenstein asks "*What* sort of ignorance does it remove? —Being sure that someone is in pain, doubting whether he is, and so on, are so many natural, instinctive, kinds of behaviour towards other human beings, and our language is merely an auxiliary to, and further extension of, this relation."[63] Quite clearly, there is nothing that we gain by saying that the child learns to associate the word "pain" with the feeling of pain since, only way we could know that the child does this is *through* its pain behaviour and in order to grant that the child is in pain we have to form our attitude towards it. Thus, this account does not help us to modify our attitude towards the child since, the account that the child has pain is itself based on our attitude towards the child.

We may want to use the behavioural aspects for predicting the future behaviour of the person. Speaking of a frightened man, Wittgenstein says "we may also be interested in his behaviour as an indication of how he will behave in the future."[64] If appropriate context reproduced and if the behaviour is repeated, we need a word to account for this behaviour. We may say then that the man is in fear looking at the circumstance and his behaviour. Without knowing the context, it is difficult to know whether the child's cry is due to fear or due to pain. For instance, the child may cry if the mother leaves it alone due to sadness, or it may cry because of some fall and got hurt. Without knowing the context, it is not possible to say why the child has cried and the context helps us to form our attitude.[65]

Understanding and Its Expression

Wittgenstein speaks of understanding and manifestation of understanding. Giving the example of the series, 1, 5, 11, 19, 29 one may understand the series in terms of formula $a_n = n^2 + n - 1$, or he may work out the series of the difference, he finds the series 4, 6, 8, 10 and says that he can go on, or he watches and says "Yes, I know that series" and continues. All the manifestations of understanding can be taken equally seriously.[66]

Kripke's skeptic would find the above example quite appropriate. He would now say, which rule did we follow when we produced the series 1, 5, 11, 19, 29...? Did we follow $a_n = n^2 + n - 1$, or the series of the difference 4, 6, 8, 10... is worked out and then the next number is generated? Only by looking at the behaviour of the pupil, one would not be in a position to conclude whether he has followed either of the above rule or yet, another one. There is no fact that would justify either answer. And if we make the hypotheses, the behaviour of the person would fit equally both the hypotheses. No record of past behaviour could be of any help here either.

Wittgenstein poses a skeptical question as to whether I know to whom I am writing the letter if there are two friends of the same name. The content of the letter might fit perfectly either. Can one be in doubt to whom the letter is being written. He asks could not there be an illusion of the following kind: "I believe I am writing to one of them when in fact I am writing to the other?" In clarifying the issue, Wittgenstein rejects the possibility that I go by the situation when I say that I did or did not mean a particular person.[67]

Given the above difficulty, Wittgenstein speaks of grasping the rule as against the following the rule. It is not enough to say that one is capable of following the rule to claim that one has understood the rule, but if one has understood the rule, it is adequate to claim that he could follow the rule.

Understanding is not something that we can say if the student is able to use the rule up to 100 cases. This is not understanding, but application of one's understanding. "The understanding itself is a state which is the *source* of correct use."[68] We take the correct application as the criterion of understanding.[69] We may test the ability of a pupil whether he understands the word 'to determine' by giving the example $y = x^2$.[70]

Understanding is not a mental process, but mental process is characteristic of understanding.[71] Wittgenstein suggests that when we fail to understand the use of a word, we take it to be an expression of some mental process.[72] He remarks "It becomes queer when we are led to think that the future development must in some way already be present in the act of grasping the use and yet, is not present."[73] This is a problem because "we say that there is not any doubt that we understand the word, and on the other hand its meaning lies in its use. There is no doubt that I now want to play chess, but chess is the game it is in virtue of all its rules (and so on)."[74] He remarks further "To understand a sentence means to understand a language. To understand a language means to be master of a technique."[75]

And So On *Ad Infinitum*

We notice this expression 'and so on' quite often in the writings of Wittgenstein especially in the context of rules and their following. Wittgenstein clearly states that there are two senses of this expression, one 'and so on' as abbreviation where we want to cut short of some more instances which we do not want to spell out. The second sense he explains in terms of 'so on *ad infinitum*' which means that up to infinity. Especially, while speaking of the rules, one has to speak of their applications and the applications of a rule are infinite. While giving a rule one has to give the instances and indicate that one should follow the rule in this manner. Here, it is not an abbreviation but the expression of a rule which has infinite application.

A rule has to be stated in terms of its application. There are two things which apparently seem to be the same. The distinction between rule formulation and the application of the rule has to be maintained. But this is not so evidently separate. If we notice the behaviour at the empirical level, one cannot so easily claim whether the rule is being explained or being applied without knowing the context. The ambiguity in the behaviour of a teacher can lead to some misunderstanding of the functioning of language. If it is a context of a teacher teaching a pupil how to calculate, then we assume from the context that the teacher knows the rule and teaching the pupil. He can explain the rule by giving the paradigms and the paradigms are not the application of the rule. It is the explanation of the rule. But when the teacher is taking the test of the student and asking him to solve the problem of calculation, it would not be a paradigm case, it would be rather application of the rule. There is no way a teacher can teach the rule to a pupil without taking some instances, paradigms. However, paradigms should not be taken to be application of the rule. It is the process of rule-formulation.

But we need to add in the process of teaching the phrase 'and so on' to teach the student. If we do not add this phrase, the teaching of the rule would remain incomplete. It would remain incomplete because, till that time the pupil would not have made an attempt to decide about the next step in the process of calculating for example. Any response based on the cause or habit is not the one that would be rightly recognized as rule-following. The pupil might answer a certain question based on his memory or association in the past, but that cannot be considered as understanding the rule at all. Understanding begins where the teacher is in the position to speak of the pupil that he is able to follow the rule. Success in expression of a rule is what indicates the understanding of the rule by the pupil.

There could be various forms of expression of the understanding of the rule. Wittgenstein cites an interesting example of 1, 5, 11, 19, 29 and the pupil has learnt to go on. There could be various expression of this understanding. One could be to come up with an algebraic formulae which says $n^2 + n - 1$, or the series worked out on the difference, or simply the intuitive knowledge of the series etc. All these techniques of how to work out the next number that the pupil learns is the expression of understanding.

Is it not the case that 'and so on' adds the normative component to a rule? Consider what description according to Wittgenstein is. He after a long discussion on how to describe a teacher teaching a pupil comes to the following conclusion. If our account does not add any judgement: "and the pupil learnt the rule" the description seems to be incomplete, and if we add this judgement to our description, then we are saying something more than what actually happened. Wittgenstein recognizes this to be our weakness and says that we are not able to stop at the level of description alone, even though that is enough. Thus, Wittgenstein seems to think that description alone would do, yet, he indicates the inevitable tendency in man to add the normative component to the description.

It seems to us that this is not an accident at all. The expression used in 'and so on' at the end of teaching a rule is not an accidental part at all. Not only that it is not teaching of the rule either. This is not an abbreviation, if it were it would have been part of our description or explanation. And so on *ad infinitum* is the one which gives the normative component to the rule, which Wittgenstein seems to fail to notice. And that is the reason he seems to think that a rule, if paradigms are given, the rules are given. If that were the case an abbreviation of the rule would have been enough to teach a rule and there would have no role for "and so on *ad infinitum*". The fact that when we teach the rule, we do not use the abbreviated form of 'and so on' is the indication that the rule has to be universal, and by making the rule universal we establish the rule. And once we establish the rule, we have given the status of a norm. This part Wittgenstein seems to overlook or decided against it.

Induction

Teaching, which is not meant to apply to anything but the examples given, is different from that which "points beyond" them.[76] Wittgenstein considers that it is quite natural to wonder how our understanding reaches beyond all the examples. Is it the case that I interpret something that is not there in the examples that makes me go beyond the examples.[77] When we explain giving some instances and saying "and so on", we mean different things in different contexts. There is much that is assumed of the hearer that he knows how to generalize from the given examples, that he has done such things earlier when we use this expression.[78]

The expression "and so on *ad infinitum*" is also governed by the linguistic rules. For instance the four dots in "1+1+1+1...." are signs for which there are some rules. And any sign cannot say anything more than what the rules of the sign permit it to say. Wittgenstein thus, remarks "That is, the expression "and so on" does not harbour a secret power by which the series is continued without being continued." Of course, "and so on" contains the meaning of infinite continuation.[79] That is to say, we have the capacity to distinguish the limited series "1+1+1, 1+1+1" from the series "1+1+1, 1+1+1 and so on".[80] The paradoxical situation is that the expression "and so on" has to occur even in the rules for the sign "and so on". For instance, 1, 1+1 and so on = 1, 1+1, 1+1+1 and so on, and so on.[81]

Causality depends on an observed uniformity claims Wittgenstein. Of course, he immediately cautions us by saying that it does not follow that uniformity so far observed will always continue. What cannot be denied is that events so far have been uniform.[82] Speaking of the law of inertia, Wittgenstein says that it is an *a priori* proposition in the following case. The law of inertia speaks about what a body does when it is not interfered with. But the criterion for its not being interfered with is not very clear. Is it ultimately that it moves uniformly in a straight line? Or is it different? he asks. If it is different, then it is not a matter of experience whether the law of inertia holds; and if it is the case that it moves uniformly in a straight line, it is not a law, but a definition. Thus, we may note that a definition cannot express a law.[83]

Wittgenstein considers this to be reasonable to expect that a rule we have observed up to now will continue to hold.[84] This is something like the law of inertia. Unless there is some reason to modify our hypothesis, we can continue to believe that the hypothesis would work. Wittgenstein writes: "Induction is a process based on a principle of economy."[85] He also remarks: "I am certain that I am able to continue the series, as I am that this book will drop on the ground when I let it go"[86] are learnt on the basis of induction.

Citing the example of the squirrel, Wittgenstein says that it stores food for the winter, but does not infer by induction that it is going to need it for the winter. Similarly, we do not need the law of induction to justify our actions or our predictions.[87] It is quite obvious to Wittgenstein that it is impossible to find in our ordinary day experience something of this kind happening that a book remained hanging in the air instead of falling and similarly he feels that it is from induction that I am as certain that I shall be able to continue the series. Wittgenstein opines that success is the measure of certainty.[88] He asks what is the certainty attached to the fact that the fire will burn me? He is sure that the kind of justification for the belief that the fire will burn me is reflected in our action and he feels that invariably every one believes that fire burns and act accordingly. This would be on the basis of previous experience and the faith in the system of hypothesis concerning natural laws.[89]

The law of induction is not grounded on matter perceived in experience says Wittgenstein. He adds further that it would be nonsense to say that I know that the law of induction is true. However, what may be said appropriately is that I believe that the law of induction is true. The major reason for this is that no one can know all the instances of induction and hence, no one can speak of the knowledge of induction.[90] There is a hint that Wittgenstein gives whether we should say only a certain regularity in occurrences makes induction possible.[91] He goes to the extent of saying that even if we find irregularity in natural events suddenly, we still would continue to make inferences just as before. Whether we would continue to call it "induction" or no is another matter he says.[92]

Hypothesis

Just because one is able to go on does not mean that one has understood the sequence is the right manner. Wittgenstein gives an example where A writes some numbers and B has to discover the rule. A writes 1, 5, 11, 19, 29... at this point B says he has understood how to go on. B gives the formula that it is n^2+n-1 and the next number confirms his hypothesis.[93] Of course, there is the alternate hypothesis that is possible. You add 4 to the first number, 6 to the next number to generate the third number, and 8 to the third number to generate the next number, 10 to the fourth number to generate the fifth number and so on. Following the second hypothesis, one can generate the next numbers as 41, 55, 71, 89 and so on. If there are two hypotheses equally fitting the same empirical data, a possibility which is entertained by Kripke, Goodman and Quine, which one has to be chosen remains an important issue. Moreover, which formulation of the hypothesis is the correct one? Are both of these equally acceptable?

A hypothesis goes beyond immediate experience of ours whereas a proposition does not and a hypothesis works or fails to work whereas a proposition is either true or false. A hypothesis is a law for inferring propositions which are instances of this law. If these propositions which are inferred are true, then we say that the hypothesis works and if they are not then the hypothesis does not work. In other words, we may say that a hypothesis constructs expectations which are expressed in the form of propositions which can be verified or falsified. The same words may express a proposition to me and a hypothesis to you says Wittgenstein.[94]

A hypothesis cannot be verified or falsified because it is a law or a rule for constructing the propositions. Thus, only the observation categorical which is derived from hypothesis is verifiable.[95] A proposition can take a truth value and this is true of hypotheses. "There seems to be a man here" is a proposition, "There is a man here" is a hypothesis. Wittgenstein writes, "When we distinguish propositions from hypotheses and mathematical propositions we mean that some grammatical rules apply to the one and not to the other."[96]

Hypothesis is not capable of definite verification in experience. Most of the propositions about physical objects which we make in ordinary life are hypotheses. For instance all men are mortal is a hypothesis. All men are mortal is true even if there is no single man. But we never say this kind of thing that all men are mortal even if there is no single man. By "If... then" we mean something quite different from implication in the sense in witch Russell defines implication says Wittgenstein.[97]

We do make use of hypothesis in order to describe the use of words satisfactorily. But sometimes it may happen that observation does not enable us to see any clear rule. If someone is willing to modify his definition and withdraw the definition, then he is not offering the rule for the use of the word.[98] If there is a judgement about sense data, no further verification is needed. For instance "This is red". A hypothesis is an expression of the form "This man is ill", "The sun will rise tomorrow" or "This is a chair". The hypotheses are confirmed or rejected by empirical science.[99]

We have a pragmatical angle to what we accept. Wittgenstein says that the hypothesis that there are electrons is taken as being true because in practice you can work as if it were the case. So, also Einstein's Theory of Relativity is accepted because it works in practice. Thus, Euclidean space is used for everyday purposes, and relativity for immeasurable and astronomical distances, though the Reinmeanian space is also equally possible. To decide between them would need a great deal of empirical evidence, and this is certainly the sense of truth we apply to them.[100] The earth is round is only a hypothesis. "There is no fact that the earth is round over and above the various facts such as shape of the shadow on the moon at an eclipse, ships disappearing over the horizon etc.; just as there is no fact that this is a physical object over the above the qualities and judgements of sense-data about it."[101] Wittgenstein gives a good example of thunder and lightning. He says that "Thunder comes after lightning" is a proposition based on our sense-data, whereas "Lightning causes thunder" is an hypothesis and needs verification which may be true or false.[102]

A proposition can be *apriori* or empirical and an expression can be a hypothesis or a proposition. Take 2 + 2 = 4, as an example. It has sense to say of visual space that two objects + two other objects make four objects. In physical space, 2 + 2 = 4 is an hypothesis and needs verification. "If you see two objects in one room and then two objects in another room, it is a hypothesis to say that they make four, because when you come to put them together they may make five objects."[103]

In a sense there can be a certain relationship of appearance and reality when we draw the distinction between visual and physical space. Visual gives us the necessary propositions where as the physical may not as is the case with two drops of rain water + two drops of rain water. Wittgenstein also gives the example of a perfectly round circle is not physically round object always. But this is not a hypothesis which can be verified, he cautious.[104]

Wittgenstein notices that there is a tendency in us to make the relation between physical objects and our sense-data a contingent one. However, he opines that the world is not composed of sense-data and physical objects. The relationship between the sense-data and the physical object is one in language, and this relationship is necessary one. He gives a *reductio ad absurdum* argument: if such a causal relation existed between the physical object and sense-data, it would have been sensible to ask the question whether someone has seen physical object causing sense-data. We can talk of the same object either as an hypothesis or in terms of sense-data.[105] Further, Wittgenstein says that we are inclined to say that the greater the number of instances conforms to the hypothesis, the more the "probable" the hypothesis is. What is meant by this is that it is more difficult to abandon the hypothesis and frame another if the hypothesis is conformed by a number of instances.[106]

If all the evidences are in favour of a hypothesis and nothing goes against it, then we can take the hypothesis to be true. But if we ask further the question whether the hypothesis agrees with reality, then one is going round in a circle opines Wittgenstein.[107] If everything that we regard as evidence goes in favour of hypothesis and nothing contrary is noticed, then we may count it as objectively certain. We find it difficult to imagine it to be false.[108]

Wittgenstein claims that a hypothesis is a law for forming propositions and it can be considered as the law for forming expectation as well. And he considers a proposition to be a particular cross-section of an hypothesis.[109]

Speaking of the relation between a hypothesis and the fact that is connected by a proposition, Wittgenstein claims that there is nothing hypothetical about it. In a metaphorical way of saying this is "The hypothesis, if that face of it is laid against reality, becomes a proposition." The experience cannot be doubted. It is possible to doubt whether the body I see is a sphere or not. But what cannot be doubted is whether it looks spherical from here or not. If that were doubtful, then Wittgenstein says that we would not have any mechanism of forming a hypothesis at all. Thus, at least appearance cannot be doubted.[110]

Perspectives

In the context of ostensive definition, Wittgenstein introduces several possible interpretation of the sentence 'this is tove'. "The ostensive definition can be interpreted to mean:

'This is a pencil',
'This is round',
'This is wood',
'This is one',
'This is hard, etc."[111]

Wittgenstein uses the duck-rabbit picture example,[112] to show how we perspectivise what we perceive. This he calls as seeing an aspect of what is presented to our senses. The picture presented can be seen as a duck's head or as a head of a rabbit. The picture could also be seen as a 'picture-rabbit' and so is true of 'picture-duck'. "But the *impression* is not simultaneously of a picture-duck and a picture-rabbit," says Wittgenstein.[113] He further notes that "You only "see the duck and rabbit aspects" if you are already conversant with the shapes of those two animals."[114]

There would not be a better example for the possibility of two extreme perspectives which any one could give. Wittgenstein has chosen the example of black and white which are normally considered to be opposed to each other. And he finds that some philosophers do not admit any change even if it is evident that the change has taken place, and some others would consider minutest change to be sufficient change to recognize the changed situation as different from the earlier one. He remarks: "When white turns black some people say "Essentially, it is still the same"; and others, when the colour turns a shade darker: 'It is *completely* different'."[115]

Wittgenstein makes us aware of the fact that our perspective makes difference to the knowledge that we gather. He writes "It makes a difference whether I think of something as a deception of my senses or an external event, whether I take this object as a measure of that or the other way round, whether I resolve to make two criteria decide or only one."[116]

Doubting certain proposition might warrant modifying our belief only in a limited manner, whereas doubting certain other propositions might warrant rejection of the whole web of beliefs. If one doubts Napoleon did not exist that makes us reject only a part of our belief system, but if we doubt whether earth existed before 150 years, then we need to doubt our whole system of evidence.[117]

Wittgenstein believes in the systemic approach to knowledge. He writes: "When we first begin to *believe* anything, what we believe is not a single proposition, it is a whole system of propositions."[118] He further remarks by speaking about axioms like this: "It is not single axioms that strike me as obvious, it is a system in which consequences and premises give one another *mutual* support."[119]

Giving the example of a child how it swallows even unreliable information along with the reliable ones, Wittgenstein remarks: "It doesn't learn *at all* that that mountain has existed for a long time: that is, the question whether it is so doesn't arise at all. It swallows this consequence down, so to speak, together with *what* it learns."[120] The following passage is quite comparable to the one which Quine has written about how the progress in science is achieved. Here, the narration is of a child how it develops a perspective. Wittgenstein writes: "The child learns to believe a host of things, i.e., it learns to act according to these beliefs. Bit by bit there forms a system of what is believed, and in that system some things stand unshakeably fast and some are more or less liable to shift. What stands fast does so, not because it is intrinsically obvious or convincing; it is rather held fast by what lies around it."[121]

Assertion of a Statement

Circumstances justify me saying he knows how to go on is a situation where I can say that he understands.[122] This is to say that we have adequate grounds on which we could assert that he understands the rule. This is what is known as assertive condition as opposed to truth conditions. We do not have grounds on which we can claim that this is true, yet, we have the grounds to say that he can go on.

Wittgenstein speaks of an interesting example where after teaching the natural numbers, one teaches him the cardinal numbers and let us assume that we have taught him and given the exercises up to 1000. Now, we give the series of + 2 beyond 1000 and he writes 1000, 1004, 1008, 1012. After some attempts to explain, we conclude that perhaps "It comes natural to this person to understand our order with our explanations as we should understand the order: "Add 2 up to 1000, 4 up to 2000, 6 up to 3000 and so on.""[123]

Wittgenstein remarks "*That* will be how meaning it can determine the steps in advance" after giving a sign unknown to us: "If by *'x–2'* you mean x^2, then you get *this* value for y, if you mean *2x*, *that* one,'""[124] What is interesting to note here is that we understand the unknown language in terms of what we are familiar with. And this can happen because translation can only translate within the framework of meaning or sense which our language can permit. This is the reason why when a poem from one language is translated into another language, the translator finds it difficult to choose the words because of the subtleties involved in the finer distinctions that are made in one language is not available in another language. Before the translation is attempted into our own language, we need to make the required distinction in our own language and then translate. For instance, if we were to translate certain sentences which refer to a subtle meaning of snow, we need to make that distinction in our own language first and then translate that sentence into ours. Quine seems to have overlooked this requirement.

Every sign is capable of interpretation, but the meaning must not be capable of interpretation, and therefore, it is the last interpretation. Let us consider translating a sign from one language into another equivalent sign. And yet, this would not give us the meaning. If it is a telegram for instance, then by translating one sign language to another, one does not give the meaning.[125]

Suppose we followed a rule and calculated upto a certain point and suppose someone else taught us to calculate using different technique. We will not admit that the calculation would work this way too, rather we would hold the view that the new technique is identical to the old one because we have to give the same sense to the rule, and recognize the rule to be the same though we have adopted two different techniques. By giving the example of green Wittgenstein wants to emphasize the fact that the difference in technique would not necessarily indicate difference in rule or sense.[126]

A rule limits the possibility of interpretations. It allows certain possibilities and does not allow others. Wittgenstein writes: "The rules of a symbolism give it a certain degree of freedom which is expressed in the rules of its grammar, which tells us which combinations are allowed and which are not allowed. Explanation increases the multiplicity of the system by distinguishing between possible interpretations. Understanding a symbolism is correlated to an explanation, and explanation removes misunderstanding. When the right multiplicity has been given, no further explanation is wanted or possible."[127]

Wittgenstein considers that the unpredictable occurrence of the prime number is obvious enough example of mathematics having synthetic character. However, that they are synthetic in this sense does not make them any less *a priori*, he claims. Thus, he writes: "The distribution of primes would be an ideal example of what could be called synthetic *a priori*, for one can say that it is at any rate not discoverable by an analysis of the concept of a prime numbers."[128]

Philosophy is not Normative

If someone wonders how he manages always to use a word correctly, one should point out to him that the fact that he is able to mean something, the thing that referred to by the word, prevents him from talking nonsense. Meaning something by the words would be nothing, but applying the words in accordance with the rules in a context, and the context does not permit certain combination of words in describing it.[129] Wittgenstein cautious us by saying that, "I may however believe I can apply them, when it turns out that I was wrong."[130] This is the reason why Wittgenstein believes that a rule which is not followable is not a rule at all. A metaphysical rule for instance at times is not followable, and for that reason it cannot be considered to be a rule.

For instance, time is unreal is something which we cannot use in our life at all and therefore this is non-sensical says Wittgenstein. And similarly, with reference to one's own sensation, one cannot use the word 'I know'. To follow a rule means, there ought to be provision to obey and not to obey the rule.

What is a complete description and what is not cannot be decided in abstraction. Wittgenstein opines "Whether this or that belongs to a complete description will depend on the purpose of the description, on what the recipient does with the description."[131] We have overwhelming temptation to say something further after everything has already been described.[132] When we have to choose between description and interpretation, Wittgenstein sides the pure description part. He feels that often we are tempted to interpret, to say something more, but one ought not. We wrongly expect an explanation after the description. Solution of the difficulty lies in description. One should not try to get beyond the description. Our difficulty is that we cannot stop even when complete description is given, claims Wittgenstein.[133]

We grasp the whole use of a word is not an astonishing thing. We often describe what happens in these words says Wittgenstein. It becomes surprising if one says that "the future development must in some way already be present in the act of grasping the use and yet, is not present." Wittgenstein adds further: there is no doubt that we understand the word, and also that the meaning of the word lies in its use.[134] Speaking of explanations, what does one to do with the word 'five' for instance, I assume that the person acts as I have described. There is no question of what is the meaning of the word "five", we do not give explanation in terms of meaning, but in terms of its use. "Explanations come to an end somewhere."[135]

Grammar gives the possibility of the combination of words. But one could say that grammar describes the reality. But would this also mean that if reality were different, the grammar would have described it differently? Wittgenstein remarks "As reality is so and so, the rules must be such and such". But this presupposes that I could say "If reality were otherwise, then the rules of grammar would be otherwise".[136] What is important to note here is that if the grammar had to describe the world which were otherwise could not have been described by grammar because those are the forbidden possibilities. If grammar tries to say those things which the grammar itself has forbidden, then it would produce only nonsense. Limit to language is limit to sense.

Is it not the case that 'and so on' adds the normative component to a rule? Consider what description according to Wittgenstein is. He after a long discussion on how to describe a teacher teaching a pupil comes to the following conclusion. If our account does not add any judgement: "and the pupil learnt the rule" the description seems to be incomplete, and if we add this judgement to our description, then we are saying something more than what actually happened. Wittgenstein recognizes this to be our weakness and says that we are not able to stop at the level of description alone, even though that is enough. Thus, Wittgenstein seems to think that description alone would do, yet, he indicates the inevitable tendency in man to add the normative component to the description.

Philosophy does not perform the normative function, it leaves everything as it is. It does not interfere with the actual use of language. Its function is to describe the rules of the language so that clarity prevails.[137] This is because philosophy cannot give foundation for science either.

Normative Aspect of Language

It is important to note that an empirical proposition can be turned into a norm of description. Thus, all empirical propositions do not have the same status. When someone uses it as a norm, it becomes part of the world-picture, i.e., the empirical proposition merges with his theory. Thus, a world-picture is something like the possible world to which one assents.[138]

Wittgenstein describes a paradoxical situation. We describe the process of a teacher teaching the pupil and how the pupil reacts. But can the description be complete without using the expression such as "Now, he can count". If this has to be the part of the description, then I have added my own judgement: "the pupil can count now". If I do not include such a judgement as a part of the description, is the description complete? And if I do include it, am I not going beyond pure description?[139]

Wittgenstein says that F.P. Ramsey once emphasized that logic was a "normative science". Now, he understands what Ramsey must have meant at that time and thinks that language with its rules behaves like a calculus. What we are talking about is not an ideal language, but the ordinary language with all the attributes of an ideal language. Therefore, Wittgenstein refuses to use the word "better" or "ideal" for this purpose.[140] Wittgenstein says that this point is not easy to grasp since, it would require better grasp of the concepts of understanding, meaning and thinking. It is only after having understood these concepts, does one realize that what a sentence means can be understood in terms of "operating through a calculus according to definite rules".[141]

Speaking of rules Wittgenstein says "Following a rule is analogous to obeying an order. We are trained to do so; we react to an order in a particular way."[142] It is important, therefore to note the normative element that is there in a rule. An order expects us to behave in a certain way and similarly, a rule guides our behaviour claims Wittgenstein. This act of guiding is said to be due to the norm attached to the rule. A rule, since, it is based on agreement and regularity in its use becomes a norm for us and by virtue of that it guides our behaviour.

We may note here that any rule is taken to be the part of the custom, and custom is an institution for Wittgenstein.[143] Any institution for that matter would be governed by rules. Since, the very existence of the institution serves some purpose for the society, the rules also acquire norms as means. Thus, language by virtue of being a social institution has its values and rules as constitutive of language would also have the norm for the use of language. Thus, the rules are essentially normative since, they guide the behaviour of individuals.

It is quite surprising that Wittgenstein would like to take his activity as describing as against any other value related activity. No doubt that prescribing has its own danger, but normative component of a perspective cannot be separated from a perspective and still consider it to be a perspective. If anything that ties different components of a perspective, it would be the normative element that is attached to it in the form of agreement, practice and the form of life within which it has its place. Therefore, we are surprised to note that despite being aware of the normative nature of the rules, Wittgenstein recognizes philosophers function as only descriptive.

Notice for instance a rule being only descriptive. As long as rules are being explained, they would remain descriptive. But we add the phrase 'and so on' to make these descriptive rules universal. Once, the rule is made universal, then there are only two options for us: either accept the rule along with its guiding element or reject the rule. All rules, though do not determine our actions, but guide our actions. Wittgenstein himself noted that if there is no guiding aspect to rule, every action can be considered to be in accordance with any rule. This is an absurd position since, the distinction between accord and going against it would loose the meaning totally. Therefore, even for Wittgenstein it becomes necessary to add normative elements to his rules so that he remains consistent.

NOTES AND REFERENCES

1. Wittgenstein, L., 1969, *On Certainty* (hence, forth *OC)* (ed.), G.E.M. Anscombe, Basil Blackwell, Oxford, §1.
2. *OC*, §15.
3. By a state of mind one may mean dispositions. Wittgenstein adds qualifications: "But there are objections to speaking of a state of the mind here, inasmuch as there ought to be two different criteria for such a state: a knowledge of the construction of the apparatus, quite apart from what it does." Wittgenstein, L., 1963. *Philosophical Investigation*, (henceforth *PI*) (ed.), G.E.M. Anscombe, Basil Blackwell, Oxford, *PI*, §149. He remarks "The grammar of the word 'knows' is evidently closely related to that of 'can', 'is able to'. But also closely related to that of 'understands'." Distinguishing the disposition use of the word 'to know' Wittgenstein speaks of the other use of the word 'to know': "we say 'Now I know!'- and similarly 'Now, I can do it!' and 'Now, I understand!'" etc., *PI*, §150.
4. *Ibid.*, §90.
5. *Ibid.*, §95.
6. *Ibid.*, §90.
7. *Ibid.*, §15.
8. *Ibid.*, §16.
9. *Ibid.*, §54.
10. *Ibid.*, §4.
11. *Ibid.*, §23.
12. *Ibid.*, §10.
13. *Ibid.*, §19.
14. *Ibid.*, §93.
15. *Ibid.*, § 245. Anthony Kenny 1994, in his book *The Wittgenstein Reader* (hence forth *WR*), Basil Blackwell, Oxford, has compiled Wittgenstein's works thematically and has provided a handy reference book on Wittgenstein. Also see *WR* p. 257.
16. *OC*, § 253. Also see *WR*, p. 257.
17. *Ibid.*, § 282. Also see *WR*, p. 259.
18. *Ibid.*, §163. Also see *WR*, p. 252.
19. *Ibid.*, §284. Also see *WR*, p. 259.
20. *PI*, §197 "For we say that there is not any doubt that we understand the world, and on the other hand its meaning lies in its use." Also see *PI*, §561.

21. *Ibid.*, §208. Also see *PI*, §§ 218, 224-227, 693. Also see *WR*, pp. 93-95.
22. *Ibid.*, §145, Also see *WR*, p. 88. Kripke's skeptic would ask the question here as to how does one know whether one has followed the same rule at all?
23. *Ibid.*, §208.
24. *Ibid.*, §208.
25. *Ibid.*, §139.
26. *Ibid.*, §140.
27. *Ibid.*, §198.
28. Wittgenstein, L., *Zettle* (henceforth *Z*) (ed.), G.E.M. Anscombe, Basil Blackwell, Oxford, 1967. *Z*, p. 58/320, Also see *WR*, p. 227, *PI*, §372. Also see Wittgenstein, L., *Philosophical Grammar* (henceforth *PG*), (ed.), R. Rhees, Basil Blackwell, Oxford, 1956. *PG*, p. 184/133. *PG*, p. 192/140.
29. Because every application of a rule requires a decision and every time we calculate the next number, we need to decide how to apply the rule. *PI*, §186. Also see *WR*, p. 94.
30. See, Malcom, N., 1989, "Wittgenstein on Language and Rules", *Philosophy*, Vol. 64, pp. 5-28. And Baker, G.P. and Hacker, "Malcom on Language and Rules", *Philosophy*, pp. 167-179, see especially pp. 170 ff.
31. Wittgenstein, L., 1956. *Remarks on the Foundations of Mathematics* (hence forth *RFM*), (ed.), G. H., von Wright, R. Rhees and G.E.M. Anscombe, Blackwell, Oxford, *RFM*, IV, p. 237/29. Also see *WR*, p. 237.
32. *PI*, §147. Also see *WR*, pp. 88-89.
33. *Z*. pp. 53/294. Also see *WR*, p.104.
34. While learning the rule, one does not apply the rule. That is the reason why Wittgenstein remarks after giving the series, one says you should "go on like this". "For at *this* level the expression of the rule is explained by the value, not the value by the rule. Z., pp. 55/301. Also see *WR*, p.105. There is no point at this level of saying "But do not you *see*...?" the rule is no use says Wittgenstein, because it is the rule that is explained, not what does the explaining. Z., pp. 55/302. Also see *WR*, p.105.
35. *PI*, §201.
36. *Ibid.*, §201.
37. *Ibid.*, §485.
38. *Ibid.*, §1.
39. *Ibid.*, §217. Also see *WR*, p. 102.
40. *OC*, §253. Also see *WR*, p. 257.
41. *WR*, p. 254.
42. *Ibid.*, §217. Also see *WR*, p. 102.
43. *PI*, §326. Also see *WR*, p. 113.
44. *WR*, p. 254.
45. *PI*, §219. Also see *WR*, p. 103.
46. One may want to contrast this against the contention of Malcom, that when we give the rule, we do not give all its applications. *Cf.* footnote 30.

47. *PI*, §293. Also see *WR*, p. 153.
48. *Ibid.*, §302. Also see *WR*, p. 154.
49. *Ibid.*, §311. PI, §302. Also see *WR*, p. 156.
50. *Ibid.*, §313. Also see *Ibid.*, p. 157.
51. *Ibid.*, §304. Also see *Ibid.*, p. 155.
52. *Ibid.*, §304. Also see *Ibid.*, p. 155.
53. *Ibid.*, §307. Also see *Ibid.*, p. 155.
54. *Ibid.*, §310. Also see *Ibid.*, p. 156.
55. *Ibid.*, §310. Also see *Ibid.*, p. 156.
56. *Z*, pp. 98/567.
57. *Z*, pp. 104/603 & 604.
58. *Z*, pp. 66/369.
59. *Z*, pp. 102/591.
60. *Ibid.*, pp. 97/557.
61. *Ibid.*, pp. 94/540.
62. *Ibid.*, pp. 91/526.
63. *Ibid.*, pp. 95/545.
64. *Ibid.*, pp. 90/523.
65. *Ibid.*, pp. 86/492.
66. *PI*, §151. Also see *WR*, pp. 89-90.
67. *Z*, pp. 1/7 & *Z*, pp. 6/27.
68. *PI*, §146. Also see *WR*, p. 88.
69. *Ibid.*, §146. Also see *Ibid.*, p. 88.
70. *Ibid.*, §189. Also see *Ibid.*, p. 96.
71. *Ibid.*, §154. Also see *Ibid.*, p. 91.
72. *Ibid.*, §196. Also see *Ibid.*, p. 97.
73. *Ibid.*, §196. Also see *Ibid.*, p. 97.
74. *Ibid.*, §197. Also see *Ibid.*, p. 97.
75. *Ibid.*, §199. Also see *Ibid.*, p.98.
76. *Ibid.*, §208.
77. *Ibid.*, §209.
78. Wittgenstein, L., 1979: *Wittgenstein's Lectures* (henceforth *LWL*), Cambridge 1932-35, from the notes of Alice Ambrose and Margaret MacDonald (ed.), Alice Ambrose, Blackwell, Oxford, *LWL*, p. 89.
79. Wittgenstein, L., 1974. *Philosophical Grammar* (hence forth *PG*), (ed.) R. Rhees, trans. A.J.P. Kenney, Basil Blackwell, Oxford, *PG* pp. 282-283.
80. *PG*, p. 283.
81. *Ibid.*, pp. 283-284.
82. *Ibid.*, p. 227.
83. *Ibid.*, p. 230.
84. *Ibid.*, p. 231.
85. *Ibid.*, p. 224.
86. *PI*, §§ 324 & 325.
87. *OC*, §287.

88. *PI*, §324.
89. *Ibid.*, §325.
90. *OC*, §499.
91. *Ibid.*, §618.
92. *Ibid.*, §19.
93. *PI*, §151. Also see Wittgenstein, L., 1958. *The Blue and Brown Book* (hence-forth *BB*), Row Publishers, New York, *BB*, §§ 62-64, pp. 112-113 for further details of the example.
94. *LWL*, p. 110.
95. *Ibid.*, p. 16.
96. *Ibid.*, pp. 49-50.
97. *Ibid.*, p. 50.
98. *PI*, §82.
99. *LWL*, p. 66.
100. *Ibid.*, p. 75.
101. *Ibid.*, pp. 80-81.
102. *Ibid.*, p. 79.
103. *Ibid.*, p. 77.
104. *Ibid.*, pp. 78-79.
105. *Ibid.*, p. 81.
106. *Ibid.*, p. 111
107. *OC*, §191.
108. *Ibid.*, §203.
109. *PG*, p. 219.
110. *Ibid.*, p. 222
111. *BB*, p. 2. Also see *WR*, p. 58.
112. *PI* (part II), pp. 194-197, 205-208.
113. *Ibid.*, p. 199.
114. *Ibid.*, p. 207.
115. *RFM*, IV, pp. 245/38. Also see *WR*, p. 241.
116. *Ibid.*, IV, pp. 243/34. Also see *WR*, p. 239.
117. *OC*, §§184-188.
118. *Ibid.*, §141. Also see *WR*, p. 250.
119. *Ibid.*, §142. Also see *Ibid.*, pp. 250-251.
120. *Ibid.*, §143. Also see *Ibid.*, p. 251.
121. *Ibid.*, §144. Also see *Ibid.*, p. 251.
122. *PI*, §154. Also see *Ibid.*, pp. 90-91.
123. *Ibid.*, §185. Also see *Ibid.*, pp. 93-94.
124. *Ibid.*, §190. Also see *Ibid.*, p. 96.
125. The *BB*, superscript 2 in the original.
126. *RFM*, IV, pp. 244/36. Also see *WR*, p. 240.
127. *LWL*, p. 41.
128. *RFM*, IV, pp. 246/43. Also see *WR*, p.241.
129. *Z*, pp. 54/297. Also see *WR*, p. 104.

130. *Ibid.*, pp. 54/297. Also see *WR,* p.104.
131. *Ibid.*, pp. 55/311. Also see *Ibid.*, p. 107.
132. *Ibid.*, pp. 55/313. Also see *Ibid.*, p. 107.
133. *Ibid.*, pp. 55/314. Also see *Ibid.*, p. 107.
134. *PI*, §197.
135. *Ibid.*, §1.
136. *LWL*, p. 47.
137. *PI*, §124.
138. *OC*, §167.
139. *Z*, pp. 56/310. Also see *WR,* p. 107. Please note that unless the judgement is added, the normative component is missing in the description. And similarly, 'and so on' gives this normative component to any description. That is the reason why description of any rule is incomplete without the normative component attached to it, for instance we need to add so on *ad infinitum*.
140. *PI*, §81.
141. *Ibid.*, §81.
142. *Ibid.*, §206. Also see *WR,* p. 99.
143. *Ibid.*, §199. Also see *Ibid.*, pp. 98-99.

6

The Straight-Solution to Skepticism

Introduction

We have examined that there are different attempts by different philosophers to answer the skeptic. Kripke has succumbed to the argument of his skeptic and agreed with the skeptic that his question cannot be answered, but made a compromise with him that life should go on and for that grant man the status of man by adopting a humane attitude. Goodman was tired of the uncertainty that followed from his '*grue*' problem and tried to avoid the skeptic by saying that he is not agreeable to anything that is short of time tested concepts. He found entrenchment a convenient way of keeping his skeptic at bay. Quine having found no satisfactory answers to his own skeptical arguments in the form of three indeterminacies and eventually compromised with whatever best was available and adopted the scientific outlook. Wittgenstein, of course, as a wise man granted everything to the skeptic to only to show him that he lacks sense. Using skeptic as a tool for rejecting nonsense, Wittgenstein answers skeptic very satisfactorily. However, the answer he provides was only partially better than the attempts made by the other three since, he also settles for less ideal: a descriptive account of meaning and rule-following. We take a bold step, of course standing on the shoulders of Wittgenstein and try to answer the skeptic directly.

Wittgenstein, like Quine, would adopt the behaviouristic criteria in understanding the sentence uttered by others; he would refer to the rules of philosophical grammar in order to interpret a sentence. By adopting this method, Wittgenstein is able to achieve objectivity through inter-subjectivity. There would be no scope for interpretation other than the one which is evident in the application of words. This is because, rules guide the interpretation. In the case of Quine, because of the ontological relativity or what he calls the indeterminacy of the reference, he is not able to fix the ontology of a sentence fully. For Wittgenstein, it is not extension that determines meaning, but for Quine, unless one knows all possible applications of the use of terms one cannot understand the in use in complete sense. Wittgenstein would not face such problems.

On induction, both Quine and Wittgenstein literally hold the same view. The difference lies in the use of vocabulary. Hypothesis, expectation, projection and verification all are linked to the perspective we adopt for both. However, Wittgenstein does not speak of scientific theory the way Quine does. Wittgenstein's language as the form of life would include even science as part of it. There is nothing which is superior and nothing which is inferior for Wittgenstein, whereas for Quine anything that has already become part of the theory is more respectable in the form of a backlog theory. This may be true of Wittgenstein as well, but he does not mention scientific theories explicitly. He is also of the opinion that certain habit formation does not permit change in perspective so easily. For instance, he says we are accustomed to see a table in a particular way and we do not comprehend all that well if the table is upside down. Both Wittgenstein and Quine do not want to make the distinction between philosophy and science.

Again both scholars agree that the similarity between two things is constituted by language in general. Quine attributes this similarity to the innate ability in the mankind including animals, and subsequently, he introduces the notion of theoretical kind and these theoretical kinds help us to see the similarity among the members of a group. Wittgenstein's scheme would allow us to go beyond the immediately perceived as he has made room for the distinction between appearance and reality[1] within the domain of language. It is possible to work out, for instance, the rise in temperature on the basis of the change in the level of mercury of the barometer. Similarly, one would know toothache by knowing the symptom of toothache. For Quine, the differences in the stimuli is not counted at the level of perceiving the similarity, whereas for Wittgenstein these differences filter out and one cannot speak of difference in these sense impulses since, language cannot capture them.[2]

Meaning and Rules

Kripke's clearly indicates that one of the reasons why the skeptic finds the rule-following account unsatisfactory is that he is not happy with the dispositional theory of meaning. We cannot think of meaning as something dispositional either in the form of habit or in the form of mental content. A normative element to the meaning would have guided the person to the next step, but that guiding factor is missing in any rule-following as there are no facts, physical or mental that helps us to take decisions that what we follow now is the same old rule. While rejecting the dispositional theory, Kripke's skeptic finds the lack of normativity. The rules used by the skeptic, therefore, at best descriptive and lack the capacity to guide the behaviour of a person.

To identify the rule that the Kripke's skeptic has followed in the past, one may make use of the provision of projecting in the past. Using the technique of projecting a hypothesis, an observer can conclude that the skeptic has behaved exactly in a similar fashion which he did in the past.[3] Thus, the rules of language would give us some basis of identifying the present following of the rule with that of past actions by the agent. However, this remains inconclusive for Kripke's skeptic. Since,, the hypothesis needs to be confirmed, all that one could do is to confirm the hypothesis by providing paradigms or instances. The past projection does not have any evidence other than the present one. And therefore, Kripke's skeptic would find our assertion of the past behaviour as a present *interpretation* of the past behaviour. He would insist that we have no fact or reason to believe that our present interpretation of past behaviour is true to the fact of our past behaviour.

Even the theory of nominalism would also fail on this account. This is so because, Goodman too, bases much part of his theory of meaning in the context of community. His theory of projection is based on the history of the projection or entrenchment of a term or word in the society. He would base his projection on the basis of the purpose served by use of words in society. As we have noted, a term is projectable if and only if it has the descriptive meaning, i.e., it has a cognitive component. Moreover, a term which has been found often used for projection has a greater chance of projection because he calls such term to be more entrenched in the culture. In other words, Goodman goes by the strength of the history of a word and its natural place in the society. Since, it is a descriptive theory, it cannot be considered to be a normative theory if norm is opposed to fact.

Even if the theory of meaning that Quine subscribes to is by and large dispositional and behaviouristic, it has other important components as well. For instance, with respect to natural kinds, we could say that his theory would admit innatism. And when it comes to the issue of normativity in epistemology, of late he is very clear that normativity is part of his epistemology. Naturalized epistemology not only describes what the true situation is, it would guide our epistemic advancement. Given these two elements in Quine's philosophy, Kripke's skeptic cannot outright reject Quine's epistemic claims. For instance, Quine's view on natural kinds cannot be rejected by the skeptic. What is water, for instance, cannot be doubted even by a skeptic.

Wittgenstein's theory of meaning is popularly known as the 'use theory'. However, use of a word is not the same thing as meaning. Wittgenstein wants to replace the problematic question of what is meaning with that of what is the use of the word. in our language. The former sometimes prompts us to answer the question in terms of mental entities, since, mental entities are problematic, Wittgenstein wants to reformulate the question about meaning in terms of the use of those terms. It serves most of our purpose of the question of meaning if we replace it by use.

The use of a word is stretched over time and hence, use itself creates another problem which we have noted in the previous chapter. How is that I am able to grasp the rule in a fraction of a moment while the rule has infinite applications? However, this formulation would not lead to strange thing like mental entities. 'Use theory' is taken to be descriptive by most philosophers, even by Wittgenstein. Wittgenstein considers his grammar to be descriptive and points out that the task of philosopher is to describe. He leaves everything as it is says Wittgenstein. Why Wittgenstein opposes normative aspect of meaning is not clear to us, though he had clearly recognized the normative aspects of rules. He says that the rules guide and not determine our next step. That is to say, rules would be used for deciding the next step, yet, human beings have the freedom to decide. Thus, while admitting the freedom of the users of language, he recognizes the normative elements embedded in the rules of language. Moreover, Wittgenstein clearly recognizes the commitment to rules. Social agreement leads to commitment and this is the base of the normativity of the rules. Despite all these, Wittgenstein prefers to call the philosophers' task descriptive and the function of grammar descriptive. It, seems that there is no way, but to conclude that the theory of meaning is by and large descriptive for Wittgenstein.

Why do we need a normative theory of meaning needs to be addressed more clearly. We do not think that the Kripke's skeptic is demanding for a normative theory without much purpose. In fact, the skeptic has the right to demand such a theory. However, it may be a mistake on the part of the skeptic to believe that such a theory cannot be forthcoming. In fact, Wittgenstein had everything to answer the skeptic. Somehow, he chose to answer the skeptic differently as discussed in the previous chapter. We need to consider the need for a normative theory of meaning in the context of skepticism.

A good theory of meaning should reasonably point out how these cluster of concepts, namely, the notions of rule, induction, prediction, expectation, projection, justification and rule governed behaviour work well. One needs to identify the place of these notions in the context of society where knowledge acquisition, transition and preservation take place. There is no denying of the fact that the four philosophers that we have studied so far, have contributed immensely in drawing our attention to the different aspects of these epistemic requirements. One should say Kripke's skeptic has drawn our attention to the element of the requirement of normativity, *grue* has drawn our attention to the entrenchment and the indeterminacies of Quine have drawn our attention to the need for naturalizing epistemology.

A descriptive theory of meaning can at best give an account of what is happening at present or at best what has happened in the past. A dispositional theory or emotive theory of meaning would have in some sense edge over the descriptive theory of meaning. Yet, because of some technical problems, one tends to interpret even these theories in the line of a descriptive theory. Of course, the motivation to do this is evident. The logical advancement would be faster if we try to find a descriptive account of meaning rather than any other form. However, the theory of meaning would lose the capacity to prediction and explain if the theory of meaning is descriptive. This is not something so evident because of the kind of thinking that prevails today. Ask the question where does a theory of meaning derive the explanatory power? Let us take an example in terms of explaining a simple rule of addition. Wittgenstein, for instance, is clear that the number of cases that a pupil has to demonstrate before it claims that "now I know how to go on" vary from person to person. This is because, we can explain the rule of addition only in terms of examples. Given this constraint, if the pupil is only a descriptive theorist, he would insist that what he has learnt so far is the examples that have been demonstrated to him. In other words, he can refuse to use the expression 'so on *ad infinitum*' since, there is nothing in the teaching that can teach him this expression.

The very moment the pupil or the teacher use this expression appropriately, they have indicated the universal nature of the rule. What follows from the universal rule is that the law of excluded middle would be immediately applied to it. That is to say, given certain behaviour, the behaviour is either in accordance with the universal rule or it is not. There is no third option. And once we have this binary value of accord or fail to accord, the norm is set in. We are in a position to judge the behaviour as something that is in accordance with the rule or has failed to be in accordance with the rule. The whole universe is now divided into two, the ones which are in accordance with the rule and the ones which are not. However, it is worth noting that if a rule is not universal, then there is the scope for concept like *grue* where the rule is applicable to certain class of objects only when they meet certain conditions, say before 2000 A.D. Such restricted rules, may not have the normative value and will not have infinite applications.

It is only the rules which have the normative element built into them would help us to predict the behaviour. What Kripke's skeptic wants is the assured behaviour of the rule-follower. Since, rules are arbitrary and we could interpret the rules the way we want given the freedom, how to have the predictable use of words is the question. Wittgenstein also recognizes this fact that man is free and remarks that the necessity is part of language. There is no way, one can have linguistic rules which have the attribute of natural laws. There is no way one can coerce the behaviour of a human being the way rails would do to a locomotive. Therefore, the kind of certainty or necessity that one is looking for is logical or linguistic kind and not of mechanical type.

Since, necessity has to be found within the framework of freedom of man, the expectation that is built on the rules of the language would be expectation which is different that can be built on the laws of nature on the one hand and psychological on the other. We could distinguish expectation built on the scientific ground. For instance, a man would die one day is the expectation built on scientific ground, since, everyone has to age and eventually die. But psychologically, one may not believe in this at all. Like the example of Russell where the hen believes that she would not be killed since, her master nurses her, loves her and feeds her well. This expectation is purely psychological, and has no scientific nor linguistic basis. Expectation built on linguistic rules is of a different kind. For example, your sister is a female is expectation built on a linguistic rule. Cuckoos are birds can also be recognized as based on linguistic rules. If we observe a cuckoo, we expect it to have the features of a bird. A being with four legs or with no feather will not be a cuckoo.

In the act of rule formation, a generalization takes place. In fact, Wittgenstein does not favour the rule of induction as a separate entity. In his scheme of things there is no room for induction as a separate entity. It is not necessary that we need to have a rule of induction first and then it has to be applied to a context where generalization is made on the basis of paradigm cases or examples. For instance, in learning the rule of addition, we do not need to apply the rule of induction. The rule of induction is redundant for Wittgenstein. The process through which we establish the rule of induction is the same for rule formation of the rule of addition. Instead of first establishing the rule of induction and then applying to the rule of addition, why not consider directly formulating the rule of addition, asks Wittgenstein? In fact, we formulate different rules on the basis of paradigm cases independently of the rule of induction.

We may note that what an explanation of meaning be like. Wittgenstein has realized the difficulty of attempting to answer the question of meaning and he turns to the explanation of meaning. Explanation of meaning is done in terms of the use of words and use of words is explained with examples adding in the end 'and so on'. This situation of terminating the explanation of a term by saying 'and so on' presupposes that the rule is universal and has unlimited examples. Of course, one should not mistake 'and so on' appearing in the context of explanation of rules to be the abbreviations of some more cases. It is evident that explanation of a rule would not have been possible, if the rules were not universal.

Once the rule is formed, it helps us to predict, expect, and project the behaviour both natural and human. A normative theory of meaning thus, would be in a position to speak of expectation, prediction, and projection in the context of human behaviour. However, there is no guarantee that our expectation would be fulfilled by the human being, and similarly, there is no guarantee that our prediction about a natural event would necessarily come through. This is because, it is possible that the individuals do not stand by their commitments and it is possible that certain surprise in nature awaits. There is no surprise in language and logic opines Wittgenstein since, everything is open in language. There does not seem to be something that is hidden in language which is revealed only to a select few. Language is the resource available to everyone equally, if it can be revealed to one, it is revealed to all. Given this, a discovery is possible only in the world. World gives us shocks at times and surprises by behaving differently than what we expect. Of course, these surprises lead to new discoveries and formation of new laws and new terminologies along with their rules for use of those terminologies.

How a normative theory could be objective and descriptive needs to be clarified here. One of the reasons why philosophers have hesitated in accepting a normative theory of meaning is that it eventually turns out to be relativistic. This is because, it is somehow felt that everything that is not truth-conditional is subjective and being subjective varies from person to person and thus, the theory is dubbed as relativistic. What we need to show is that a normative theory need not be relativistic and it need not be subjective in the derogatory sense either. The only example that we have in this connection which could lend some hope is the Kant's categorical imperative. Let us use this analogy to understand the outline of such a normative theory of meaning.

The Normative Theory of Meaning

Why do we think that a theory of meaning be normative? This issue should be addressed carefully. We speak of rules, and their normativity, we speak of explanation of meaning, we speak of justification, prediction, expectation etc. are also part of the epistemological vocabulary. A theory of meaning should be adequate and what we want to show is without the normative element attached to a theory of meaning all these things cannot be accounted.

Let us first consider how we can explain the meaning of a term. It is clear from the place given to 'so on *ad infinitum*' to the process of learning the use of a term, remains incomplete till one has reached the stage where he is in a position to go on his own. Learning of the rule has to take place with particular paradigm. One cannot say at what stage of giving the next step the student would grasp the rule. Yet, all the cases of demonstration would not exhaust the application of rule. That is to say, the examples provided are always less than the total applications the rules would have. This process of grasping the rule in a moment consists of the following elements.

The rule now appears to be having unlimited application, if not in real life at least in imagination. The rule may have exception, but it is universal. At least it is applicable to all objects of a certain kind. Notice that the rule has already given the sense of a kind to the person who has grasped the rule. The rule gives the sense of boundary, it permits the person to classify the cases where the rule is applicable and where it is not. The person is in a position to provide new imaginative examples where the rule would be applicable, i.e., he can provide new contexts where the rule is applicable. The person is in a position to judge correct application and is able to point out wrong application. He is in a position to verify if he is asked to do and is able to explain the rule using paradigms. All these activities are possible because rules have normativity and the person grasped the normative aspect of rules while grasping the rule.

This grasping of the rule has one striking similarity with Kant's categorical imperative. As the name itself suggests, the imperatives that Kant wants to consider are categorical not conditional. Our descriptive theory of meaning has to be categorical here yet, must have an element of normativity tied to it. Kant achieves this categorical imperative by universalizing the maxim. When he tries to universalize, if the maxim reduces itself to absurd position, then any rational man feels repulsive exactly in the manner the *reduction-ad-absurdum* argument works with all rational individuals. All those maxims which can be universalized without leading to absurd conclusions are said to be rational by Kant.[4] A rule, when grasped by a rational person would have this universal character.

By no means should one think that there are no restricted rules. Quite a few rules can be cited in favour of this. However, these restricted rules alone cannot form a language. No grammar would work with restricted rules alone. This is because, the grammar would lose all its universal character in such an event and would lose its autonomy and thus, would not be comparable to any genuine language. So, the restricted rules, can work only in the language where universal rules are there as constitutive of the grammar.

The rules that are thus, accepted in the form of universal rules having the element of rational commitment would have the guiding force as pointed out by Wittgenstein. And having this guiding force it would exert on a rational person and would govern his behaviour.

Thus, we would be in a position to predict the behaviour of a person who is thus, rational. This is like saying that one can predict the behaviour of the truthful and trustworthy person. Expectation of the behaviour of the person and the prediction of the same is possible because rules are accepted and they have the normative component. Given this normative element, interpretation of the rule in all possible ways does not take place. If interpreted in bizarre manner, language would fail to serve its purpose.

The Notion of Philosophical Grammar

Why grammar is fundamental is that grammar is made up of conventions. All conventions are true by the very act of invoking the convention. For instance, it would not make sense to say that why should a meter be the length of the meter rod kept at Paris. Simply we have taken the length of that rod as one meter. Of course, this does not mean that our notion of a meter is dependent on the contingent fact of the length of the meter kept at Paris. For instance, one can very well imagine that the rod is stolen or gets destroyed because of an earthquake, yet, we will be able to use the notion of a meter. Therefore, once conventionalised, a rule does not depend on the empirical fact whatsoever which was taken as an empirical base of our convention.

The foundation of a normative theory of meaning can be provided only by a universal language. The concept of a universal language is difficult since, there are different languages spoken by different societies. Even if one language is imposed on all societies that would only contingently become a universal language. The concept of universal language required by the normative theory of meaning would not be this contingent achievement, it should be truly universal without any constraint. Logic was thought to be universal language, but it was found to be limited to only certain type of sentences. Being aware of the limitation of the natural language, Wittgenstein conceived grammar to be the base of such a universal language. The notion of philosophical grammar which Wittgenstein speaks of is truly universal cutting across all the linguistic and geographical barriers. Languages having this philosophical grammar would permit translation, projection, expectation, induction and forming of hypothesis, verification and all that can be called epistemic activity. One may speak of therefore, philosophical grammar which has the wider base than that of logic.

Language being an autonomous calculus of rules, the possibilities in language is not explained in terms of some logico-syntactical rules connected to the reality by the logical proper names whose meanings were simple objects that constitute the substance of the world. Wittgenstein considers that grammar consists of only two things: rules and symbols. Thus, philosophical grammar as a tool of clarification is concerned with the language only, every thing then go within language and our explanation and understanding is confined within the limits of grammar.

Wittgenstein believes that language and 'form of life' are pre-given. We do not invent language, but we are born within the institution of language. Having born in such an environment, we adopt the language that is prevalent there. Human beings of course are governed by their linguistic rules, but what one can do is to describe the behaviour in terms of the rules. When we give a rule, we give it by describing how to use it. At times, we give examples and explain how to use them.

For instance, one can describe how a marriage takes place within a particular culture. This description is not a norm. Norm would lie in the rules of the marriage. For instance if the custom says that the marriage can take place only in the Church, it is not possible to conduct marriage in a hotel for instance. Thus, though the rules of grammar are normative, not all acts performed using grammar or a rule needs to be normative. For instance, one ought to pay income tax. This would be a normative judgement, but one can describe an act by saying "he paid his income tax". A rule is applied when we describe, but a rule can also be used for disapproving certain actions. Income tax should be paid on time is action guiding. All rules which govern human behaviour have both the aspects: they can be used to describe human behaviour; they can be used to guide human behaviour or evaluate human behaviour. Both the uses of rules are not the same, the former is descriptive and the latter is normative.

How does the grammar that is so much depended on the form of life can provide the necessity and normativity to its following. The conventional and relativistic nature of rules can be manipulated in any way one likes. The explanation of behaviour based on such arbitrary rules, it is very difficult to go 'beyond the rules': the whole process of rule-following has become a routine. The mechanical process where the creativity, discovery, invention and the meaningful deviation from the scope of rule are virtually impossible. A rule as it is heavily dependent on the conventional practice of the members of the community is whimsical, subjective and is subject to change at will, therefore, it is natural to wonder how such relativistic rule can provide the ground for the justification of our meaning and communication. Rules formulated within the framework of grammar provide the necessity for three reasons: (1) commitment, (2) regularity and (3) conformability.

First, rules are stipulated for certain purposes, approved and followed in the community by its members. Therefore, rules are very much objective and collective in nature and there should be no problem of inter-subjective communication. Though the assumption that community view of justification is arbitrary and always fallible this does not force us to embrace relativism, a very common charge leveled against any theory based on convention. This is because, once we invoke a rule, we are committed to follow it; are supposed to be faithful to it. Though rules are arbitrary, their applications are not.[5] The application of a rule becomes a social necessity. The community view of rule and faith to honour the accord as a *normative constraint* determines our choices. Systematic and consistent use of rules along with commitment to rule gives us the required parameters to judge the epistemic behaviour of other members in the community. Rules, thus, are predictable, they tell us in advance which behaviour would fit which rules. In a sense, a rule determines its extension. Thus, on the strength of the knowledge of the rules used in the communities, one member understands the behaviour of the others in the society. An important point of rule is that commitment to a rule is an inevitable part of any conventional rule. The commitment to rule is essential part of our very institution of language is best exemplified by the fact that one has no freedom to question the truth of a statement expressing a definition. Having defined a week consisting of seven days, I cannot further ask the question why a week should consist of seven days. This is the implication of Wittgensteinian thesis that rules cannot be justified further though we justify our actions and judgements in terms of rules.[6]

However, we do not deny the possibility that there can be a rule for instance a time table, totally designed and followed by an individual isolated from the society. But this fact does not make such a rule mysterious. What we object, following Wittgenstein, is that we cannot follow a rule privately. This is because rules are not mental facts and it is not the case that an individual who possesses this mental state alone is privileged to follow it. Rules may be formulated by an individual, but it makes sense only when they are followed publicly or at least the conditions of those rules should be clear enough for somebody who is willing to follow. The agent can disobey a rule or even can stipulate contradictory rule for there is no right or wrong rule, only convenient or inconvenient rules to follow. Therefore, though rules are merely conventional, that does not license the user to change the agreement unless and otherwise there is a case for either giving up the convention or introduce a new convention which is in some way opposed to the present one, otherwise we do not change the existing conventions as they are already part of our way of life. There is force of a promise attached to every rule because we have committed to the rule and, thus, if we are violating them, which we can very much do, it amounts to cheating the society in a subtle manner by not keeping our promise; and the result would be a conceptual confusion.

However, the commitment to rule may not be so visible when it is the case of a complex rule. For instance, though it is a commitment that one should keep one's promises, in extra-ordinary circumstances, it may not be obvious why one should do so. It is possible to question the very rule instead of accepting the commitment. For example, one can question the very institution of money lending and hold the view that the money borrowed need not be returned. However, we notice that even questioning the institution of money lending is possible because there is already an institution of promising. Following Kant, one can show that if no one were to keep one's promise, the world order would have been so different that the word 'promise' would have lost its meaning and the word would have been out of currency.

If language has to work, commitment to rules cannot be overlooked. Assume that every sentence that I utter, one word in the sentence is used in a deviant manner. I explain my deviant use of the word in the sentence. However, the sentences that I use to explain the previous one itself contains one word which again has been used in a deviant manner. Notice that no amount of explanation is going to bring any clarity as long as there is no commitment to social norms. Commitment would fundamentally break down if there is no commitment to rules. It is a fact that we are members of a community who speak language and this is made possible because we accept commitment to rules.

Let us now turn to the second aspect of rules: the systematic and regular use of rules. Note that even the worst skeptic has to grant that if something is true by definition, it is true. Even the skeptic does not have the freedom to blatantly contradict himself. This is because, if the skeptic is advancing a point for our consideration, he needs to have minimum commitment to rules, otherwise communication breaks down. The skeptic will grant us the point that if a week consists of seven days by definition, it would consist of seven days. However, he will fully exploit the linguistic licence he has as a member of the society and claim that it is possible to offer a new definition of a week consisting of only six days. Of course, this new definition could be offered only after withdrawing commitment to the other definition of seven days a week otherwise we are making the word 'work' ambiguous and if in this manner everyone exercises his freedom to define this term, the term would be totally useless.

Thirdly, rules must be followable. If a rule has no application, it cannot be a rule. There is no point in prescribing rules which the agent cannot follow and are not within the cognitive reach of the finite human beings. Though we can very much stipulate a very arbitrary traffic rule like "jump over the road when there is a red light", we do not formulate such an unpractical rule, for if it cannot be practiced, it would not be a rule at all. Consequently, the conformability requirement constraints us to stipulate arbitrary rules.

The notion of grammar thus, is kernel concept in Wittgenstein. Grammar relates our language with reality through conventional rules. This being so one wonders what is the place of syntax and semantics in Wittgenstein's philosophy. A rough outline could be given as follows. The syntax of language is considered as the part of grammar. It exists in the form of conventions in language. Since,, it is the grammar that gives the possibilities of combining different words in a sensible manner; we should say that it is the grammar that inherits the rules of syntax. But the view regarding the semantics is relatively more difficult to understand. We need to speak of assertability-condition and truth-condition. Assertability-condition should be met in order to justifiably use sentences regarding other minds, and truth-conditions should be met to justify the statements about the external world. Thus, grammar is the one which provides us with justifications whether it is of assertability-condition or truth-condition type.

Rules and Their Extensions

There is no surprise in language and logic holds Wittgenstein. This is because everything in language is predictable and rule governed. As we have noted earlier, if we know the rules, we know their extension. This is the reason why language cannot give us anything that we might be surprised with. If reality surprises us, that is because, our language and vocabulary are limited. For instance, when Aluminum was discovered, it was a surprise to scientists. Similarly, when water was discovered to be a compound, there was a surprise. All these surprises were possible because reality were not the way the humans thought them to be. These situations made the scientists invoke new rules to describe these unanticipated events and realities. Thus, with the advancement of science and human history, there would be many surprises which are made part of human knowledge with additional vocabularies. But once, they are made as part of human knowledge, they are not the sources of surprises.

The philosophical analysis of rule points out two important aspects of rules and their following: first, rules and their following are internally related and thus, rules are not mysterious and hidden from the view of the users. This aspect of the rules show that rules cannot be identified with some mental states or physical process to be discovered. Second, rules are understood in their use and mastering the technique how to use the rules. The rules without any application are pseudo rules and applications if they are not applications of some rules are meaningless.

It does not make sense to presuppose any metaphysical intermediaries between rules and their extension, for the rules of grammar are not grounded in reality. The grammar of rules can be characterized by the following facts: the relationship between rules and their applications are immanent and internal, yet, transparent, for we have to acknowledge the use of the rules for using them and we should be willing to cleave them, otherwise rules cannot act as reason for its applications. The grammar of rules involves the understanding of the rules and fixing the different actions in accordance with or in conflicting with the rules. The understanding of the rules is a conscious act in which the followers intentionally know what rules he is following and mastering the technique to defend the rules in the time of criticism and debates. The grammar of the expression rule will render a rule non-sensical if we cannot use it or it is impossible to violate in principle.

The reason for the internal relation between a rule and its application is that, the use of the rule is very much contained in the rule itself. Nothing would be counted as a rule independently of being used as a rule. There is nothing as our following a rule without our being able to explain or justify our actions by reference to them, for the calculus of rule is nothing but the uses of rule. A rule without any application is a meaningless expression.[7]

The practice and custom are essential for understanding the rules and how to follow the rules. Wittgenstein validly argues that "a person goes by the sign-post only in so far as there exists a regular use of sign-post, a custom."[8] The mastering of the technique is possible because we have a common language and some uniform practices. The other frameworks within which the successful following of the rule is dependent are that, the world is substantially unchanging and uniform in nature, there is harmony between language and reality and human beings have their own limitation. Thus, we are not expected to jump the road when there is red light, though such a rule can be formulated. We simply cannot say that we have violated such a rule. This is what Wittgenstein say the 'forms of life'. However, the forms of life is not the definition of the rule and its following, in the sense that they provide the minimum requirements to conduct our rule-governed activity smoothly, but they do not define or constitute rule-following. The forms of life provide the frame work through which we operate our grammar. This is because the applicability is "not an agreement in opinions but in the forms of life."[9]

Objectivity of knowledge is possible because the rule is objective. Rules are objective because, their essence lies in their application. And a rule and application of rule are internally related, i.e., we need nothing else to connect a rule and its application. Given these, it follows that any two persons in possession of any particular rule will have identical prediction. For instance, any two persons having known the rule of addition of 2 of real numbers would have eventually had the same series of numbers, e.g., both of them would have had 1004 after 1002.

A rule has infinite applications, and the two individuals who possess the rule also would know these infinite applications. And therefore, there is no gap between the knowledge of A from B with respect to the rule. Similarly, if one knows that within the Euclidean geometry a triangle is a figure with three straight lines that would be the same for the other too. Not only that both of them would have agreed that the statement is true of any triangle what so ever of the past and of the present and of the future.

The rules are objective irrespective of how one has comprehended a rule and how often one has used the rule or followed it. This is because, the rule determines its extension and its determining extension does not depend on any other external factor other than rule itself. Therefore, if two rules are such that one rule is subsumed within another rule, they would be related in a particular manner irrespective of their referents or extensions. For instance, the rule that identifies a triangle is a rule within the Euclidean geometry and it would necessarily include the rule of what is a straight line. It is not possible to determine what a triangle is without knowing how to use the term "straight line". Thus, if ABC is a triangle, it would consist of straight lines. We can say that a straight line and a triangle are necessarily related without knowing the extensions of these two expressions: triangles and straight lines.

The requirement that rules ought to be surveyable or followable makes the rules determinable in advance. That is the reason, we do not require to employ some introspection or look into the inner process which goes inside the mind of the follower to determine the future step of the applications. It should be determinable or identifiable by a finite follower independently of any particular application-condition under which a particular rule is first used. The conformability condition of rules also incorporates fallible nature of rules.

Grammar and Necessity

Logicians thought that the laws of thought are obeyed by mind and Russell inquired whether the laws of thought are also the laws of reality. However, Wittgenstein in his later works has made the laws of logic conventional as well, i.e., logic as a form of language and the laws of logic as the rules within that language. He invokes the notion of philosophical grammar which is different from the traditional notion of grammar. The philosophical grammar is the foundation of rules in language. Symbols and rules which constitute the language and both of them are accepted conventionally.

There is no language having some functional significance, which does not reflect reality. This is because, language without application would be a useless language and if there ought to be some application then it is to the world that we apply the language. Therefore, there is no way that we can have language which in some sense comes in conflict with reality. This is because, language is developed against reality. Wittgenstein says there are only two possibilities: either we obey the rules or do not, there is no third possibility. This is the reason that we are able to decide the truth values of the statements that we make of the world. But Wittgenstein would not accept truth as a concept and hence, there is no rule for establishing which statement is true. We use a statement and then decide its truth value says Wittgenstein.

Given the harmony between language and reality, and given the universal nature of grammar, only certain combination of words can be permitted in language. If we try some other possibilities, the sentence turns out to be nonsense. Wittgenstein finds the limit to language this way. What should be noted is the necessity that follows from this. Grammar, in a sense, imposes certain restrictions on us on the matter of what is sensible and what is not. It is not that we have freedom to choose between sensible and nonsensical. But within the sensible which includes both the sets of statements true and false can be asserted accordingly. If language were to contain only true propositions, then every sentence in that language would have been necessary. But in that case language would have lost its autonomy. Therefore, Wittgenstein says that every statement about the world is contingent and every statement about the world can be denied. This is because language is autonomous.

It is not possible to have such a statement in language which reflects the reality and yet, is true necessarily. Wittgenstein believes that the essence of the world cannot be described in language because if such a possibility exists, then such a description cannot be negated. This is so because anything that is essential to a thing when negated, it should result in a self-contradiction. For this reason, both tautologies and contradictions are considered to be useless since, they have no application to the world, and even if they are necessary in some sense, that necessity is of no use when it is a matter of application.

Going by the traditional criterion, if there are synthetic *a priori* statements, then they ought to be necessary. Even the skeptic has no option but to accept the synthetic *a priori* statements. Wittgenstein admits the possibility of synthetic *a priori* propositions. He considers "Bismarck" has 8 letters to be both synthetic and *a priori*. It is synthetic because we have to know empirically that it consists of 8 letters and it is *a priori* because it does not depend on our experience.[10] Another example he considers is that the unpredictable occurrence of the prime number is obvious enough example of mathematics having synthetic character. However, that they are synthetic in this sense does not make them any less *a priori*, he claims. Thus, he writes: "The distribution of primes would be an ideal example of what could be called synthetic *a priori*, for one can say that it is at any rate not discoverable by an analysis of the concept of a prime numbers."[11]

We need to make the distinction between a tautological and an analytical sentence on the one hand and contradiction and a self-contradiction on the other. A sentence is tautologous by virtue of the structure of the sentence itself. We require a compound sentence in order to have a structure such that the sentence is true by virtue of its structure. We call "P V ~p" a tautologous sentence. Here, the logical connective has played an important role. However, if we take a singular sentence having a subject and a predicate, we can speak of analyticity or self-contradiction. A contradiction has the form "P . ~P" while a self-contradiction can be ascribed to a singular sentence having a subject and predicate. Wittgenstein has opined that tautologies and contradictions are of no use to us as descriptions of the world; however one cannot deny their importance as logical tools in inferences.

A skeptic cannot deny any tautology, yet, he can reject it as useless even if it is necessary since, it directly does not apply to the world. However, he cannot so easily dismiss the analytic statements which are true by virtue of their meaning. However, he would perhaps invoke the notion of linguistic truth and claim that these analytic sentences are true by virtue of conventions. That is to say, we have invoked the linguistic rules in such a manner that the statement ought to be true. For instance, "Cuckoos are birds" is an analytic statement which even Quine admits, but this statement is true by virtue of the rules of the language. We need not have to know facts about the world in order to know that the sentence in question is true.

We have the difficulty of distinguishing the lawlike statements and the analytic statements. The difficulty arises because both the sentences have the universal character and hence, the logical structure of these seems to be the same.[12] Certainly, the analytic sentences are universal and if we admit certain use of words in a certain manner, then we are forced to admit that these sentences are true by virtue of their meaning or use. However, a law and a lawlike sentence both can be denied without getting the feeling of self-contradiction. It is obvious then, there is no relationship of linguistic kind between different terms that constitute the law or the lawlike statement. From this what follows is that both laws and the lawlike statements have to be necessarily synthetic. This is the reason why their denial does not result in a self-contradiction.

All the linguistic rules would have the universal character and have the structure of a lawlike statement. They are normative and hence, they do not allow formulating certain sentences in certain manner. If we insist on forming certain sentences in certain manner, they produce nonsense. This is the reason why Wittgenstein calls them grammatical nonsense. For instance, "it is 5 O'clock on the sun now" is such a nonsense because the talk of time in this manner is not permitted by grammar of our language. Or the statement "people on the other side of the hemisphere walk upside down" cannot be considered to be a sensible combination of words.[13]

If our language has to be applied to the world and if we have to formulate the laws of nature in our language, then the sentences that express the laws of nature should not be of the following kind: (1) The sentences should not be tautologies or contradictions. (2) They should not be analytical sentences since, their truth is decided by the conventional rules of language. If we eliminate these two types of sentences from our list of the type of sentences which can express the laws of nature, then we are left with only two types of sentences which are actual laws of nature and which look like laws of nature, i.e., the lawlike sentences.

Goodman has taken pains to carefully distinguish between lawlike statements and the actual laws or hypothesis which can be projected. However, we cannot be happy with that method since, finally what he claims amount saying that what has already been accepted in science ought to be accepted till they are rejected. Therefore, we need to think of a method which is more convenient and pragmatic. Our method should not restrict our investigation to the historical perspectives, though should make use of what our history can offer in the efforts of building the knowledge system. Such a thing would be possible if and only if we are able to show how empirical knowledge can be objective and universal. Let us now clarify our notion of objective knowledge.

By all means, a necessary statement gives us the objective knowledge. However, all necessary statements are necessarily not of the world and hence, they cannot give us the required necessary knowledge about the world. What a skeptic is seeking seems to be that kind of statement which is empirical and yet, is necessarily true of the world. Let us see whether one could have such a statement at all.

We claim, perhaps no one would disagree with us, that a necessary statement is one which is true in all possible worlds, or in all possible perspectives or in all possible interpretations. The notion as defined is very general and is not clear at that. It has been often stated that a necessary statement in the metaphysical sense has to be true in every possible world. Even if a statement is false in one particular world, then that statement is called contingent. However, possible worlds do not exist out there. Since, this talk is misleading, we should rather speak of the possible perspectives of the same world, or world-views. When we use this expression, then a statement is necessary when it is true in all world-views. One could express the same sentence in a slightly different manner by using the expression 'interpretation'. A sentence is necessary if it is true in all interpretations. However, there are some difficulties here. Many objects that exist in the world are themselves contingent, and hence, any statement about them cannot be necessary since, these contingent things do not exist in all possible worlds or perspectives necessarily. If they would exist necessarily in all possible worlds, then they are no more contingent objects, they would be one like unmoved mover.

Let us assume that the numbers of possible worlds are Ws, then that statement is necessary which could take the value true or false in W_1, W_2, W_3 and so on. But it is epistemically impossible for any one to know the truth of any single statement in all the possible perspectives since, all the possible perspectives are not known to any one. Then are we seeking for something impossible? If there is a mechanism to know whether a synthetic statement is true in all possible worlds without actually verifying whether the statement is true in all these possible worlds? What could this mechanism be? If we bank on the linguistic rules, then the statement would turn out to be analytic one, and if we bank on tautologies, then they are not applicable to the world. Except some mystical and speculative method, there does not seem to be any uncontroversial method to establish the truth of such necessary statements. Unfortunately, we cannot epistemically establish a synthetic statement about the world and yet, think that it would be true in all possible perspectives. What a skeptic asks is for such a sentence.

In the wake of such difficulty, let us reconsider analytic statements, whether they can be synthetic as well as analytic in some sense. Let us see whether some synthetic statements turn out to be analytic in the long-run and thus, have the cake and eat it too.

Analytic sentences are true by virtue of the linguistic rules, but can they be also true synthetically? To say that a sentence is true by linguistic rule need not make us think that they are not true synthetically because language does not contradict reality. Since, language and reality are in harmony, since, they belong to different realms, there is no reason to believe that an analytic statement which is true by virtue of language cannot be true in any other sense. Double citizenship can be permitted, one linguistic and the other empirical. What is important, therefore, is to see whether there is any sense in saying that one and the same sentence is true for two independent reasons. Kripke has remarked that analyticity and syntheticity are the linguistic distinction, *a priori* and *a posteriori* are epistemic distinctions and necessity and contingency are metaphysical distinctions.[14] It seems Kripke has shown us the possibility of combining, as Kant and Wittgenstein have done already two items from two different categories, namely synthetic *a priori* judgements. If analytic statements can be synthetic as well, there seems to be much hope for philosophers.

There is no reason to believe why truth cannot have many criteria. Wittgenstein believes that truth is not a concept, meaning thereby there is no single rule to use this word. Thus, we can speak of various criteria unless these criteria are mutually exclusive. Criteria of truth, especially the pragmatic, correspondence and linguistic or coherence need not be mutually exclusive, since, the ground on which a particular statement is decided to be true are different and are not mutually exclusive. Therefore, it would be unreasonable to claim if an analytical statement is true by virtue of linguistic rules, it cannot be true empirically. Thus, we need to consider analytical statements which apply to the world whether they meet the condition of a necessary synthetic statement.

One such example which Wittgenstein discusses is that there are four primary colours. The example is a perfect one because, theoretically also there are only four primary colours (we have accepted this as our conventional truth) and practically, or empirically also there are only four primary colours. Thus, the statement "there are four primary colours" is at once true because of the convention, as well as because of the experience or fact of nature. Though it is possible to logically deny the statement and have a false statement, it is not a statement that is true by definition. Even if one argues that in future, this may turn out to be false, that argument has no meaning because our rules are normative. Rules determine their extension and four colours which include red, blue, green and yellow would include these colours and these colours alone as primary colours and nothing else. Since, rule and its extension are internally related, there is no chance of even future course changing the matter of fact. Hence, we would like to say that this is the strongest sense of necessity, i.e., empirically as well as logically that man has ever thought of.[15]

The question that might trouble a philosopher is: Can a proposition be both logically and empirically true? This question arises with the assumption that the realm of logic is different from the realm of experience. However, Wittgenstein has tried to show the relation between logic and experience *via* his notion of philosophical grammar. Grammar is conventional and yet, can be empirical in the sense anything empirical can be conventionally taken as the symbol in language. Ostensive definition incorporates our experiential aspect into language. Similarly, colour charts play important role in our language game of colours. Models are part of the language of advertising. Drawings, graphs and photographs are part of our reports. All these indicate how perception can be part of our language.

The assumption that if empirical truths and logical truths are mutually exclusive is held forcefully, then we need to say that logical principles are not true of empirical world. The consequence of holding this view would be unpleasing since, the conclusions that we derive from inference should not be applicable to the world. This is against the very spirit of logic. We study logic for pragmatic reasons and to say that the two are mutually exclusive is to strip the logic of its importance.

Yet, there is the serious reservation as to how the logical relationship if any can be empirically discovered. If logical truths can be empirically discovered, why do we need logic after all? All the functions that logic can perform, our experience could also perform then.

Either we need to maintain that the term "true" is ambiguous or we need to maintain that a proposition can be both logically and empirically true. For example, the law of excluded middle wherever it applies should be true both logically as well as empirically. For instance, "either this table is furniture or it is not" is certainly a case in point. This sentence we can declare to be true on the basis of our experience that it is a table and since, one of the components is known to be true, the whole sentence is true. We could also declare the sentence in question to be true on the basis of the very logical structure without involving any sense perception. This certainly indicates that what is logically true need not be excluded from our empirical investigation and *vice-versa*. Since, the exercise is redundant, we may not use empirical method to explore the truth known through logic. By no means, we claim that everything that can be known by logic can be known by experience.

Objectivity of Knowledge

Wittgenstein has spoken of assertability-conditions and truth-conditions. This distinction he had to invoke while speaking of statements pertaining to mental states. He recognized that we speak of someone else's pain intelligibly without having the problem of private language. He thought that we have every right to talk about others the way we have been doing. This was made possible by explaining what an assertability-condition is. An assertability-condition is nothing, but the adequate linguistic condition based on which one decides to apply a term.

Note that Wittgenstein spoke of criteria and symptom distinctions and the nature of criteria is such that given the criteria, one can logically use the word which has been satisfied by the criteria. Thus, a criterion is sufficient even if it is not necessary. To speak of truth-conditions, one must be able to speak of necessary and sufficient conditions, whereas to speak of assertability-condition, one needs to speak of only sufficient condition and not necessary one. Thus, Wittgenstein has modified drastically the logical requirement before ascribing certain mental attributes to someone else.

The assertability-condition is a wider concept in comparison to the concept of truth-condition. All truth-conditions are assertability-conditions in this sense, but all assertability-conditions are not truth-conditions. This is because, all sufficient conditions fulfill the requirement of necessary conditions for the use of words anyway, whereas terms which require to meet both necessary and sufficient conditions for their use cannot be used in the context where sufficient conditions are met. Given this reason, it is possible to present all the truth-conditional statements in the mode of assertability-conditions.

Speaking of assertability-condition, one may wonder how that can give us the objectivity of knowledge, since, there is no question of necessary and sufficient condition that is met in order to justify our judgement about the experiences of others. The onus is on us to prove that objective knowledge is possible and the skeptical issue can be avoided. Let us take up the issue of objective knowledge about the external world first and then turn to the issue of objective knowledge about other minds and private experiences by showing the possibility of rule-following despite the problem of memory, extension and projection issues.

First, note that if we accept the regularity in nature conventionally as a rule, there is no reason to believe that the necessity achieved would be of a lesser kind. For instance, fire burns and this simple fact of fire, or that of the property of fire can be conventionally accepted as a rule for the use of the term "fire". And having accepted it conventionally as a rule, it is true by definition that "fire burns" is true. If it is true by definition, even a skeptic cannot doubt it. If a skeptic doubts a truth by definition, then he is refusing to use a language which has sense and if a skeptic is a person speaking of no sense, nothing needs to be proved to him. Therefore, "fire burns" is a necessary statement of the highest order and hence, it is true empirically and logically necessary. Thus, one can generate numerous examples to provide straight solutions to a skeptic.

The analytic sentences are true in all possible worlds wherever they are applicable. If there are no sticks at all in a possible world, or possible perspective, our statement that every stick has two ends would turn out to be a statement without any reference. Similarly, every individual has two parent turns out to be having no instance if in a possible world no mortals of our kind exist. Similarly, if an object is not supported it would fall would not have any instance in a possible world where there are no objects of the kind of our world.[16]

Having noticed the possibility of analytic statements being true of the world, i.e., they are applicable to the world; we may extend the notion of analyticity to cover statements involving more than two terms. Normally, an analytic statement expresses the relationship between two terms, a subject and a predicate, but there can be relationship between three or more terms. Why should we not call them analytic if there exists the linguistic relationship? Consider for instance, there is some relationship among volume, weight and density. Or consider the Boyle's law. There are three terms which are related in a particular manner in this case: temperature, pressure and the volume. If there can be analyticity having definite relationship between two terms, why there cannot be analyticity among these three terms? Perhaps, we find it difficult to answer this question because of two reasons: first, any subject predicate sentence can take only two terms, one as the subject and another as the predicate, second the way Kant had introduced the term 'analytic' had something to do with the meaning of these two terms and we could speak of three terms yet, with the same meaning. For instance "A = A = A" as analytic with three terms. The difficulty is more fundamental than this.

Going by the general thrust of Quine and Wittgenstein that there does not seem to be any language including the scientific one which is not governed by our linguistic rules, we could conclude that even the terms in formulation of laws and scientific theories are governed by linguistic rules. If there can be analytic sentences in ordinary language, there could as well be analytical sentences in the language of science. A good example would be "Water is H_2O", or "Heat is molecular agitation".[17] But why is it that we do not speak of analytic relationship among three terms?

Having spoken about the analyticity not in terms of meaning, but in terms of rules,[18] we should be speaking of analyticity in terms of linguistic rules. This mode of speaking of analytic relationship would permit us to find the linguistic relationship among more than two terms. For instance, cuckoos are birds, so are the crows. We now know that cuckoos are not crows on the basis of the linguistic rules and this follows that "cuckoos" and "crows" are mutually exclusive yet, they are the species of the genus "birds". Similarly, we can speak of the linguistic relationship among the terminologies that are involved in the formulation of a scientific law. For instance, in the Boyle's law, the three terms, namely, pressure, temperature and volume have a definite relationship. And moreover, when we speak of the relationship among force, mass and acceleration in the Newton's law, again there is the definite relationship among these three terms which can be considered to be linguistically related.

The main difference between the linguistic rules applied to objects of the world having linguistic relationship and the laws of nature having three or more terms which are inter-related is that we speak of quantitative aspects in the case of terms that are involved in the laws of nature, but not in the case of analytic sentences based on linguistic rules. Thus, we may be guided to say that the words that constitute natural laws are also governed by linguistic rules, yet, linguistic rules themselves do not yield natural laws. True enough, yet, what is important to note is that the induction that is involved in science whether that follows the pattern of the linguistic generalization or that of empirical generalization needs to be examined. We are inclined to think that the generalizations in science take the model of rule formation in language. Though, one may think that we are generalizing on the basis of empirical observation, it does not happen that way. Philosophers, for having failed to notice the fact that language is also playing crucial rule in generalizing the natural laws, conclude that there are conjectures and refutations of various kind. Popper, Goodman and Quine all seem to believe that hypothesis are somehow formed having no logic. We think that there is logic to hypothesis formation; the logic is comparable to the rule formation in language. Having observed some cases of a certain type, we may propose a hypothesis on the analogy of our proposing the rule of addition after doing some examples of addition.

To claim that grammar is the bounds of sense is to claim that there is a limit to our way of thinking. For instance, sensation and the inner experiences cannot be captured by language and this is the limit of language. Similarly, we cannot speak of certain things for they are grammatically forbidden. For instance, we have noted earlier that it would be meaningless to say that it is 5 O'clock on the sun. This is the reason why Wittgenstein has chosen to speak of assertive condition as against the truth conditions. Since, language seems to have its own limitations, our thought and perceptions are also limited by the limits of the language. This being so, all that we can speak as humans can be spoken of within the language. If a skeptic demands for something that cannot be met by any language, then the skeptic is unrealistic. This is the reason why we cannot have the mechanistic necessity in the realm of humans.

If we have formulated our rules on the basis of our observation in the regularity in nature, what happens is that the rules that are formulated provide us the linguistic necessity. If in case we discover the regularity in nature in such a way that two rules that we formulate in language have such a relationship that they are related necessarily, then certain analytic statements would be applicable to the world exactly the way that natural laws are applicable to the world. There is nothing that stops a natural scientist accepting the natural laws to be linguistic laws. All that he requires to do is to align himself to the laws of nature while formulating linguistic rules to govern natural laws.

If we speak of natural laws which have been adapted in our language, the instances of the laws can be equally predicted well in advance. There is not any element of uncertainty in our prediction. Moreover, a skeptic cannot fail to obey the laws of nature. Given the fact that laws of nature are already embedded in our language, skeptic has no scope to disobey the rules.

Since, language is in perfect harmony with reality and since, natural laws have been part of our culture and since, skeptic cannot contradict himself there are at least some cases where rule-following is certain, I cannot be saying that a cup of tea is hot and mean that it is cold. For instance, if I have dropped an object and the object fell down, this cannot be doubted by a skeptic. Even if the skeptic is not very happy about the example, one can construct several examples carefully choosing the cases where natural laws have been adapted culturally by invoking certain conventions to prove the point. Thus, we have given a straight solution to the skeptical paradox.

Second, we may now discuss how objectivity can be attained regarding the other minds and private experiences. Let us recapitulate the problem of rule-following skepticism and examine the genesis of the skeptical paradox. Among other things, the paradox is based on the assumption that one ought to know the rule-governed behaviour of one's own past so that one can judge whether one has acted in accord with the same rule at present. But this is an impossible condition to be met holds the skeptic, because first, one cannot be sure of one's own past intentions; second, one cannot read off the rule from the behaviour of a person since, in any context multiple rules fit the behaviour equally.

Contrary to our normal belief, Wittgenstein and following Wittgenstein, Kripke believed that one cannot know one's past intentions. And the argument in support of this is the following: intention is always in the present. This being so, when one speaks of the intentions of one's past actions, it is the same whether one speaks of one's own intentions of past behaviour or some one else speaks of the same. One does not have any added advantage in being the agent of the action while identifying the intentions of one's past behaviour opines Wittgenstein. According to him, what one normally does while identifying the intention of one's own past behaviour is that one recollects one's past behaviour and assigns what one now thinks *appropriate intention* to it. And one's present act of *assigning a particular intention* to one's past behaviour is one's *present intention*, and there is no way one can circumvent the role played by one's present intention. Therefore, in a manner of speaking, all my descriptions and explanations of my past intentions are in true sense my present conceived intentions of my past behaviours.

On the above interpretation, it is impossible to know the intention of our past behaviour and that is the reason why Kripke's skeptic asks: How do I know that I followed the same rule in the past? And the same question is reformulated with reference to meaning: How do I know that I used the word with the same meaning in the past?

Intention of a person is not an event in time, whereas, mental events of taking decisions are. Nothing happens whether in the mental world, or in the physical just because I intend to give a lecture on Wittgenstein. But if this intention is executed in the form of action, i.e., I actually gave a lecture on Wittgenstein, then it is an event in time and it can be stored and retrieved from my memory.

It is possible to know whether I followed the same rule in the past and now, but not in the manner Kripke's skeptic wants us to do, but in an entirely different manner. For instance, we need to remind ourselves of the Wittgensteinian thesis that if a rule is given its application is given, i.e., the rules determine their extension. However, this thesis should not be interpreted in the manner in which the thesis is obviously false i.e., all the contexts of the application of rules are given when the rules are given. The thesis rightly asserts that given a context with necessary details, we would be able to know whether the rule applies or not if we know the rule. This thesis of internal relation between a rule and its application can be fruitfully made use of in assessing our past and present actions in terms of rules.

All that we need to do is to re-assess our past and present behaviour in the light of the rule in question. I remember what I did in the past and I also know what I should do if I were to follow the same rule again by simply knowing what are the two situations in which I would apply the same rule. If rule determines its extension, it is possible for me to know whether I followed the same rule then and now if they are the instances of following the same rule. Kripke's skeptic assumes that the rules and their extensions are not necessarily related (internally) and therefore, he needs to know whether present rule is the same rule which he has followed in the past. This is one like putting the cart before the horse. The right way of knowing whether one has followed the same rule then and now is by raising the issue: If last occasion where I behaved in a certain manner is an appropriate context where one can say that I followed a certain rule, can my present behaviour too be a right context where the same rule be applied? Or can a rule have past and present correct applications? And every one knows that the answer is clearly "Yes".

Similar analysis can be offered in the context of meaning. "Meaning" like "intention" can only be spoken of in the mode of present. This can be demonstrated with an example. When I say "By democracy I meant....", my use of past tense does not refer to anything that was past. It indicates my continued use of the word in a particular manner. The issue of identity of meaning across time rests on a mistake. Even when I say that I meant "such and such" it is only with reference to present that I mean such and such. That is to say, one cannot attach temporal dimension to meaning.

There can be no history to meaning, however there can be history of words. There is no sense in which we can speak that meaning has changed, though we do often speak of the change of meaning of words. When we speak of change of meaning, it is only in the contexts of words changing the meaning: being associated with different meanings with certain interval of time. Instances of an unequivocal term becoming equivocal, and an equivocal term becoming unequivocal etc. are many. This is a unique feature of meaning that it never changes; while the words do undergo changes, and most importantly words are associated with different meanings which we call change of meaning in common parlance.

Another common belief which is questionable is that intention is the meaning of the word. Consider the example: I wanted to warn my friend by saying "you are irresponsible". Here, intention is not the part of the meaning of the sentence. "You are irresponsible" is a value judgement and my intention to warn my friend is not part of it at all. A descriptive sentence might coincide with the intention of the speaker provided the sentence is used for asserting something. And similarly, "be careful!" can be a warning provided it is used in the right context to warn someone. But multiple uses of these sentences are possible and multiple intentions cannot be embedded in the sentence. Thus, meaning of the sentence is unquestionably different and is distinguishable from the intention of the one who uses the sentence.

If this is so, how do we speak of our past at all? What is not noted is that we do remember events that have happened in the past. And this includes any event that has happened to me as a person including my experiences and feelings, and the events that have happened which I have witnessed or heard of. Memory stores an experience which is an event which has a temporal dimension.

It is not absurd to refer to yesterday with regard to our decisions and commitments. When we say "yesterday I decided to work on my research paper, but today I decided not to work on that research paper" is not a contradiction in terms, because there are no two intentions in some way conflicting with one another. It would be a contradiction if and only if I want to work on my research paper and also do not want to work on my research paper just now. But that can never occur-together.

My decision to work on my research paper yesterday remains in the form of a commitment. In this sense all my lasting promises remain in the form of commitments. And we should not mistake commitments to be our intentions or past intentions. We do remember our commitments and if we have accepted a rule, Wittgenstein claims that we have a commitment to it. Since, commitment can be over a period of time, it is possible to have commitment to a rule across the time. And if rule determines meaning, it is possible to speak of identity of meaning across the time by speaking of commitment to a rule across time. Thus, though we cannot know our past intentions and meaning, we can still know our past commitments and obey the rule as per our old commitment.

The skeptic believed that it is impossible to establish the link between what is known as "private language" and the public, since, we are not in a position to know the intention of others. However, we may note that this again rests on a mistake. We are told that the early stage of our economy depended largely on the barter system where people exchanged their commodities for one another. That is to say, even though their commodities are different, they have valued them equally. This analogy is applicable to our problem of interpersonal meaning. Even if the physical feeling and the physical impact the sound makes on our ear drums are different, the value attached to what is heard in the form of meaning for different people is often the same.

When I have the so-called private experience of fire I say "fire!" and I have a certain visual experience. When someone else looks at it and says "Oh! fire" he also has some visual experience. We both meant fire when we said "fire", i.e., there are two experiences which are spatio-temporally separated, yet, the meaning of the word uttered by both of us is the same. The word "fire" which is used ostensively is functioning like a demonstrative pronoun. There is the meaning equivalence[19] even though the personal experiences of the fire are different since, our personal experiences depend on various factors such as the distance between the person and the fire, the angle, the shape of the eye and so on. No two persons have the same hand-writing, yet, what is written can be the same.

Since, perception is dependent on various conditions such as attention, sense organ of the perceiver and physical conditions such as the distance between the subject and the object of perception and other conditions like the adequate light in the case of visual perception and so on, it is quite difficult to achieve identical physical conditions to use an expression with the same meaning. If one has to create identical physical condition in order to use an expression with identical meaning in language, we would have never developed our language beyond a traffic language. Meaning communicated does not normally depend on such physical features of mode of communication unless it is in a special kind of context such as shouting.

Language is recognized as a social institution, and all social institutions are built on agreement. Agreement is nothing but agreement in intention on various constitutive components of the institution. In the case of native speakers of a language, there is general agreement on the vocabulary of language, what is grammatical and what is not grammatical in the context of sentences, what is formal and what is colloquial and so on. Once, we have the institution of language which is based on agreement it is possible to have expressions having meaning independent of the personal factors of the members of that institution.

For instance, we can consider the institution of telegraph services. There are certain rules and regulations in availing telegraph services and as a member of the society, one can avail of these services by adhering to the rules and regulations. However, the institution of telegraph services will not be concerned with individual intentions and feelings at a given point of time. For instance, a member of the society sends a telegram to someone wishing him a happy and married life by writing a number on the prescribed telegraph form and paying prescribed fee. The telegram would be delivered at the other end to the addressee by decoding the coded number into the text form following the rules by the telegraph department. The telegram communicates certain intention which is institutionally recognized; but this communicated intention may not match with the intention of the person at this end. The intention of the person might not have been to actually wish the person but to acknowledge the receipt of marriage invitation card. The meaning of a sentence and the intention of the speaker may not match always. For instance, "Who are you?" is a sentence which indicates that the speaker is making certain query, but in some context the speaker might use the sentence to question the authority of someone else. And this intention of the speaker may not be obvious if the meaning of the sentence is different from the intention of the speaker.

Communication failure occurs if the meaning intended and the meaning of the sentence do not match, and occasionally the meaning of the sentence is not obvious because of ambiguity. However, what is obvious is that one can communicate one's intention through language and that is what we do when we write letters and declare our intentions through an affidavit etc.

Can we mean something else than what the words mean? Is a sensible question within a framework and is a non-sensical question in another framework. Those who believe that we cannot, are the ones who believe that language is an institution and we need to be a member of the institution even to make an attempt to change the institution, i.e., this group does not believe that you can be an outsider and still change the meaning of the words in a language. Those who claim that it is possible to mean something different than what the words mean, are the ones who do not believe in the institution of language as given and eventually face the paradox of rule-following as the following analysis shows.

If intention can be different than the meaning of a sentence, how is it that we are able to assign new meanings to words and sentences even by arbitrarily defining them? It is possible because, normally we take the term to have the normal meaning in ordinary usage and whenever we assign new meanings, we define these terms; and in the written form we indicate this difference by putting the word which is used as a technical term deviating from the normal usage by putting the word into inverted commas. In the context of verbal communication, there are various ways that one can communicate this fact that one is using a term in a unique manner. A hermeneutician or for that matter everyone who claims that intention is the meaning of the sentence or word should put each and every word into inverted commas and thus, make the language an impossible one. That is to say, only while arbitrarily defining a word, or assigning the meaning to a word, our intention and the meaning are the same. However, subsequently, we can separate our intention and meaning. If we want to abide by ourselves by the rules of the society, we can continue using the words without any special meaning and if we do not want to abide by the norms of the society, we can use the terms in our own way. The thesis that intention is the meaning of the term or the sentence has, to fail. And it is demonstrated by the following example.

Let us assume that two of us are familiar with English and one holds the view that intention is the meaning of the words and sentences and the other holds the view that intention is independent of the meanings. The former, is well within his scheme to use each and every word the way he wants, as there is no social constraints that he should care for; while the latter who believes in the social theory of meaning cannot do that. However, it is well within the scheme of things for an intentionalist to imagine a situation where he for a moment is willing to take the social theorist seriously and abide by the rules within a certain context of say, playing chess. If both of them agree on rules, it is possible to play several games of chess where one wins and the other loses. Let us now introduce an element in this chess game from the intentionalist's point of view. What is checkmate is decided by the player. It is possible to imagine a context where one willfully loses, and if a person willfully loses, he wins. For instance while teaching chess to one's own child, one may willfully loose the game just to encourage the child and by loosing one has succeeded in what one wanted to achieve. Thus, in this modified context, if intentional theory of meaning is correct, then no one can loose the game of chess unless the player himself wanted to loose. For the meaning of what is to win is offered by the person concerned. The player might decide to give up, which is in his own scheme of things winning.

Let us further stretch the example and imagine that both the intentionalist and the proponent of the social theory converse on a mundane topic for sometime. Let us also assume that intentionalist being considerate would speak words with normal meaning most of the time yet, he fails because of the influence of his theory and uses one word in his own peculiar way in every sentence he utters. The social theorist asks for clarification to which the intentionalist responds in his usual manner. However, being consistent with his own theory the intentionalist uses a term in his own unique manner while explaining the peculiar use of the sentence in his previous utterance. If the intentionalist continues with his own style of speaking, there is no way that the social theorist would ever understand anything that is uttered by intentionalist.

Intentionalist can produce a sample or two only to argue that his theory is correct. He cannot practice his own theory while demonstrating the validity of his theory. If one thinks that every time one utters a sentence one offers a definition, it would be a gross mistake. Kripke's skeptic believes in the validity of this intentional theory and demands the demonstration of the type which we have indicated is impossible. The skeptic's demand rests on a mistaken theory of meaning that meaning lies in intention.

If our understanding is correct, it is possible to learn the meaning of an expression simply by imitating others. Since, intention is not part of the rule and part of the meaning of a word, it is possible to imitate the behaviour of others without knowing the intention of the other person. As a consequence, one learns the use of words and the meaning of those words. Thus, we have understood the meaning of the word "week" without knowing what the intention of the speaker is.

Thus, we may note that one can speak about the experience of others, their thoughts as well as about the facts of nature in an objective manner. Even then, it would not be a contradiction to negate a statement about other minds that does not prove that our knowledge is not objective. Regarding the knowledge about the world, the strongest sense of necessity that one could have is the sentence which is found to be true on three counts: linguistic, empirical and metaphysical. Are there such sentences? We tend to say yes. As we have mentioned above, fire burns, water boils, birds fly, individuals have parents are all the examples of statements which are true on these counts. Linguistically, if you call someone a human being, you need to presuppose that he is born to his parents, this is found to be empirically true and scientifically justified. Moreover, any possible perspective or world we imagine where we speak of the individual in question, we need to grant that he has parents and hence, is true even in the metaphysical sense. Therefore, one could demonstrate there are many examples of this kind and the notion of necessity is the strongest possible one. Yet, Wittgenstein might say that the world may behave differently than what we think!

Thus, our theory of meaning based on Wittgenstein's notion of grammar having the element of categorical imperative of Kant in order to have the normative aspect of a rule has succeeded in demonstrating how knowledge can be objective, necessary and normative. Statements that are necessary in the strongest possible would not give any chance even to the Kripke's skeptic to doubt the validity of the knowledge. This is because if he does, he would not be speaking sense.

Summary

An innovative way of posing the skeptical issue can be found in the work of Kripke. He poses a radical and all pervasive skeptical problem in the context of rules and their following by hypothesizing another rule just like our arithmetical rule of addition with one important difference. The other rule which he calls *quus function* is different from the plus function in some unobserved cases, while it is identical to the *plus function* on all observed cases. Kripke demonstrates that any rule governed behaviour of an individual in the act of adding numbers is equally a rule-governed behaviour of using *quus function*. By generalizing from this, Kripke is in a position to claim that any rule governed behaviour of a person can be interpreted in more than one way since, the behaviour fits many competing rules. There are no facts physical or mental which can lend us help in identifying the rule that is being followed. Moreover, even the person who follows the rule cannot be sure of which rule he had followed in the past since, even he cannot have access to his own past intentions.

Rule-following skepticism is a very powerful form of skepticism for it strikes the very vital cord of knowledge, i.e., it makes language impossible. It denies ascription of meaning to any symbol and makes understanding, thought, and communication impossible. Thus, it enters every segment of human life leaving no room for rule-governed activity.

What the Kripke's skeptic is demanding is that, first, we should be in a position to identify the rule that we follow now is the same as the one which we have used up till now. Second, we should have some mechanism to determine the infinite future applications of rules which are yet, to take place independent of the actual applications we have made so far. In other words, skeptic is demanding a *normative guideline* to determine infinite applications of rules in the future.

Kripke concedes the argument of his skeptic and argues that skeptic cannot be answered on his own conditions. However, he provides a *skeptical-solution* to the skeptical problem by compromising with the skeptic on the ground that the life should go on and for that the man should be granted the status of human by adopting the right attitude towards him. Kripke is of the opinion that we cannot provide always truth-conditions, i.e., necessary and sufficient conditions for certain sentences. He claims that truth-conditions have to be replaced by assertive conditions, i.e., whether the situation is linguistically fertile to assert certain statements irrespective of whether we are able to discover whether the statement is true or false. This requires change in attitude immediately after observing the pain behaviour, instead of asking whether someone is really in pain, we do ask now: what can we do to help the individual?. On the skeptical-solution, we have the ways of ascribing concepts to others and claim whether the rules followed are the same with reference to present and past behaviours of an agent. However, this cannot silence Kripke's skeptic, since, the assertive condition of a rule provides only the history of the use of the rule, but does not have any guiding force for future applications. Thus, Kripke's assertive condition is nothing more than a descriptive answer to a normative question.

Since, this form of skepticism operates at the level of language, it has far-reaching consequences on other issues, namely, hypothesizing, induction, generalization, projection, prediction, scientific theory, etc., and in nutshell, every walk of rational activity where rules and rule-following is inevitable. On this background, the thesis makes an attempt to interpret and evaluate Goodman's *new riddle of induction* as a rule-following skepticism in the context of induction, hypothesis and projection, Quine's *three indeterminacies* are interpreted as problems of rule-following arising in the issue of knowledge, theory and translation and Wittgenstein's use theory of meaning in the case of meaning and use of the words.

Making use of the linguistic liberty, Goodman defines the term *grue* in such a way that each and every observation of emerald after specific time support two incompatible hypotheses equally, namely, "all emeralds are green" and "all emeralds are grue", similar to the problem of multiplicity of rules. From this Goodman argues that there is no syntactic and semantic criterion to differentiate lawlike statements from contingent generalizations.

Goodman's theory of projection adopts a descriptive attitude to the problem of skepticism, as it is based on the history of the projection or entrenchment of a term in the given society. He would base his projection on the strength of entrenchment and the purpose served by the use of words in the society. Goodman's theory of projection as a solution to skepticism would remain inconclusive as it offers a descriptive answer to the skeptic.

Quine entertains three main skeptical issues. First, the indeterminacy of reference which shows that ontology cannot be fixed since, it is relative to the perspective. This leads to the problem of deciding as to what we mean by a sentence if its scope is different when perspectives change. Second, the indeterminacy of translation which shows that the notion of proposition as sentence meaning is untenable, since, translation depends on the manual of translation. And third, what the empirical under-determination of theory shows is that there are various defensible ways of conceiving the world.

All the three skeptical issues share the same feelings of Kripke's skeptic: Given the behaviour or data which rule or theory do we fit to the context? In the context of indeterminacy of reference, the issue is: how do we interpret the quantified sentence if the predicate term refers to different ontologies or different perspectives? In the context of translation, the issue is that of finding the exact translation from one language to another given the verbal behaviour in addition to the individual's sense perception. And if a theory is never deduced from the data and if the theory is transcending the observations, and if two theories are empirically equivalent, the underdetermination of theory may be interpreted as: how do we choose one theory against another?

Quine attempts to answer skeptic by establishing objectivity on the basis of unification of science through theoretical kinds and naturalization of epistemology. He hopes to achieve unification on the ground that natural kinds can eventually evolve into theoretical kinds, and predicate logic would take over natural language. Though, Quine speaks of normative element in his naturalized epistemology, because of the problem in theoretical kinds and his immanent theory of truth, his goal of the unification of science remains ideal.

The Wittgensteinian formulation of the paradox of rule is this: How is it that we can say that we have grasped the meaning of a word when meaning lies in use and use is spread over time? We argue that Wittgenstein presents the skeptical problem to reject it as part of his method of *reductio-ad-absurdum* argument. Though, Wittgenstein's *philosophical grammar* and *form of life* can very much accommodate the normative aspects of rules, he considers his grammar and the task of philosopher to be descriptive one, and thus, fails to meet the requirement of Kripke's skeptic.

What the skeptic doubts is the possibility of objective and necessary knowledge. If we can establish the objectivity of knowledge, and make it the foundation of science, then this would be an adequate answer to all forms of skepticism, i.e., the riddle of induction, indeterminacies etc. Objectivity of knowledge can be the foundation of our value system as well. It can be the basis of communication, induction, prediction, explanation, translation etc. And it would, in fact, touch all the aspects of engineering and sciences on the one hand, culture and value on the other.

We have tried to achieve the normativity, thus, the necessity and objectivity in rule by inducting universal character and commitment into linguistic rules. It should be noted that we have accepted the Wittgensteinian framework of philosophical grammar to establish the objectivity and normativity of knowledge with only one minor modification. As is known, grammar is a set of free-floating conventional linguistic rules which are descriptive. As it stands, the arbitrary set of rules cannot provide the basis of the objectivity and necessity. But once, we infuse our commitment and universalize its use, a rule acquires normativity. For example, the simple rule of addition becomes normative rule when we universalize it by adding 'so on *ad infinitum*' to the explanatory examples.

But the question is how can we utilize the linguistic rule to explain the world? In other words, if rules of grammar are merely conventional set of guidelines, how it can be used to explain the laws of nature, which are supposed to be independent of our thought and language? To say that a sentence is true by linguistic rule need not make us think that they are not true synthetically because language does not contradict reality. Since, language and reality are in harmony, since, they belong to different realms, there is no reason to believe that an analytic statement which is true by virtue of language cannot be true in any other sense. If we accept the regularity in nature conventionally as a rule, there is no reason to believe that the necessity achieved would be of a lesser kind. For instance, fire burns and this simple property of fire can be conventionally accepted as a rule for the use of the term "fire". And having accepted it conventionally as a rule, it is true by definition that "fire burns" is true. If it is true by definition, even a skeptic cannot doubt it. If a skeptic doubts a truth by definition, then he is refusing to use a language which has sense and if a skeptic uses the language which lacks sense, nothing needs to be proved to him. If there can be analytic sentences in ordinary language, there could as well be analytic sentences in the language of science. A good example would be "Water is H_2O" or "Heat is molecular agitation".

We may be permitted to say that the words that constitute natural laws are also governed by linguistic rules, yet, linguistic rules themselves do not yield natural laws. Philosophers, for having failed to notice the fact that language is also playing crucial role in generalizing the natural laws, conclude that there are conjectures and refutations of various kind. Goodman, Quine and Popper all seem to believe that hypothesis are somehow formed having no logic. We think that there is logic to hypothesis formation; the logic is comparable to the rule formation in language. Having observed some cases of a certain type, we may propose a hypothesis on the analogy of our proposing the rule of addition after doing some examples of addition. If we have formulated our rules on the basis of our observation in the regularity in nature, what happens is that the rules that are formulated provide us the linguistic necessity. If in case we discover the regularity in nature in such a way that two rules that we formulate in language have such a relationship that they are related necessarily, then certain analytic statements would be applicable to the world exactly the way that natural laws are applicable to the world. There is nothing that stops a natural scientist accepting the natural laws to be linguistic laws. All that he requires to do is to align himself to the laws of nature while formulating linguistic rules to govern natural laws.

Since, language is in perfect harmony with reality and since, natural laws have been part of our culture and since, skeptic cannot contradict himself there are at least some cases where rule-following is certain, I cannot be saying that a cup of tea is hot and mean that it is cold. For instance, if I have dropped an object and the object fell down, this cannot be doubted by a skeptic. Even if the skeptic is not very happy about the example, one can construct several examples carefully choosing the cases where natural laws have been adapted culturally by invoking certain conventions to prove the point.

To conclude, the strongest sense of necessity that one could have is the sentence which is found to be true on three counts: linguistic, empirical and metaphysical. Are there such sentences? We tend to say yes. As we have mentioned above, fire burns, water boils, birds fly, individuals have parents are all the examples of statements which are true on these counts. Linguistically, if you call someone a human being, you need to presuppose that he is born to his parents, this is found to be empirically true and scientifically justified. Moreover, any possible perspective or world we imagine where we speak of the individual in question, we need to grant that he has parents and hence, is true even in the metaphysical sense. Thus, one could conclude that there are many examples of this kind and the notion of necessity involved is the strongest possible one.[20]

NOTES AND REFERENCES

1. Wittgenstein, L., *Philosophical Investigation*, (henceforth *PI*) (ed.), G.E.M. Anscombe, Basil Blackwell, Oxford. *PI*, §354.
2. *PI*, §304. Anthony Kenny in his book *The Wittgenstein Reader* (henceforth *WR*), Basil Blackwell, Oxford, 1994, has compiled Wittgenstein's works thematically and has provided a handy reference book on Wittgenstein. see *WR*, p. 155.
3. We had already some occasion to know how this is possible. Please see chapter 2, section 2.9, "Immediate Response to Kripke's Skeptic".
4. Please see Kant, I., *Fundamental Principles of the Metaphysics of Ethics*, trans. T.K. Abbott, Longman, (10th ed.) 1959, pp. 87 ff.
5. *PI*, §241.
6. *Ibid.*, §482.
7. Wittgenstein remarks: "every sign by itself seems dead. What gives it life? — in use it is alive.... Or is the use its life.", *PI*, §432. Again, "one cannot guess how a word functions, one has to look at its use and learn from that", *PI*, §340, for example, "a lever is a lever only in use, disconnected it is a rod" and "the signpost is an order — if, under normal circumstances, it fulfils its purpose", *PI*, §87.
8. *PI*, §198.
9. *Ibid.*, §241.

10. Wittgenstein, L., 1956, *Remarks on the Foundations of Mathematics* (henceforth *RFM*), (ed.), G. H., von Wright, R. Rhees and G.E.M. Anscombe, Blackwell, Oxford, pp. 245/39.
11. *RFM*, pp. 246/43.
12. Though Goodman seems to deny this. See Goodman, Nelson, 1965, *Fact, Fiction and Forecast*, 2nd edition, Bobbs-Merrill Co. Inc., Indianpolis, p. 83.
13. Goodman might insist that we need more stringent criterion to distinguish bogus lawlike sentences from the genuine ones.
14. See Kripke, S., "Identity and Necessity", 1997, in *Naming, Necessity and Natural Kind* (ed.), S.P. Schwartz, Cornell University Press, Ithaca, pp. 84-85.
15. Wittgenstein, L., 1967, *Zettle* (ed.), G.E.M. Anscombe, Basil Blackwell, Oxford, pp. 60/331.
16. Notice that when we speak of object falling, we consider falling as the attribute of an object, not due to gravitational force. If we invoke the concept of gravitational force which operates on the concept of mass and mutual attraction, then the statement loses its normal sense of ordinary language.
17. Kripke calls them to be identity statements between two rigid designators. See *Naming and Necessity*, pp. 90-91.
18. Wittgenstein has replaced the issue of meaning with that of rules as we have noted earlier.
19. This view is different from Quine's stimulus theory of meaning; but is comparable to his notion of similarity of 1981. For Quine's view, 1981, see his *Theories and Things*, Harvard University Press, Cambridge.

Bibliography

Abel, Gunter, 1991, "Logic, Art, Understanding in the Philosophy of Nelson Goodman", *Inquiry*, 34, pp. 311-21.

——1994, "Indeterminacy and Interpretation", *Inquiry*, Vol. 37, pp. 403-419.

Anscombe, G.E.M., 1985, "Wittgenstein: On Rule and Private Language", *Ethics*, Vol. 95, pp. 342-352.

Baker, G.P. and Hacker, P.M.S., 1984, *Scepticism, Rule and Language*, Blackwell, Oxford.

——1986. *Wittgenstein: Rules, Grammar and Necessity*, Vol. 2, Basil Blackwell, Oxford.

Baker, G.P. and Hacker, P.M.S., 1990, "Malcolm on Language and Rules", *Philosophy*, Vol. 65, pp. 167-179.

Barker, S.F. and Achinstein, P., 1968, "On the New Riddle of Induction", in P. Nidditch (ed.), *Philosophy of Science*, Oxford University Press, London, pp. 149-161.

Barrett, R. and R. Gibson (eds.), 1990, *Perspectives on Quine*, Basil Blackwell, USA.

Bergstorm, Lars, 1993, "Quine, Underdetermination and Scepticism", *Journal of Philosophy*, pp. 331-358.

Blackburn, S., 1984. *Spreading the Word: Grounding in the Philosophy of Language*, The Clarendon Press, Oxford.

Blich, Baruch, 1987, "Natural Kind as a Kind of 'Family Resemblance'", in Weiberger, Koller, Schramme, A. (ed.), *Philosophy of Law, Politics and Society, The Proceeding of the 12th International Wittgenstein Symposium*, 7th-14th August, pp. 284-289.

Bloor, David, 1983. *Wittgenstein: A Social Theory of Knowledge*, MacMillan, London.

Boghossian, Paul, A., 1989, "The Rule-Following Considerations", *Mind*, Vol. 98, pp. 507-549.

Boorse, C., 1975, "The Origin of the Indeterminacy Thesis", *Journal of Philosophy*, pp. 369-387.

Brown, H.I., 1988, "Normative Epistemology and Naturalized Epistemology", *Inquiry*, 31, pp. 53-78.

Byrne, A., 1996, "On Misunderstanding Kripke's Wittgenstein", *Philosophy and Phenomenological Research*, pp. 339-343.

Chisholm, R., 1977, *The Theory of Knowledge*, 2nd ed., Prentice-Hall, Englewood Cliffs.

Churchland, P.S., 1987, "Epistemology in the Age of Neuroscience", *Journal of Philosophy*, pp. 544-53.

Coates, Paul, 1986, "Kripke's Sceptical Paradox: Normativeness and Meaning", *Mind*, pp. 77-80.

Cook, John W., 1983, "Moore and Scepticism", in Carl Ginet and Sydney Shoemaker (ed.), *Knowledge and Mind*, Oxford University Press, Oxford, pp. 3-25.

Davidson, D., 1986, "A Coherence Theory of Truth and Knowledge", in E. LePore (ed.), *Truth and Interpretation*, Blackwell, New York, pp. 307-19.

——1994, "What is Quine's View of Truth", *Inquiry*, Vol. 37, pp. 437-440.

Descartes, R., 1984, *The Philosophical Writings of Descartes*, trans. J. Cottingham, R. Stoothoff and D. Murdoch, Vol. 2, Cambridge University Press, Cambridge.

Earman, John, 1994, "Concepts of Projectibility and the Problems of Induction", in Stalker, D. (ed.), *Grue! The New Riddle of Induction*, Open Court Publisher, La Salle, pp. 97-115.

Elder, C.L., 1990, "Goodman's 'New Riddle' — A Realist's Reprise", *Philosophical Studies*, 59, pp. 115-135.

Ernie, LePore, 1995, "Quine, Analyticity and the Transcendent", *Nous*, pp. 468-480.

Feyerabend, P., 1975. *Against Method*, NLB, London.

——1991. *Three Dialouges on Knowledge*, Blackwell, Oxford.

Frege, G., 1972, *Conceptual Notation and Related Articles*, Clarendon Press, Oxford.

Fuller, Steve, 1988. *Social Epistemology*, Indiana University Press, Bloomington,

Gemes, Ken, 1991, "The Indeterminacy Thesis Reformulated", *Journal of Philosophy*, pp. 91-108.

Gibson, R.F., 1994, "Quine and Davidson: Two Naturalized Epistemologists", *Inquiry*, Vol. 37, pp. 449-63.

Godel, K., 1962, *On Formally Undecidable Propositions of Principal Mathematics and Related Systems*, trans. B. Mehtzer, Oliver and Boyd, London.

Goodman, N., Schwartz, R. and Scheffler, I., 1970, "An Improvement in the Theory of Projectibility", *Journal of Philosophy*, pp. 605-608.

Goodman, N., 1951. *The Structure of Apperence*, Harvard University Press, Cambridge, Mass.

——1952, "On Likeness of Meaning", in Linsky, L. (ed.), *Semantics and the Philosophy of Language*, University of Illinois Press, Urbane, pp. 67-74.

——1965. *Fact, Fiction and Forecast*, 2nd ed., Bobbs-Merril, Indianapolis.

——1968, "Positionality and Pictures", in P. Nidditch (ed.), *Philosophy of Science*, Oxford University Press, London, pp. 162-164.

——1968, "Safety, Strength, Simplicity", in P. Nidditch (ed.), *Philosophy of Science*, Oxford University Press, London, pp. 121-123.

——1972, Problems and Projects, Hackett, Indianapolis.

——1978, *Ways of Worldmakings*, Bobbs-Merrill, Indianapolis.

——1979, "Credence, Credibility and Comprehension", *Journal of Philosophy*, pp. 618-619.

Hacking, Ian, 1994, "Entrenchment", in Stalker, D. (ed.), *Grue! The New Riddle of Induction*, Open Court Publisher, La Salle, pp. 193-223.

——1993, "On Kripke's and Goodman's Uses of 'Grue'", *Philosophy*, Vol. 68, pp. 269-295.

Harman, Gilbert, 1994, "Simplicity as a Pragmatic Criterion for Deciding What Hypotheses to Take Seriously", in Stalker, D. (ed.), *Grue! The New Riddle of Induction*, Open Court Publisher, La Salle, pp. 153-171.

Holtzman, S. and Leich, C. (eds.), 1981, *Wittgenstein: To Follow a Rule*, Routledge and Kegan Paul.

Hookway, C., 1990. *Scepticism*, Routledge and Kegan Paul, London.

Hume, David, 1975. *Enquiry Concerning Human Understanding* (ed.), L.A. Selby-Bigge, Clarendon Press, Oxford.

Jackson, Frank, 1975, "Grue", *Journal of Philosophy*, pp. 113-131.

Kant, I., 1959. *Fundamental Principles of the Metaphysics of Ethics*, trans. T.K. Abbott, Longman.

Katz, J.J., 1990. *The Metaphysics of Meaning*, The MIT Press, Cambridge, Mass.

Kennedy, R. and Chihara, C., 1975, "An Improvement on Zabludowski's Critique of Goodman's Theory of Projection", *Journal of Philosophy*, pp. 137-141.

Kenny, A.J.P., 1994, *The Wittgenstein Reader*, Basil Blackwell, Oxford.

Ketchum, R.J., 1991, "The Paradox of Epistemology: A Defense of Naturalism", *Philosophical Studies*, Vol. 62, pp. 45-66.

Kitchner, R.F., 1986. *Piaget's Theory of Knowledge: Genetic Epistemology and Scientific Reason*, Yale University Press, New Haven.

Kornblith, H. (ed.), 1985, *Naturalising Epistemology*, The MIT Press, Cambridge.

Kripke, S.A., 1977, "Identity and Necessity", in S.P. Schwartz (ed.), *Namining, Necessity and Natural Kinds*, Cornell University Press, Ithacca, pp. 66-101.

——1982, *Wittgenstein: On Rule and Private Language*, Harvard University Press, Cambridge, Mass.

Kuhn, T., 1972. *The Structure of Scientific Revolution*, University of Chicago Press, Chicago.

——1977. *The Essential Tensions*, University of Chicago Press, Chicago.

Laudan, L., 1988, "Are All Theories Equally Good? A Dialogue", in Robert Nola (ed.), *Relativism and Realism in Science*, Kluwer Academic Publishers, The Netherlands, pp. 117-139.

Laudan, L. and Leplin, J., 1991, "Empirical Equivalence and Undetermination", *Journal of Philosophy*, pp. 449-472.

Lewis, D.K., 1974. *Convention: A Philosophical Study*, Harvard University Press, Cambridge.

Malcolm, Norman, 1986. *Wittgenstein: Nothing is Hidden*, Blackwell, Oxford,

——1989, "Wittgenstein on Language and Rules", *Philosophy*, Vol. 64, pp. 5-28.

Martin, R.M., 1990, "It is not that Easy to Being Grue", *The Philosophical Quarterly*, Vol. 40, pp. 299-315.

McGinn, Marie, 1984, "Kripke on Wittgenstein's Sceptical Problems", *Ratio*, pp. 19-32.

Mulhall, S., 1989, "No Smoke without Fire: The Meaning of Grue", *The Philosophical Quarterly*, Vol. 39, pp. 166-189.

Moore, G.E., 1959. "A Defence of Commonsense", in G.E. Moore, *Philosophical Papers*, George Allen & Unwin. London.

——1959. "Proofs of an External World", in G.E. Moore, *Philosophical Papers*, George Allen & Unwin. London.

Musgrave, Alan, 1993. *Common Sense, Science and Scepticism*, Cambridge University Press, Cambridge.

Nagel, Thomas, 1986. *The View From Nowhere*, Oxford University Press, New York.

Nemirow, L., 1995, "Understanding Rules", *Journal of Philosophy*, pp. 28-43.

Nidditch, P.H. (ed.), 1968, *The Philosophy of Science*, Oxford University Press, London.

Papineau, D., 1992, "Reliabilism, Induction and Scepticism", *The Philosophical Quarterly*, Vol. 42, pp. 1-20.

Peacoke, C., 1989, "What are Concepts?," *Midwest Studies in Philosophy*, pp. 1-28.

Pettit, Philip, 1990, "Affirming the Reality of Rule-Following", *Mind*, Vol. 99, pp. 433-439.

——1990 (a), "The Reality of Rule-Following", *Mind*, Vol. 99, pp. 1-21.

Popkin, R.H., 1964. *The History of Scepticism From Erasmus to Descartes*, Assen, New York.

Popper, K.R., 1965. *Conjectures and Refutations*, Routledge and Kegan Paul, London.

——1959. *The Logic of Scientific Discovery*, Hutchinson, London.

——1972. *Objective Knowledge: An Evolutionary Approach*, The Clarendon Press, Oxford.

Putnam, H., 1979, "Reflections on Goodman's Ways of Worldmaking", *Journal of Philosophy*, pp. 603-619.

——1990, "Why Reason Cannot be Naturalized?", in David, J. Cole *et al.* (ed.), *Philosophy, Mind and Cognitive Inquiry*, The Kluwer Academic Publishers, The Netherlands, pp. 283-303.

Quine, W.V., 1953. *From a Logical Point of View*, Harper and Row, New York.

——1963, *Word and Objects*, Harper & Row, New York.

—-1969, "Two Dogmas of Empiricism", in T.M. Olshewsky (ed.), *Problems in the Philosophy of Language*, Holt, Rinehart and Winston Inc., pp. 398-417.

——1975, "The Nature of Natural Knowledge", in Guttenplan (ed.), *Mind and Language*, Clarendon Press, Oxford, pp. 67-81.

——1981. *Theories and Things*, Harvard University Press, Cambridge.

——1985, "Epistemology Naturalized", in Kornblith, H. (ed.), *Naturalising Epistemology*, The MIT Press, Cambridge, pp. 15-29.

——1985. "Natural Kinds", in Kornblith, H. (ed.), *Naturalising Epistemology*, The MIT Press, Cambridge, pp. 31-47.

——1990, "Three Indeterminacies", in Barret, R. and Gibson, R. (eds.), *Perspectives On Quine*, Basil Blackwell, USA, pp. 1-15.

——1993, "In Praise of Observation Sentences", *Journal of Philosophy*, pp. 101-11.

——1994, "Responses", *Inquiry*, Vol. 37, pp. 495-504.

——1995. *Pursuit of Truth* (revised edition), Harvard University Press, Cambridge, Mass,

——1995. *From Stimulus to Science*, Harvard University Press, Cambridge, Mass.

Roth, M.D. and Ross, Gleen, (eds.), 1990. *Doubting: Contemporary Perspectives on Scepticism,* The Kluwer Academic Press, The Netherlands.

Sanford, D.H., 1994, "A Grue Thought in a Bleen Shade: '*Grue*' as a Disjunctive Predicate", in Stalker, D. (ed.), *Grue! The New Riddle of Induction*, Open Court Publisher, La Salle, pp. 173-192.

Searle, John, R., 1969, "How to Derive 'Ought' from 'Is'", in Hudson, W.D. (ed.), *The Is-Ought Question*, The MacMillan Press, London.

Shimony, A. and Nails, Debra, (eds.), 1987. *Naturalistic Epistemology: A Symposium of Two Decades*, D. Reidel Publishing Company, The Netherlands.

Shoemaker, S., 1975, "On Projecting the Unprojectible", *Philosophical Review*, Vol. 34, pp. 178-219.

Sober, Elliot, 1994, "No Model, No Inference: A Bayesian Primer on the Grue Problem", in Stalker, D. (ed.), *Grue! The New Riddle of Induction*, Open Court Publisher, La Salle, pp. 225-240.

Stalker, D. (ed.), 1994, *Grue! The New Riddle of Induction*, The Open Court Publisher, La Salle.

Stevenson, C.L., 1944, *Ethics and Language*, Yale University Press, New Haven.

Strawson, P.F., 1985, *Scepticism and Naturalism: Some Varieties*, Methuen, London.

Stroud, Barry, 1984, *The Significance of Philosophical Scepticism*, Oxford University Press, New York.

Summerfield, D.M., 1990, "On Taking the Rabbit of Rule-Following out of the Hat of Representation: A Response to Pettit's 'The Reality of Rule-Following'", *Mind*, 99, pp. 425-432.

——1987, "Wittgenstein on 'Rules' and Representation", in Weiberger *et al.* (ed.), *Philosophy of Law, Politics and Society, The Proceeding of the 12th International Wittgenstein Symposium*, 7th-14th, August, pp. 336-341.

Suppes, P., 1994, "Learning and Projectibility", in Stalker, D. (ed.), *Grue! The New Riddle of Induction*, Open Court Publisher, La Salle, pp. 263-272.

Takeo, J., 1987, "Following a Rule in Making Inference in Natural Language", in Weiberger *et al.* (ed.), *Philosophy of Law, Politics and Society, The Proceeding of the 12th International Wittgenstein Symposium*, 7th-14th, August, pp. 350-353.

Teghrarian, S., 1987, "Rule-Scepticism and Wittgenstein's Theory of Meaning" in Weiberger, *et al.* (ed.), *Philosophy of Law, Politics and Society, The Proceeding of the 12th International Wittgenstein Symposium,* 7th-14th, August, pp. 342-345.

Ullian, J. and Goodman, N., 1975, "Bad Company: A Reply to Mr. Zabludowski and Others", *Journal of Philosophy*, pp. 142-145.

Unger, P., *Ignorance*, 1975. *A Case Study for Scepticism*, Oxford University Press, Oxford.

Williams, M., 1991. *Unnatural Doubt: Epistemological Realism and the Basis of Scepticism*, Blackwell, U.K.

Williamson, C., 1989, "Following a Rule", *Philosophy*, Vol. 64, pp. 487-504.

Wittgenstein, L., 1956, *Remarks on the Foundations of Mathematics*, (ed.) G.H. von Wrigth, R. Rhees and G.E.M. Anscombe, trans. G.E.M. Anscombe, Basil Blackwell, Oxford.

——1958, *The Blue and Brown Book*, Harper & Row Publishers, New York.

——1961, *Tractatus-Logico-Philosophicus*, trans. Pears. D. and B. McGuinness, Routledge & Kegan Paul, London.

——1963, *Philosophical Investigation*, (ed.) G.E.M. Anscombe, Basil Blackwell, Oxford.

——1967, *Zettle*, (ed.) G.E.M. Anscombe, Blackwell, Oxford.

——1969. *On Certainty*, (ed.) G.E.M. Anscombe, Basil Blackwell, Oxford.

——1974. *Philosophical Grammar*, (ed.) R. Rhees, trans. A.J.P. Kenney, Basil Blackwell, Oxford.

——1974. *Philosophical Remarks*, (ed.) R. Rhees, trans. R. Hargreaves and R. White, Blackwell, Oxford.

——1939, *Wittgenstein's Lectures on the Foundations of Mathematics*, Cambridge (ed.) C. Diomand, Harvester Press, Sussex, 1976.

——1979. *Wittgenstein's Lectures*, Cambridge 1932-35, From the notes of Alice Ambrose and Margaret MacDonald (ed.), Alice Ambrose, Blackwell, Oxford.

——1980. *Wittgenstein's Lectures*, Cambridge 1930-32, From the notes of John King and Desmond Lee, (ed.) Desmond Lee, Blackwell, Oxford.

Yalcin, U.D., 1992, "Sceptical Arguments from Underdetermination", *Philosophical Studies*, Vol. 68, pp. 1-34.

Zabludowski, A., 1994, "Concerning a Fiction about How Facts Are Forecast", in Stalker, D. (ed.), *Grue! The New Riddle of Induction*, Open Court Publisher, La Salle, pp. 57-78.

Index